design | culture | identity

THE WOLFSONIAN COLLECTION

Issue 24,
Design, Culture, Identity:
The Wolfsonian Collection,
The Journal of Decorative and
Propaganda Arts, published
by The Wolfsonian–Florida
International University.
ISBN 0-9631601-9-2.

Editorial Offices:
The Journal of Decorative
and Propaganda Arts
The Wolfsonian–Florida
International University
1001 Washington Avenue
Miami Beach, Florida 33139
Telephone: (305) 535-2612
Fax: (305) 531-2133
e-mail: dapa@thewolf.fiu.edu
www.wolfsonian.org

The Journal of Decorative
and Propaganda Arts
Issue 22, Cuba Theme Issue;
23, Florida Theme Issue; and
24, Design, Culture, Identity:
The Wolfsonian Collection
are distributed by
The MIT Press
Massachusetts Institute
of Technology
Cambridge, Massachusetts
02142
http://mitpress.mit.edu.

For information on the
availability of other back
issues, contact *The Journal's*
editorial offices.

Cover:
Leon Gilmour, *Cement*
Finishers, woodblock print,
38 x 30 cm, 1939. The
Mitchell Wolfson Jr. Collection,
The Wolfsonian–Florida
International University,
Miami Beach, Florida.

Printed in Spain by Grafos S.A.

Exploring the period 1875 – 1945

24

The Journal of Decorative and Propaganda Arts

Publisher and Wolfsonian–FIU Director
Cathy Leff

Guest Editor
Joel M. Hoffman

Senior Editor
Leslie Sternlieb

Editorial Assistant
Jacqueline Crucet

Art Director
Peter Roman
PrimalLabs

Defining the Wolfsonian Collection through Objects, Presentations, and Perceptions
Joel M. Hoffman
8

Stalin as Isis and Ra: Socialist Realism and the Art of Design
John E. Bowlt
34

Modernity and Tradition in Hungarian Furniture, 1900–1938: Three Generations
Juliet Kinchin
64

W. A. S. Benson, Machinery, and the Arts and Crafts Movement in Britain
Alan Crawford
94

Feast of Dutch Diversity: Nieuwe Kunst Book Design
Alston W. Purvis
118

Mobilizing the Nation: Italian Propaganda in the Great War
Thomas Row
140

The Tripoli Trade Fair and the Representation of Italy's African Colonies
Brian L. McLaren
170

From World War I to the Popular Front: The Art and Activism of Hugo Gellert
James Wechsler
198

Looking at Labor: Images of Work in 1930s American Art
Erika Doss
230

"Painting Section" in Black and White: Ethel Magafan's *Cotton Pickers*
Susan Valdés-Dapena
258

Cathy Leff

Introduction

With this issue, The Wolfsonian–Florida International University (FIU) celebrates the integration of *The Journal of Decorative and Propaganda Arts* into its publishing program. We could think of no better way to initiate this relationship than by dedicating the first volume published under the auspices of FIU to scholarship conducted on The Wolfsonian's collection.

Although the authors included in this volume came to The Wolfsonian in diverse capacities, the majority embarked upon their research through the museum's fellowship program. Established in 1993 to encourage a multidisciplinary approach to research in the material culture of the late nineteenth to mid-twentieth centuries, The Wolfsonian's fellowship program has hosted an array of scholars from North and South America, Europe, and Australia and has supported a variety of projects examining the aesthetics, production, use, and cultural significance of decorative arts, design, and architecture.

This program exemplifies The Wolfsonian's and the university's commitment to advancing international scholarship in the fields of visual and material culture; the current volume gathers just a sampling of the research that has been conducted to date. It was difficult to select so few contributors from among the dozens who have entered The Wolfsonian's intellectual milieu, but additional compilations will undoubtedly follow.

Guest Editor Joel Hoffman, The Wolfsonian's former associate director for programs and administration, opens this volume with an interpretive framework for defining and approaching the museum's extraordinary holdings, amassed by its founder Mitchell Wolfson Jr. and donated to FIU in 1997. Analyzing both quantitative and qualitative constructions of the collection in press coverage, independent research, exhibitions, publications, and programs, he points to the difficulty of objective classification and the rich opportunities for future investigation.

Four articles then explore diverse aspects of design in modern Europe from equally diverse perspectives. While some consider broad cultural phenomena and others focus on individual artists, all examine the nexus between design and its context.

Soviet Socialist Realism under Joseph Stalin—especially that in the decorative or applied arts—is the focus of John Bowlt's essay. In an effort to move beyond the negative stigma of this style, Bowlt provocatively compares "Stalin culture" with the ostensibly remote regimes of ancient Egypt, Louis XIV, and Peter the Great. In the process he identifies the primary strategies of the Socialist Realists, including their reliance on images of sunshine and optimism to counteract the often harsh realities of life in the Soviet Union during the 1930s and 1940s.

Juliet Kinchin explores Hungarian design in the first third of the twentieth century, stressing that the nation's evolving political climate and identity fostered dramatic aesthetic change. She sheds light on this process through the successive stories of three eminent designers—Pál Horti, Lajos Kozma, and Ernö Goldfinger—in telling case studies of the deceptively simple furniture they designed—a long-case clock, a cabinet, and a sideboard.

British Arts and Crafts movement metalworker, furniture designer, and architect W. A. S. Benson is the subject of Alan Crawford's contribution. Analyzing biographical information, Crawford offers insight into the life and work of Benson and demonstrates that his use of machinery represented a complexity within—rather than a contradiction of—the Arts and Crafts movement.

Alston Purvis provides a valuable introduction to Dutch Nieuwe Kunst (Art Nouveau) bookbindings in The Wolfsonian's collection, roughly spanning the period from 1890 to 1920. This article surveys the work of numerous designers and considers the impact of Dutch enchantment with Javanese design, including batik. A special emphasis is placed on Nieuwe Kunst bindings commissioned by the publisher Lambertus Jacobus Veen for the literature of Holland's best-known nineteenth-century author, Louis Couperus.

The next two essays look specifically at Italian material culture. Thomas Row offers a compelling introduction to the development of Italian propaganda during World War I. Explaining that propagandistic images took on increasing importance as Italy's losses escalated, Row presents the sources, the media, and the targets of that nation's propaganda and carefully analyzes the iconographic implications of propaganda paintings, posters, and postcards.

Considering a slightly later chapter in early twentieth-century Italy is Brian McLaren, who examines the Tripoli Trade Fair, an annual display of Italian and colonial goods held between 1927 and 1939. Arguably the most important of Italy's colonial exhibitions, the Libyan event was intended to enhance economic ties between the European nation and North Africa, while communicating the Italian colonial project to a wider audience. McLaren shows how the fair evolved in concert with the political objectives of Fascism in Italy.

The final three essays provide insight into American art of the 1920s and 1930s. James Wechsler follows the career of Hungarian-born artist Hugo Gellert, whose work was inextricably linked to his support of the communist ideal in the United States. Not only did Gellert produce a vital, socially engaged body of work, he also occupied a crucial position in the important artists' organizations that proliferated during the Great Depression.

Erika Doss, also looking at the relationship between art and politics, considers how and why labor was visualized by American artists during the 1930s, the decade of the depression. She argues that the frequent representation of working-class men as eroticized and objectified subjects stems from longstanding and largely unresolved tensions regarding class, masculinity, and American identity that especially flourished during this time.

The representation of African Americans in New Deal mural art is the focus of Susan Valdés-Dapena's study — the last in this volume. She considers the career of young American artist Ethel Magafan and, specifically, her post office mural *Cotton Pickers*, examining closely the highly mediated sphere of commissions by the Treasury Department's Section of the Fine Arts.

This volume is the result of the labor, commitment, and collaboration of many individuals and organizations, both inside and outside of the museum.

Guest Editor Joel Hoffman was responsible for shaping the content of this volume. His intellectual contribution was pivotal to this project. As former associate director of the museum, he helped develop and nurture our fellowship program. I am confident that the insights provided in his essay on the nature of the collection as well as into the mind of the collector, museum founder Mitchell Wolfson Jr., will stimulate further research.

Leslie Sternlieb, senior editor, played an incomparable role in the process, working with the guest editor, the contributors, and the graphic designer. She also deserves heartfelt thanks for casting such a careful eye over the publication. I am also extremely appreciative of the conscientious coordination and attention to detail provided by Editorial Assistant Jacqueline Crucet.

I am grateful for the indispensable efforts of all of the contributors, whose inquiry and interest are vital in our ongoing quest to document, interpret, and disseminate The Wolfsonian's extraordinary collection. In residence at the museum and as emissaries beyond, these scholars hold an essential place in our institutional and intellectual advancement.

I wish to express appreciation to my colleagues at The Wolfsonian–FIU, who assisted with various phases of this project not the least of which is providing the ongoing interpretation, care, and access to the collection. I especially thank Marianne Lamonaca, assistant director of exhibitions and curatorial affairs, who not only answered numerous questions about the collection that arose during the editing process, but who also, with Francis X. Luca, associate librarian; Nicholas Blaga, assistant librarian; Jonathan Mogul, fellowship coordinator; and Kimberly J. Bergen, registrar, played a leading role in working with Wolfsonian fellows. Kudos also go to Silvia Ros, Wolfsonian photographer, for providing the needed images; Birgit Scaglione, research assistant; Claudia Mendoza and Amy Silverman, registration assistants; Joanne Leese, curatorial assistant; Angelika Tompas, administrative assistant; Mary Knapp, proofreader; and Maria Gonzalez, former editorial assistant.

Peter Roman of PrimalLabs, art director of this issue, delivered a beautifully designed volume and displayed an acute sensitivity to the intricacies required by this publication. His talent is only matched by his dedication.

Publication of this volume would not have been possible without the support and sponsorship of The Cowles Charitable Trust and the publication program of the J. M. Kaplan Fund, Inc. I wish to express my appreciation to Wolfsonian board member Charles Cowles for his fervent commitment to *The Journal*.

I want to thank Roger Conover and The M.I.T. Press for their recent association with The Wolfsonian–FIU. Distribution of *The Journal* by this very distinguished press acknowledges the international relevance and reputation of this publication and enables us to reach audiences as broad and diverse as our collections.

Our readers—scholars, collectors, designers, architects, and material-culture enthusiasts—and the FIU community deserve thanks for their ongoing support, without which continuation of *The Journal* would not be possible.

And finally, thanks to Mitchell Wolfson Jr. for assembling such an extraordinary collection that will continue to provide a powerful lens through which to view and understand the momentous history of the modern world.

Through this volume, we hope to provide a mere glimpse into our holdings and the possibilities they hold for future examination and exploration. ✧

Joel M. Hoffman

Defining the Wolfsonian Collection through Objects, Presentations, and Perceptions

Joel Hoffman is vice-director for education and program development at the Brooklyn Museum of Art. He formerly served as associate director for programs and administration at The Wolfsonian–Florida International University, where he oversaw the institution's research fellowship program and other educational activities. Hoffman holds a Ph.D. in art history from Yale University.

When my former colleagues and I began planning this issue of *The Journal of Decorative and Propaganda Arts,* the first dedicated to research emanating from The Wolfsonian, we deliberated the merits of an essay describing the institution's collection. The other essays in this volume could, of course, address only a small sampling of objects, themes, and methodologies. And, as it turned out, the contributions gleaned from individuals who had conducted research on the collection were very much skewed toward material culture of the 1930s, particularly in Italy and America. We thus wondered whether this volume could accurately communicate The Wolfsonian's enormous potential for supporting research without an overview of its extraordinary resources. We agreed that it would be difficult, and perhaps uninteresting, to describe the collection. Was it even important? I believed that an openly interpretive or subjective description would be valuable, and have sought to analyze some of the various definitions of The Wolfsonian's holdings as constructed in press coverage, in outside research, and in exhibitions, publications, and programs of the museum. This essay is in no way intended as a definitive account of the collection. I have simply selected themes of personal interest in an attempt to clarify something that eludes objective classification.

It is appropriate to acknowledge my deep connection to the subject at hand, having served as an employee first of The Wolfsonian and then of The Wolfsonian–Florida International University, when Mitchell Wolfson Jr. (b. 1939) donated his collection and the building that houses it to the State of Florida. I oversaw public and academic programs and enjoyed the opportunity of working with a rich collection and the institution it fostered. On the one hand, I am extremely close to the material and am

Detail of Renato Bertelli's *Profilo continuo del Duce* (Continuous Profile of Mussolini), 1933.

fig. 1
(right)
*Looking Back at the
"World of Tomorrow":
Programs on the 1939
New York World's Fair,*
promotional brochure for
The Wolfsonian–Florida
International University,
October 1998. Designed
by Jacques Auger Design
Associates, Inc.

fig. 2
(far right)
Program calendar for
The Wolfsonian–Florida
International University,
January–April 2000.
Designed by Jacques Auger
Design Associates, Inc.

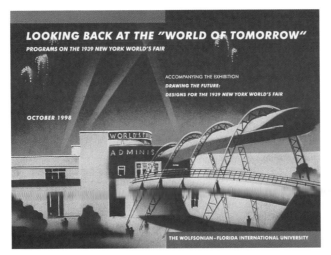

among the individuals who have been responsible for its interpretation to
the general public. While exhibitions have been documented in catalogues,
the history of educational programming is recorded in the museum's
promotional materials (figs. 1 and 2). On the other hand, I am struck by
the extent to which my job did not involve direct contact with objects,
but revolved more around the concepts of their presentation and relevance
in an institutional setting. Although I have set out to analyze the collection
critically, my views are biased by fondness for the subject and my former
colleagues who created a valued base of scholarship — and by my admiration
for Mitchell Wolfson Jr. I am, as a 1992 *Miami Herald* article described
Wolfsonian staff, among the "many who owe Wolfson parts of their careers." [1]

To paraphrase the museum's original mission statement, The Wolfsonian
was formed in 1986 to oversee the collection, preservation, research, and
interpretation of material culture of the late nineteenth to mid-twentieth
centuries. Although the museum has acquired objects from various sources,
particular emphasis has, understandably, been placed on the Mitchell
Wolfson Jr. Collection, given its status as the basis and bulk of the whole.
Until 1996, The Wolfsonian included Wolfson's holdings in Genoa, which
consist of approximately eight thousand items from Italy and elsewhere
in Europe. Although that office is no longer officially connected with the
Miami Beach museum, the two maintain an intellectual and spiritual link.
Some of the studies in this volume take advantage of both collections,
providing a model for ongoing collaboration. [2]

With regard to quantity, volume, and value, those items donated by
Mitchell Wolfson Jr. easily constitute virtually all of The Wolfsonian's
collection at this time. John Barry, a *Miami Herald* reporter who

1. John Barry, "The Collector," *Miami Herald*, 20 December 1992, 1J.

2. At present the Genoa collection is on long-term loan to the Fondazione Regionale
   Cristoforo Colombo.

fig. 3
(below, right)
Interior of the Miami
Beach Woman's Club,
designed by Russell
Pancoast, 1933.
Photograph by Thomas
Delbeck, 2000. Donated
to The Wolfsonian in 1995.

fig. 4
(below, far right)
Attributed to W. H. Knapp,
Exhibit Builders, Inc.,
sketches for various
displays, mat board,
graphite, color crayon,
paper, 61 x 48 cm, c. 1962.
The Wolfsonian–Florida
International University,
Miami Beach, Florida.
Gift of Exhibit Builders, Inc.

published a series of articles on The Wolfsonian in 1992, described the collection's genesis:

> As he travels, Wolfson collects, a hobby that began during boyhood trips with his parents, when he started what is said to be the largest key ring in the world, bearing more than 5,000 keys to hotel rooms and ocean-liner cabins.[3]

As an adult, Barry explained, Wolfson "traveled across Europe on personal scavenger hunts for old books, furniture, machines, figurines, glassware, even pieces of buildings."[4] According to Barry, "some experts say the collection owes its specialness, its extraordinariness, to the fact that it *was* amassed by a single person," while others consider that characteristic to be "limiting."[5] Though Micky Wolfson once purchased whatever he pleased, his proposed gifts are now subject to staff review. This ensures the "appropriateness" and "necessity" of collection additions, but the review process necessarily "constrains" the founder's vision. We will see below that Wolfson's identity, whether by its inclusion or exclusion, is central to that of the collection.

Over the years, a number of important items and collections have been donated to The Wolfsonian by others, particularly now that the institution is in the public trust. Gifts have included the Miami Beach Woman's Club facility (fig. 3); the rich archive of the prominent designers Florida National Exhibits/Exhibit Builders Inc. (fig. 4); and drawings, prints, and paintings by the American Ashcan-era artist Alexander Z. Kruse (1888–1972).

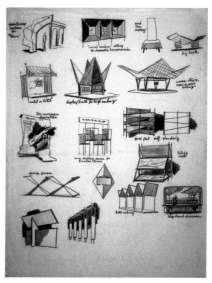

3. John Barry, "Invincible Man: The Myth and the Museum," *Miami Herald*, 20 September 1992, 4J. Micky Wolfson maintains that his collection is actually the second largest.
4. Barry, "The Collector."
5. Barry, "Invincible Man," 4–5J.

Donations from individuals other than Wolfson serve to legitimate the museum's status as a public entity and allow The Wolfsonian to diversify its holdings. On the contrary, objects are sometimes offered and generally accepted only if they complement existing collections, thereby perpetuating already-dominant themes. As Exhibit Builders, Inc. had played a pivotal role in creating Florida's world's fair exhibits, for example, their donation strengthened The Wolfsonian's focus in this area,[6] Likewise, after accepting a portion of the Alexander Kruse collection, The Huntington in San Marino, California, facilitated the offer of the artist's overtly political works to The Wolfsonian, based on the latter museum's related holdings. The Kruse donation included a drawing of Kaiser Wilhelm as a mature kangaroo, with Adolph Hitler as the joey in his pouch (fig. 5). For our colleagues at The Huntington, this work seemed patently "Wolfsonian."

fig. 5
Alexander Z. Kruse, *Two Generations*, tempera on paper board, 114 x 88 cm framed, 1936. The Wolfsonian–Florida International University, Miami Beach, Florida. Gift of Mrs. Kathreen Kruse in memory of Martin Alexander Kruse.

Although this essay does not focus on objective description of the collection, I do feel compelled to provide some empirical data at the outset. Chronological and geographical parameters are probably most essential to understanding the collection's identity in the broad sense, for the vast majority of artifacts date to the period 1885 to 1945 and hail from North America and Europe. The nations most comprehensively represented are the United States, Great Britain, Germany, Italy, the Netherlands, and Russia/the former Soviet Union. Objects include furniture, industrial design and decorative arts, rare books, periodicals, ephemera, works on paper, paintings, textiles, and medals.

To explain the sixty-year framework for the collection, The Wolfsonian's 1995 exhibition catalogue, *Designing Modernity,* defined 1885 as "the age of New Imperialism, the peak of Europe's political and economic hegemony over the rest of the world." The collection's theoretical end date of 1945 is clearly linked to the conclusion of World War II.[7] William Booth, writing for the *Washington Post,* opined that The Wolfsonian's period "tracks the tremendous transformation of the world from the agrarian to the industrial… the rise of mass communication…, mass transportation…and mass movements, such as fascism and communism."[8] Just a few years ago, Wolfsonian director Cathy Leff characterized the collection as particularly well suited to the community in which it resides, stating: "This collection

6. See the author's research on Exhibit Builders, Inc., in "From Augustine to Tangerine: Florida at the U.S. World's Fairs," *The Journal of Decorative and Propaganda Arts* 23 (1998): 58–82.

7. Peggy Loar, "Preface," in *Designing Modernity: The Arts of Reform and Persuasion, 1885–1945,* ed. Wendy Kaplan (New York: Thames and Hudson, 1995), 8.

8. William Booth, "A Museum Takes Shape, Buy and Buy," *Washington Post,* 12 November 1995.

fig. 6
Installation view of the
exhibition *Print, Power,*
and Persuasion: Graphic
Design in Germany,
1890–1945, **The**
Wolfsonian–Florida
International University,
Miami Beach, 2000.
Photograph by Thomas
Delbeck, 2000. The image
on the far right depicts an
anti-Hitler poster produced
at the conclusion of
World War II.

couldn't be a better fit for Miami-Dade County. We're a 20th century city and everything in the collection is about the themes that drove the 20th century…"[9] Comfortably ensconced in the twenty-first century, we must now consider the implications of working with a collection that dates to an earlier century in the previous millennium: what was once the recent past now seems significantly more distant. In addition, one might argue that the end date of 1945 is arbitrary, artificial, and sometimes frustrating. Note, for example, that most every Wolfsonian narrative on German culture inevitably culminates in the catastrophic Third Reich, providing little evidence of that nation's postwar evolution—including the 2000 exhibition *Print, Power, and Persuasion* (fig. 6). Various stakeholders have likewise questioned the institution's chronological and geographical focus, envisioning a broader collection with potentially even greater interest to a local community that is focused more on contemporary culture and Latin America than on a Eurocentric past. Moreover, as Wolfsonian staff contemplate the museum's future, they are faced with the challenge of determining whether the collection will drive the institution or vice versa. In other words, will The Wolfsonian continue to derive its identity primarily from the collection of a single individual or will the institutional mission broaden the objects and issues addressed?

As early as 1992, founding director Peggy Loar observed, "There isn't any reason why this concept couldn't go into the 1950s or 1960s."[10]

9. "Cathy Leff Pilots Activities at FIU's Wolfsonian Museum," *Miami Today*, 15 April 1999, 5.

10. Barry, "Invincible Man," 5J.

fig. 7
(right)
James Lamb, cabinet, ebonized mahogany, calamander, amboyna veneer, ivory, boxwood, brass, glass, leather, and gilt, 102 x 170 x 40 cm, c. 1875. The Mitchell Wolfson Jr. Collection, The Wolfsonian–Florida International University, Miami Beach, Florida.

fig. 8
(above, far right)
Radio lamp model no. 1260, Mitchell Manufacturing Co., Ltd., phenolic resin base and white glass, 1950. The Mitchell Wolfson Jr. Collection, The Wolfsonian–Florida International University, Miami Beach, Florida.

fig. 9
(below)
Artist unknown, *Orientals Using Obsolete Modes of Transport*, poster, 31 x 53 cm, n.d. The Mitchell Wolfson Jr. Collection, The Wolfsonian–Florida International University, Miami Beach, Florida.

Micky Wolfson, too, has considered this possibility. According to *Miami New Times* writer Judy Cantor, at the press preview of the museum's inaugural exhibition, Wolfson "announced that perhaps he should have extended the scope of his collection beyond 1945 to encompass the Cold War period, ending with the fall of the Berlin Wall in 1989."[11] The prospects for collecting, or at least exhibiting, materials of the Cold War, the information age, and more specifically the Cuban revolution and the body-oriented design culture of south Miami Beach are appealing to some, including me. But the prevailing logic holds that limited funding, staff, and space render broad expansion of the collection impractical, and even irresponsible, at this point. And as virtual museums, online collections, and global consortia redefine the field, the wisdom or necessity of developing the collection in an entirely new area is certainly questionable.

A number of objects already do fall outside of the often-repeated parameters of date and national origin. The Wolfsonian's world's fair holdings, for example, begin with the Great Exhibition of 1851 at London's Crystal

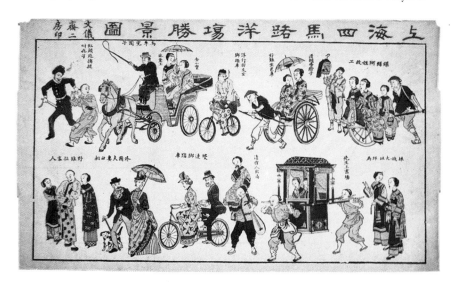

11. Judy Cantor, "Thoroughly Modern Micky," *Miami New Times*, 23–29 November 1995, 59.

fig. 10
(above)
Keshawa Dewadi,
*Mahatma Gandhi Leading
the Oppressed People
of the World to Salvation,*
**gouache on paper,
33 x 48 cm, 1943.
The Mitchell Wolfson Jr.
Collection, The
Wolfsonian–Florida
International University,
Miami Beach, Florida.**

fig. 11
(below)
**Sample architectural
ornament from
Ahmedabad, India, late
nineteenth to early
twentieth century.
The Mitchell Wolfson Jr.
Collection, The
Wolfsonian–Florida
International University,
Miami Beach, Florida.**

Palace. Many other pieces push the parameters more subtly, such as the 1870s cabinet by James Lamb (fig. 7) and the 1950 radio lamp by Mitchell Manufacturing Co. of Canada (fig. 8). There also are objects from Asia, Australia, and South America. Some works represent relatively isolated "exceptions to the rule," including an undated Chinese poster showing obsolete modes of transport (fig. 9) and a brilliantly colored Indian gouache, *Mahatma Gandhi Leading the Oppressed People of the World to Salvation* (fig. 10). Others form part of more substantial collections, such as the assemblage of late nineteenth- to early twentieth-century sample architectural ornaments from Ahmedabad, India (fig. 11); diverse materials commemorating the opening of Australia's Sydney Harbour Bridge in 1932 (fig. 12); or the many Peruvian medals on the inauguration of train lines in that nation.

Within the generally agreed-upon boundaries of time and place, several

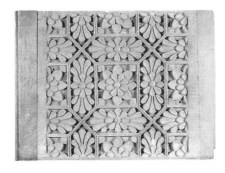

thematic or canon-related strengths may be identified. The Wolfsonian holds a large collection of objects associated with the Aesthetic and Arts and Crafts movements in Britain. It also possesses noteworthy holdings of Nieuwe Kunst and Stile Floreale, the manifestations of Art Nouveau in the Netherlands and

fig. 12
Sydney Harbour Bridge,
photograph by Deane and
Small Ltd., 20 x 25 cm,
c. 1932. The Mitchell
Wolfson Jr. Collection,
The Wolfsonian–Florida
International University,
Miami Beach, Florida.

Italy, respectively. German design reform associated with groups such as the Darmstadt Art Colony and the Werkbund also are well represented. From the United States, industrial design objects and materials produced under the New Deal emerge as significant nodes of interest. Dominant themes include urbanism and architecture, transportation and travel, advertising and political propaganda, labor, and world's fairs and exposi- tions. According to the *Miami Herald's* John Dorschner:

> What the Wolfsonian has is…well, the stuff Micky bought. He liked Italian and German and Dutch and English, not so much French or Spanish. He dislikes abstract and surreal art, so there are no recognitions of Picasso or Dalí. He doesn't like stark modernism, so he avoided the Bauhaus material.[12]

However, in defining the collection by the themes, movements, and nations most strongly represented, one runs the risk of perpetuating a narrow understanding of The Wolfsonian's holdings. Because exhibitions, programs, and publications have featured select collection highlights, they have engendered more research on these familiar areas rather than on those that are less well known.

Although it is difficult (and perhaps not that useful) to do, one can attempt to quantify the collection, for size seems to matter, either because it's genuinely important or just because it's a cultural obsession. In the past, those commenting on the collection's quantitative aspects sometimes

12. John Dorschner, "What Hath Micky Bought?," *Tropic, Miami Herald,* 29 October 1995, cover, 6.

referenced its staggering rate of growth—its velocity—rather than its size. Peggy Loar, for example, said of Wolfson in 1992: "He's just unable to resist wonderful things. That is both delicious and a problem—our acquisition rate on a monthly basis, including rare books, is close to 300 objects."[13] Most would agree that The Wolfsonian's collection as a whole is large relative to the number of items the institution can exhibit, publish, or even share with scholars in the next several decades. From an administrative perspective, Wolfsonian director Cathy Leff recently stated: "The collection is vast. While we have it all catalogued, its interpretation and documentation really requires work by the scholarly community."[14]

Compared to the collections of other internationally known museums, The Wolfsonian's is arguably modest. For more than a decade, Wolfsonian-generated literature had described the collection as having seventy thousand items. Recently the museum has increased that number to seventy-eight thousand, comprising twenty-eight thousand objects and fifty thousand books, periodicals, pieces of ephemera, and archival works. This data is based, partly, on accession numbers assigned by the museum, but some single records represent myriad objects, such as the collection of approximately eight thousand matchbook covers gathered by King Farouk of Egypt beginning in the 1940s (fig. 13) or the approximately thirty volumes of Wiener Werkstätte textiles, containing thousands of swatches. One may contend that size is moot, as only those objects of interest to a given individual at a given time actually count, unless that person is a collections manager or an insurance underwriter. And how does a massive sideboard compare with a matchbook in this ambiguously quantified inventory? In terms of physical storage, movement, display, and monetary

13. "Peggy Loar Readies Wolfson Collection for Public View…," *Miami Today*, 31 December 1992.
14. "Cathy Leff Pilots Activities at FIU's Wolfsonian Museum," 4.

fig. 14
(opposite page, above)
Installation view of
Uncommon Clay at
Miami-Dade Community
College, 1985. The
Mitchell Wolfson Jr.
Collection of Decorative
and Propaganda Arts.
In the foreground lies the
glazed terra cotta window
grille from the Norris
Theatre, Norristown,
Pennsylvania, now part of
The Wolfsonian's lobby.

fig. 15
(opposite page, below)
Installation view of
Light Opera at
Miami-Dade Community
College, 1987. The
Mitchell Wolfson Jr.
Collection of Decorative
and Propaganda Arts.

fig. 16
(above)
Installation view of the
Agostino Lauro room
in *Stile Floreale* at
Miami-Dade Community
College, 1988. The
Wolfsonian Foundation.

value, the two are, in most cases, worlds apart. In terms of their potential research interest and the number of bytes they consume in a computerized collections management system, the two are more or less equal.

In the realm of interpretive definition, Wolfsonian programs, promotional materials, and institutional statements—and media reactions to them—have played a critical role in shaping public perceptions in Miami and beyond. Mitchell Wolfson Jr.'s collection was first shown at the downtown Miami campus of Miami-Dade Community College prior to the formation of the museum. Catalogues from the nine exhibitions held at this location provide illustrations of and access to what were then his personal holdings. Among the exhibitions mounted at the college were *Modern Glass, Public Works, Uncommon Clay, Style of Empire, Light Opera,* and *The Great World's Fairs and Expositions* (figs. 14 and 15). All of these were curated by Stephen Neil Greengard (1952–1997). The final exhibition of the Wolfson collection at the college was *Stile Floreale* (fig. 16), organized by The Wolfsonian and curated by Gabriel Weisberg, a professor of art history at the University of Minnesota. The catalogues from these exhibitions demonstrate that the presentation of Micky Wolfson's collection at Miami-Dade Community College followed a variety of methodological models. According to author John Malcolm Brinnin, objects in at least the first of these exhibitions, *America's Futurist Vision,* were "certified by no philosophy but that of the man who chose them."[15] In retrospect, The Wolfsonian's then-director Peggy Loar deemed the potential at the college limiting. She felt that "without the ability and funding to develop serious educational components, the collection seemed esoteric, irrelevant and distant to the students."[16]

With the launch of The Wolfsonian as an independent entity on Miami Beach, the collection was often described by its proponents—Micky Wolfson and the Wolfsonian staff—as one formed and understood by methodology rather than content. This methodology has consistently revolved around the nexus between material objects and society. The Wolfsonian's original mission statement, for example, proclaimed the museum's focus on the meaning of objects as agents and expressions of the cultural, political, and technological changes that have transformed

15. John Malcolm Brinnin, "Mitchell Wolfson Jr.: The Man and His Mission," *The Journal of Decorative and Propaganda Arts* 10 (Fall 1988): 80–82.
16. "Peggy Loar Readies Wolfson Collection for Public View."

fig. 17
Installation view of
The Arts of Reform and
Persuasion, 1885–1945,
The Wolfsonian,
Miami Beach, Florida,
1995. Photograph
by Steven Brooke.

the world. A brochure advised prospective members that "the Wolfsonian's goal is to educate all audiences about the ways design has served as a reflection of societal values and as an active force in the shaping of human experience."[17] And the broadside describing Wolfsonian fellowship opportunities, which I reissued several times, encouraged "projects that examine the aesthetics, production, use, and cultural significance" of objects, "supporting a multidisciplinary approach to research and publication."[18] The authors whose essays follow demonstrate these principles, variously combining the visual analysis of objects and what historian Dennis Doordan calls their "design strategies," with exploration of biography, human behavior, and broader historical phenomena.[19] Those who do not adhere to this "flexible dogma" generally have limited interest in The Wolfsonian, preferring instead to study collections more likely to support more traditional art historical inquiry.

Micky Wolfson himself defined the collection as rich in ideas rather than artistic masterpieces. According to John Barry, Wolfson explained, "I was bored awfully soon with contemporary art," continuing, "and I couldn't afford the old masters in paintings. I wasn't interested in art for art's sake, but as it reflects man's aspirations." In a later article, Barry appropriated

17. "A Special Invitation," Wolfsonian membership brochure, c. 1995.
18. "The Wolfsonian Research Center," Wolfsonian brochure, c. 1994.
19. Dennis Doordan described various design strategies in a Wolfsonian-sponsored workshop for faculty at Florida International University, 2 March 2000.

Wolfson's interpretation of the collection as his own, stating, "It breaks the rules of museum collecting and sets a new standard of value for artifacts: The beauty of objects is irrelevant; their value lies in what they say about us."[20] Unconvinced of this anti-aesthetic position on the eve of the museum's official inauguration, Miami-based critic Beth Dunlop (guest editor of the Florida Theme Issue of *The Journal of Decorative and Propaganda Arts*) recast Wolfson and his collection in a slightly more conventional fashion for readers of *Elle Décor*:

> Initially, Wolfson says, he accumulated "objects reflecting a historic political context," which even included Nazi and Fascist propaganda. At that time he did not think of himself as a patron of the arts... "I was mad for history," he says. "I was not interested in aesthetics at all." But the aesthetics—and a sense of purpose—followed...[21]

Clearly, Dunlop was on the mark, for a great many of the objects would be deemed beautiful—classically so or otherwise—as well as meaningful.

Despite the apparent consonance between collector and collection, Micky Wolfson was distinctly absent from interpretation surrounding *The Arts of Reform and Persuasion, 1885–1945*, the museum's first major exhibition in its renovated Miami Beach facility, which fully opened in November 1995. Of this exhibition curated by Wendy Kaplan—former Wolfsonian staff member and current chief curator of decorative arts at the Los Angeles County Museum of Art—*Herald* journalist Barry wrote:

> This is the first time Wolfson will be answerable for his acquisitions to anyone but himself, the first time he will allow others to oversee a treasure that so intimately reflects his personal vision.[22]

The Arts of Reform and Persuasion legitimated Wolfson's holdings by placing them in a coherent and compelling historical narrative. This distanced the collection from its roots as a personal treasure trove—or what Wolfson once called "a self-portrait."[23]

The seamless narrative was divided into three sections, all examining "design at the height of the industrial age in the context of social, techno-logical, and aesthetic issues."[24] The first, "Confronting Modernity," focused on the period between 1885 and World War I, and analyzed various design and reform movements that grappled with modernity, some embracing it, others resisting it. Among the topics addressed were the Arts and Crafts movement, Romantic Nationalism, Art Nouveau, and the German Werkbund (fig. 17). The second section, "Celebrating

20. Barry, "Invincible Man," 1J.

21. Beth Dunlop, "One Man's Passion," *Elle Décor* (October 1995): 112.

22. Barry, "Invincible Man," 4J.

23. Brinnin, "Mitchell Wolfson Jr.," 82.

24. *The Arts of Reform and Persuasion, 1885–1945*, exhibition brochure, November 1995.

fig. 18
(right)
Installation view of
The Arts of Reform and Persuasion, 1885–1945,
The Wolfsonian, Miami Beach, 1995. Photograph by Steven Brooke.

fig. 19
(below)
Cover of *Designing Modernity: The Arts of Reform and Persuasion, 1885–1945* (New York: Thames and Hudson, 1995).

Modernity," examined the promotion of industrial progress in the 1920s and 1930s through advertisements, utilitarian objects, and other works (fig. 18). The final section, "Manipulating Modernity: Political Persuasion," explored the arts of propaganda from World War I through the end of World War II, notably in New Deal America, Nazi Germany, Fascist Italy, and the Soviet Union.

The exhibition consisted almost exclusively of objects culled from Mitchell Wolfson Jr.'s holdings. The text panels and accompanying brochure, however, did not mention the fact that *The Arts of Reform and Persuasion* was not simply an overview of the period but rather the layering of an interpretive framework over a collection that reflected one man's vision and predilections. Although the relationship between aesthetics and politics was explored throughout the exhibition, the narrative flow—culminating in propaganda items—subtly suggested a shift in emphasis from the former to the latter over the period 1885 to 1945. To some extent this shift reflected the collection's strengths, while creating a meaningful and comprehensible experience for visitors unfamiliar with either Wolfsonian objects or methodologies. The narrative exclusion of Mitchell Wolfson Jr.

was, no doubt, predicated on the museum's desire to provide an opportunity for addressing the broad intellectual implications of his collection. But as The Wolfsonian strove for recognition as a public institution, this exclusion also reflected concern about the fact that its collection was then privately owned by Wolfson. *The Arts of Reform and Persuasion* and its award-winning catalogue (fig. 19) provided not only the general

fig. 20
(above)
Installation view of *Art and Design in the Modern Age: Selections from the Wolfsonian Collection,* opened 1996. Photograph by Thomas Delbeck, 1997.

fig. 21
(above, far right)
Installation view of *Art and Design in the Modern Age: Selections from the Wolfsonian Collection,* opened 1996, showing a gallery dedicated to world's fairs and international expositions. Photograph by Thomas Delbeck, 1997.

fig. 22
(below, right)
Renato Bertelli, *Profilo continuo del Duce* (Continuous Profile of Mussolini), bronzed terracotta, 1933. The Mitchell Wolfson Jr. Collection, The Wolfsonian–Florida International University, Miami Beach, Florida.

fig. 23
(far right)
Walter Dorwin Teague, *Nocturne,* radio, model no. 1186, glass, metal, wood, c. 1936. The Mitchell Wolfson Jr. Collection, The Wolfsonian–Florida International University, Miami Beach, Florida.

public—in South Florida and at the various venues to which it traveled—but also staff and prospective researchers, a potent template for understanding the collection.

The Wolfsonian's evolving permanent exhibition, *Art and Design in the Modern Age: Selections from the Wolfsonian Collection,* offers interesting parallels and contrasts. Curated by Marianne Lamonaca and designed by Richard Miltner—now, respectively, The Wolfsonian's assistant director for exhibitions and curatorial affairs and its exhibition designer—the installation opened in 1996 and is periodically updated. *Art and Design in the Modern Age* is organized into fourteen thematic galleries, addressing such familiar topics as technology, transportation, labor, urbanism, colonialism, world's fairs, advertising, and political propaganda. By definition, this permanent exhibition unfolds as a well-organized sampling of collection objects rather than a seamless narrative (figs. 20 and 21). Similarly, its title, unlike that of the inaugural exhibition, does not define a broad historical thesis, but acknowledges that the exhibition is constrained by the collection from which it is drawn. Although *Art and Design in the Modern Age* is mounted in the galleries created for *The Arts of Reform and Persuasion,*

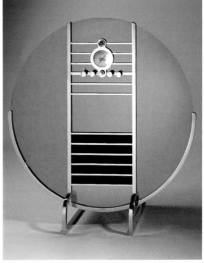

initially it included no objects from the inaugural exhibition, for these were touring the nation. In planning the permanent exhibition, it was not difficult to identify three hundred "new" objects, but it was clear that many of The Wolfsonian's most obvious "treasures" had already been showcased. Over the years, some visitors have nostalgically requested that selected objects from the inaugural exhibition be returned to public view, including Renato Bertelli's (1900–1974) *Continuous Profile of Mussolini* (fig. 22). Staff have begun to fulfill this desire by integrating into the permanent exhibition such favorites as Walter Dorwin Teague's (1883–1960) spectacular blue-hued *Nocturne* radio (fig. 23) and Irishman Harry Clarke's (1889–1931) eight-panel stained glass window created for the League of Nations (fig. 24). Much more common, however, is the public's request that curators make accessible The Wolfsonian's storage areas or that they display uninterpreted object assemblages as a means of better sharing the collection. This hunger for more objects is predicated on the perception that the collection is unfathomably large relative to the number of objects on view at any time — a condition not uncommon among collecting museums.

While it is essential to consider exhibitions when defining the collection, understanding the role of The Wolfsonian's founder, Mitchell Wolfson Jr., is central. A number of critics and historians have perpetuated the institution's perspective on the cultural meaning of objects while also decisively inserting Micky Wolfson into the mix. Such commentators, understandably, have attributed the character of the collection to its "chief acquisitor." Notable in this respect was Victor Margolin, whose review of *Designing Modernity* appeared in a special volume of the research periodical *Design Issues* dedicated to the museum and its period. Entitled "Micky Wolfson's Cabinet of Wonders: From Private Passion to Public Purpose," Margolin's essay commenced with an assessment of Wolfson's methodology for creating the collection. He described the three methods for amassing objects defined by museologist Susan Pearce: systematics, fetishism, and souvenir collecting. Margolin concluded that systematics, "an attempt to represent an ideology," was the model behind The Wolfsonian's collection, and the ideology he identified in the Miami Beach museum was that of using objects to tell the story of the cultures that produced them. He also acknowledged, however, that there was more to Micky Wolfson's collection than didactic intent, writing, "Beneath the pronouncements of his collection's cultural significance, there is a powerful desire to annex things that appeal to him for highly personal reasons." Margolin further remarked that Wolfson's accumulation of Nazi and Italian Fascist materials was intriguing, particularly "because he is Jewish." Whether, in fact, Wolfson actively identifies with or practices Judaism was not addressed by Margolin in his quest to contextualize the collection. Although he noted that other museums and libraries around the world have collected these often-shunned

materials, Margolin described Wolfson's perspective as unique in its combination of "a strong sense of aesthetic value with a keen awareness of an object's historical significance."[25]

Margolin was, by no means, alone in having commented on Micky Wolfson's interest in materials from Nazi Germany and Fascist Italy. These items have consistently captured the attention of both scholars and the general public and are important in understanding Wolfson and his collection. Not surprisingly, the German holdings have aroused more controversy than their Italian counterparts. For while it is one thing to acknowledge the awesome design sensibility of those endorsing dictatorship, it is another to do so for those enacting genocide. Following such works as Daniel Goldhagen's bestseller, *Hitler's Willing Executioners*—with its thesis of broad German complicity in the Holocaust—growing interest in the study of Nazi design is to be anticipated. Gregory Maertz of the English department at St. John's University in Jamaica, Queens, New York, has undertaken the most extensive analysis of this issue with regard to The Wolfsonian's collection. In his perceptive study, Maertz analyzed Wolfson's methods and motivations for amassing Nazi artifacts, providing information about the collection through its collector. Maertz conducted three interviews with Wolfson in 1998 and gathered these in a manuscript entitled "Museumizing Nazi Artifacts and Challenging Traditional Museum Culture: A Conversation with Mitchell Wolfson Jr."

Questioning the sanitizing exclusion of Nazi art from twentieth-century canons, Maertz observed that Wolfson sought to subvert the idealized fantasy of mainstream collectors and curators:

> In place of the established hierarchy of cultural artifacts, in which the fine arts enjoy the dominant position, The Wolfsonian validates the universality of all artisanship, including that of objects tainted by association with Nazism. In contrast to curators in Germany, where trafficking in Nazi artifacts remains illegal…Wolfson has consistently maintained that such objects are worthy of study and should be made accessible…[26]

Maertz also provided the most significant documentation to date of Micky Wolfson's view of the collection. What emerges is Wolfson's fascination with recent history and its vicissitudes, his desire—familiar to those who know him—to agitate others into seeing things differently, and his commitment to preserve the past through material culture. In these interviews, Wolfson also described the museum's methodology of contextualism as proprietary, stating in his customarily provocative manner:

25. Victor Margolin, "Micky Wolfson's Cabinet of Wonders: From Private Passion to Public Purpose," *Design Issues* 13 (Spring 1997): 67–69.

26. Gregory Maertz, "Museumizing Nazi Artifacts and Challenging Traditional Museum Culture: A Conversation with Mitchell Wolfson Jr.," manuscript, 1999.

The faith has been taken up by the believers and so the "religion," if you want, is established. And there are converts now, people who once didn't believe but who believe now, and as I go to museums all over the world I hear the liturgy, the language of our faith, that of "Wolfsonianism," and I see attempts being made to bring materials in line, methodologically and ideologically, with the context in which we operate.[27]

With regard to his interest in National Socialism and other manifestations of fascism, Wolfson compellingly argues that the recording of history is necessarily prejudiced, and that no written account has provided a satisfactory explanation of Hitler's rise to power. Artifacts, on the contrary, he feels, "don't lie," but rather hold the power to provide answers to this and other historical conundrums. Maertz, like Margolin, raised the issue of Wolfson's religious identity and its relationship to the collection. But his intense scrutiny revealed that Wolfson's sense of spirituality is not confined to a single religion but, like the collection, informed by an abiding intellectual relativism. Micky Wolfson's strongest statement to this effect comes toward the end of the Maertz interviews, when he more or less retracts the institution's methodological position on the collection and its formation, stating: "I'm not trying to influence or impose an interpretation on the viewer's encounter with the collection. I'm simply the agent of this encounter."[28]

Despite Wolfson's articulate demeanor, some journalists, writing from a more populist angle, have portrayed him as eccentric and have characterized the collection as his assemblage of oddities. From the institution's perspective, these critics have missed the point. Micky Wolfson comments instead, "I like the bad reviews even more than the good ones, especially when they personally attack me. A bad review stirs me up and gives me a challenge."[29] For me, the review most memorable in this regard was a November 1995 reference in the *New York Times Magazine*. In an article entitled "How They Spend It," Peter Passell assigned a noteworthy example of consumption to each letter of the alphabet. The letter "J" he reserved for "Junk," the term he used to characterize The Wolfsonian's collection. Attributing the collection to Wolfson's lavish expenditures, Passell referenced objects that are commonly invoked as signifiers of eccentricity: "the first Scotch tape dispenser, a Braille version of 'Mein Kampf,' and King Farouk's matchbook collection."[30]

An October 1995 article in the *Miami Herald's Tropic* magazine by John Dorschner was similarly biting in its appraisal of the collection. The cover featured an illustration of a charmingly amused "Millionaire Mitchell

27. Mitchell Wolfson Jr., interview with Gregory Maertz, 1998, in Maertz, "Museumizing Nazi Artifacts."

28. Ibid.

29. Ibid.

30. Peter Passell, "How They Spend It," *New York Times Magazine*, 19 November 1995.

fig. 25
**Pages from an article
by John Dorschner in
the *Miami Herald's Tropic*,
29 October 1995.
Photograph of Mitchell
Wolfson Jr. ©1995
Al Diaz / The Miami Herald.**

Wolfson Jr." in the museum's lobby, headlined: "Micky's Magic Kingdom…
Will the world beat a path to see the stuff that Micky bought?" At the
time, Wolfson probably led others to conclude that he had created
something that was more magical than museological. Once he had conjured
the institution, he contended, it was up to the public to support it—
or else it would vanish into thin air. Now you see it, now you don't.
Responding to Wolfson, Peggy Loar provocatively stated, "If the community
wants us, we're here. If not, we're all going away."[31] Inside, the article was
titled with another interrogative: "What Hath Micky Bought?" (fig. 25).
This question was interwoven with the statement:

> After a lifelong shopping spree, Mitchell Wolfson Jr. found himself
> loaded with Nazi beer mugs, King Farouk's matchbooks, an old museum
> turnstile, and two buildings full of other quirky stuff. Now he's hoping
> you'll pay to look at it in one of the world's most eccentric museums.[32]

Reminiscent of Wolfson's earlier reference to his holdings as self-portrait,
Dorschner interpreted the collection as a direct expression of Micky Wolfson, or what he considered Micky Wolfson to be, namely an "eccentric,
whimsical, opinionated socialite/art collector/museum creator/*bon
vivant*/international traveler."[33] A full-page photograph depicts Wolfson
peering through shelves that support his rich collection of Dutch books
with Nieuwe Kunst (Art Nouveau) bindings, visually associating the man
with his "mania."

31. Dorschner, "What Hath Micky Bought?," cover, 8.

32. Ibid., 6.

33. Ibid.

fig. 26
Detail of article by
Herbert Muschamp,
"Well-Made Surfaces
and the Conflicts
Lurking Beneath Them,"
New York Times,
3 December 1995. The
often-reproduced photo-
graph by Richard Sexton
shows Micky Wolfson
with an object used as an
automotive ornament in
conjunction with the 1939
New York World's Fair.
Copyright ©1995 by
the New York Times Co.
Reprinted by permission.

Several months later, local writer Andrew Delaplaine, in his own opinionated South Beach newspaper, *Wire,* humorously dismissed The Wolfsonian's collection and its pursuit of meaning in material culture as pseudo-intellectualism. He wrote:

> Even though to you and me an old toaster is still an old toaster, it is not an old toaster at the Museum that Mickey [*sic*] Built. No, my little cumquat, my precious ignoramus, my little bumblebee, it is an "artifact from the 1930s."[34]

While such comments were potentially deleterious to the museum's quest for public support, they were not entirely unexpected in a city without a history of museums and the veneration of artifacts they inspire. It is recurrently, and perhaps not surprisingly, The Wolfsonian's utilitarian materials—the matchbooks, propaganda posters, and toasters—that evoke the strongest commentary, confusion, and disdain, since the world's best-known art museums instead feature paintings and sculpture.

Odd it is, though, to find such comments from the likes of Dianne Pilgrim, then-director of the Cooper-Hewitt National Design Museum, an institution of kindred spirit with The Wolfsonian. Pilgrim commented on the collection's unusual focus, noting of Wolfson, "He has helped scholars and the American public to see things they've never seen before." But in the spirit of Dorschner and those troubled by eccentricity, Pilgrim continued,

"The collection is considered controversial, because the quality level runs A to Z… Art historians are a little horrified by the mix of things."[35] Old-school art historians— aesthetes and formalists—perhaps. If The Wolfsonian is a "house of horrors" for those interested only in canonical art history, it represents a resource of great intrigue for art historians with a broader intellectual scope and for scholars from disciplines less focused on highbrow aesthetics. As curator Wendy Kaplan cheerfully explained of "a bland, sentimental German portrait": "It is so fifth-rate—no art museum would display it… But for a piece of the period, to represent the Nazi image of women, it is perfect. You see, we're not just an art museum."[36]

34. Andrew Delaplaine, "Barbs," *Wire,* 1 August 1996.

35. Dorschner, "What Hath Micky Bought?," 8.

36. Ibid.

Sometimes The Wolfsonian's collection is considered bizarre only with respect to its context. Shortly after the inauguration of *The Arts of Reform and Persuasion*, Herbert Muschamp, writing for the *New York Times,* associated south Miami Beach with such skin-deep phenomena as "models, mindlessness, Eurotrash, thong bathing suits, sex, old folks, young folks…" (fig. 26). In contrast, he defined The Wolfsonian as serious, a place "not about brunettes and bikinis…, but about the meanings of things." Muschamp added, "The mission of this specialized, philosophically focused museum is to plumb the ideological depths of decorative objects."[37] Muschamp easily discerned the methodological basis for the collection. Likewise, Judy Cantor writing for the *Miami New Times* apprehended The Wolfsonian's institutionally endorsed perspective, describing *The Arts of Reform and Persuasion* as

> an uncluttered but far-reaching visual and social history of Western industrial design that effectively demonstrates how political and societal change is promoted and perceived through everyday objects, patriotic posters and memorabilia, typography and book design, and, to a lesser extent here, fine art.[38]

From the staff perspective, these critics "got it."

Ultimately, though, this methodological definition does not provide practical parameters for understanding what exactly The Wolfsonian holds. Relative to the collection's contents, there is lack of consensus on a fundamental level. John Heskett, professor at the Institute of Design at the Illinois Institute of Technology, for example, maintained: "What Wolfson has done is gone out and collected on the broadest possible scale. He doesn't attempt to be *comprehensive* in any single area."[39] But *New York Times* reporter R. W. Apple Jr., on the contrary, proclaimed that The Wolfsonian holds "the *most comprehensive* collection of early modern design in the world."[40] While Heskett's comment is self-explanatory, Apple's assertion is more abstruse and merits closer consideration as a means of understanding what this collection is and is not.

Relative to Apple's use of the term "early modern," certainly the Victoria and Albert Museum and other European collections are more comprehensive in both their depth and variety. To deem The Wolfsonian more comprehensive than the Victoria and Albert, one must and should include the persuasive or propaganda arts as an integral feature of its "design" holdings. Relative to the word "modern," I've wondered whether Apple

37. Herbert Muschamp, "Well-Made Surfaces and the Conflicts Lurking Beneath Them," *New York Times,* 3 December 1995, 38H.

38. Cantor, "Thoroughly Modern Micky," 59.

39. Barry, "Invincible Man," 5J. Italics added for emphasis in this and following quotation.

40. R. W. Apple Jr., "Art in Miami Now Extends Beyond Deco," *New York Times,* 14 November 1997, Weekend section, 33.

fig. 27
(below)
Riding Power Wheel Toy,
design drawing by
Exhibit Builders, Inc.,
color crayon, graphite,
construction paper, mat
board, 43 x 60 cm, c. 1969.
The Wolfsonian–Florida
International University,
Miami Beach, Florida. Gift
of Exhibit Builders, Inc.

fig. 28
(below, far right)
Lajos Kozma, design
drawing of a two-story
toy dollhouse, paper, ink,
watercolor, 19 x 14 cm,
c. 1930s. The Mitchell
Wolfson Jr. Collection,
The Wolfsonian–Florida
International University,
Miami Beach, Florida.

meant the era or the movement. No doubt the Museum of Modern Art holds a more comprehensive collection of design from the early Modern movement. However, MoMA does not provide an overview of nineteenth- and twentieth-century material production. Instead it perpetuates a carefully delineated canon of "Modern masters." Herbert Muschamp recognized this distinction in 1995, writing of The Wolfsonian:

> Modernity, not modernism, is the collection's focus: It traces not only the orthodox modern movement but the whole, eclectic panorama of artifacts with which designers responded to the upheavals of industry, technology, politics and global warfare.[41]

With regard to the Wolfsonian collection's comprehensiveness "in the world," one must consider its focus on North America and Europe and its minimal inclusion of Latin America, Asia, Africa, and Australia. Relative to geography, one would hardly expect The Wolfsonian's comprehensive holdings of early modern design to encompass an assemblage of early twentieth-century drinking vessels from Papua New Guinea. The Wolfsonian's collection is most likely comprehensive for its catholic approach to objects within stringently defined geographical, chronological, thematic, and methodological parameters. As Dennis Doordan wrote in his "Introduction" to the aforementioned 1997 volume of *Design Issues:*

> It is not just the sheer number of objects collected by Mitchell Wolfson, Jr. that is noteworthy; equally important is the range of this material… Exquisite and unique items fashioned out of precious materials share space with mass produced artifacts intended for popular consumption. Oil paintings appear in the Wolfsonian registry along with postcards and match book covers.[42]

41. Muschamp, "Well-Made Surfaces," 38H.
42. Dennis Doordan, "Introduction," *Design Issues* 13 (Spring 1997): 2.

fig. 29
Photographer unknown.
From A "Titanic" Hero:
Tomas Andrews,
Shipbuilder
(Baltimore: Norman,
Remington, 1913). The
Wolfsonian–Florida
International University,
Miami Beach, Florida.
Image depicts the RMS
Titanic leaving Belfast for
Southampton, England.

The collection is, undoubtedly, noteworthy for its ability to sustain thematic research across a multiplicity of media.

Ultimately, for me the collection's non-canonical quality is perhaps its defining feature. For intellectual, emotional, and, presumably, economic reasons Mitchell Wolfson Jr. (and the museum he established) would be more inclined to collect go-carts and doll houses than Beaux-Arts and Bauhaus (figs. 27 and 28). Indeed, Wolfson has a penchant for developing and promoting the peripheral, non-mainstream components and qualities of the collection. In February 2000, for example, he delivered a lecture on the museum's collection of nineteenth-century British objects in conjunction with the exhibition *Leading "The Simple Life": The Arts and Crafts Movement in Britain, 1880–1910*. Wolfson responded enthusiastically to the invitation to speak. He explained, though, that he wished to deliver a "contrarian" lecture, one that explored exclusions from the curated exhibition and that looked instead at the relationship between the exquisitely crafted Arts and Crafts items in the show and garish High Victorian counterparts. Wolfson sought to expose the collection's lesser-known or lesser-respected items. In so doing, the collector provocatively distanced himself from the Arts and Crafts material comfortably inscribed in the Modern trajectory by Nikolaus Pevsner and others.

Although material objects do not significantly change over time, perspectives and methodologies do, and so a collection defined by the way it is interpreted cannot remain static. The focus on North America and Europe in the period 1885 to 1945, while meaningful to Wolfson and those currently involved in the Wolfsonian project, will likely seem increasingly insular and arbitrary with the passage of time. Moreover,

"the Wolfsonian way" of looking at objects is clearly the method *du jour*. In November 1999, the Association of Research Institutes in Art History — to which The Wolfsonian belongs — held a conference at the Center for Advanced Study in the Visual Arts at the National Gallery entitled "The Practice of Advanced Research in Art History Today." Asked to moderate a panel on the implications of nationalism to art historical scholarship — notably one of only two panels dedicated to art historical topics — I explained that the study of national identity was fundamental to Wolfsonian exhibitions, programs, research, and publications. But what would happen if the now-dominant interest in the cultural meanings of artifacts were to give way to a revival in connoisseurship or formalism, or the development of entirely new methods? Would the museum's holdings become a monstrously empty signifier? No doubt The Wolfsonian's collection would still have much to offer, but its definition and perceived value would shift radically. It is, thus, clear that this volume is among the preliminary explorations of an under-researched collection — the tip of the iceberg. And although The Wolfsonian's objects associated with the ill-fated *Titanic* might suggest otherwise (fig. 29), prospective researchers can forge ahead with courage and optimism, knowing that many rewards lie beyond the cultures, themes, objects, and methods represented within this volume. ✧

Acknowledgments
I would like to thank Micky Wolfson, Cathy Leff, and Peggy Loar for the wonderfully stimulating opportunity of working with The Wolfsonian. I, further, appreciate Cathy Leff's kind invitation to serve as guest editor of this issue of *The Journal of Decorative and Propaganda Arts,* which has allowed me to maintain a close connection with this remarkable institution. Senior Editor Leslie Sternlieb, Editorial Assistant Jacqueline Crucet, former Editorial Assistant Maria Gonzalez, and Art Director Peter Roman deserve special thanks for their collegial collaboration, diligence, and hard work on this project. I am, likewise, grateful to my past and present Wolfsonian colleagues Annie Wharton, Gina Maranto, Wendy Kaplan, Marianne Lamonaca, Neil Harvey, Francis X. Luca, Pedro Figueredo, Nicholas Blaga, Kimberly J. Bergen, and David Burnhauser for their invaluable contribution to The Wolfsonian's fellowship program during my tenure at the museum. Heartfelt thanks also to my partner, John A. Stuart, for offering an array of insightful opinions during the editorial process.

John E. Bowlt

Stalin as Isis and Ra: Socialist Realism and the Art of Design

John E. Bowlt is professor of Slavic Studies at the University of Southern California, Los Angeles, where he is also director of the Institute of Modern Russian Culture. He has lived for extended periods in the Soviet Union/Russia and published widely on the subject of modern Russian art. He guest-edited issues five and eleven of *The Journal of Decorative and Propaganda Arts* exploring Russian/Soviet themes. Bowlt conducted research for this essay as a Wolfsonian Fellow in 1995.

T his essay focuses on the Soviet visual arts, especially the decorative or applied arts, under Joseph Stalin (1879–1953) during the 1930s and 1940s.[1] It is especially appropriate that the topic receive attention now, since a substantial part of Stalin's cultural output has been removed from history: on the one hand, many of the artifacts have been destroyed or mutilated and, on the other, what has come down to us in the way of architecture, paintings, ceramics, textiles, and knick-knacks—from ashtrays to antimacassars—is today the frequent target of ridicule or abuse. True, the last decade has witnessed a flurry of publications and exhibitions on the subject of Soviet Socialist Realism both in Russia and in the West, and these have gone a long way to reestablishing the subject as a legitimate field of academic investigation.[2] By and large, however,

1. The transliteration of Russian names modifies the Library of Congress system so that the Cyrillic ending "i + i *kratkoe*" of proper names has been rendered by "y," not "ii" (e.g., Chukovsky, Gor'ky). Where a variant spelling has long been established in the West, e.g., Joseph Stalin (not Iosif Stalin), this has been retained.

2. On the Soviet visual arts of the Stalin era see, for example, the following monographs: Vladimir Paperny, *Kul'tura dva* (Ann Arbor, Mich.: Ardis, 1985); Anders Aman, *Architecture and Ideology in Eastern Europe During the Stalin Era* (New York: The Architectural History Foundation, 1992); Matthew Cullerne Bown, *Art Under Stalin* (New York: Holmes and Meier, 1991); Matthew Cullerne Bown, *Socialist Realist Painting* (New Haven, Conn.: Yale University Press, 1998); Igor Golomstock, *Totalitarian Art* (London: Icon, 1990); Evgeny Gromov, *Stalin. Vlast' i iskusstvo* (Moscow: Respublika, 1991); Loren R. Graham, *The Ghost of the Executed Engineer. Technology and the Fall of the Soviet Union* (Cambridge, Mass.: Harvard University Press, 1993); Hans Günther, ed., *The Culture of the Stalin Period* (New York: St. Martin's Press, 1990); Hugh Hudson, *Blueprints and Blood. The Stalinization of Soviet Architecture* (Princeton, N.J.: Princeton University Press, 1994); James von Geldern and Richard Stites, *Mass Culture in Soviet Russia* (Bloomington, Ind.: Indiana University Press, 1995); also the exhibition catalogues: Tatiana Nikitina et al., *The Aesthetic Arsenal: Socialist Realism Under Stalin*, New York, Institute for Contemporary Art, 1993–1994; Alessandro De Magistris, ed., *URSS. Anni 30–50*, catalogue of exhibition at the Accademia Albertina delle Belle Arti, Turin, April–June 1997; Peter Moever, ed., *Tyrannei des Schönen. Architektur des Stalin-Zeit*, catalogue of exhibition at the Osterreichisches Museum für angewandte Kunst, Vienna, April–July 1994; Jan Tabor, ed., *Kunst und Diktatur. Architektur, Bildhauerei und Malerei in Osterreich, Deutschland, Italien und der Sowjetunion 1922–1956*, catalogue of exhibition at the Künstlerhaus, Vienna, March–August 1994 (two volumes); and Hubertus Gassner et al., *Agitatsiia za schast'e*, catalogue of exhibition at the Museum Fridericianum, Kassel, and the State Russian Museum St. Petersburg, 1994.

Detail of *Tapestry with Portrait of Stalin*, 1936.

these endeavors have focused on literature and the "high" arts of painting, sculpture, and architecture, whereas the "minor" arts of everyday life have been neglected.[3] It is often the prosaic material culture — rather than the august portrait or the palace of power — that expresses most vividly the sociopolitical aspirations of a particular regime. Consequently, any attempt to forge a conceptual link between the ideological structure of the Soviet Union and its visual production should take account of all the media as a synthetic expression and, as far as possible, afford equal attention to the decorative as well as to the fine arts, however difficult that may be.

The use of decorative arts for overtly propagandistic and didactic purposes often obscured, and still obscures, their aesthetic qualities. As with Nazi realism and, to a lesser extent, Italian Fascist realism, there still remains a disagreeable tension between the medium (which may be "beautiful") and the message (which may be "ugly"), and it is often impossible to speak of the former while ignoring the latter. Stalin and the applied or decorative arts is an uneasy subject, therefore; because in seeking an aesthetic justification for the "Stalin style" vis-à-vis the horrors of political dictatorship, universal censorship, and physical oppression, few can suspend their beliefs, prejudices, and distaste.

One way, however, in which this judgmental issue may be resolved and a contemporary appraisal of Socialist Realism may be undertaken in a more sympathetic manner is to approach the subject laterally rather than centrally, metaphorically rather than ideologically. By delineating historical precedents that, rightly or wrongly, are less distasteful to the researcher than a portrait of Stalin or a photograph of the White Sea Canal, we may establish a more favorable milieu for an evaluation of Socialist Realism. In this way some of the negative charge that still accompanies the contemporary reception of the Stalin style may be defused, even if its function as a principal vehicle of political persuasion cannot be disregarded. For the sake of simplicity, the 1930s and the 1940s are being considered here as a single time frame with an artistic and ideological constancy, cohesion, and continuity throughout, even though, of course, there *were* modulations in artistic theory and practice before, during, and after World War II. On the other hand, this chronology of particular dates and events should not proscribe comparison with other regimes and historical moments, near or far, that the art of the Stalin era may suggest. Comparison of "high"

3. For a general survey of the Soviet applied and decorative arts, see Vladimir Tolstoi, *Monumental'noe iskusstvo SSSR* (Moscow: Sovetsky khudozhnik, 1978); for specific issues see Karen Kettering, "An Introduction to the Design of the Moscow Metro in the Stalin Period: 'The Happiness of Life Underground,'" *Decorative Arts 7* (Spring–Summer 2000): 2–20; Karen Kettering, "Sverdlov Square Metro Station: 'The Friendship of the Peoples' and the Stalin Constitution," Ibid., 21–47; Jane Friedman, "Soviet Masters of the Skies at the Mayakovsky Metro Station," Ibid., 48–64; and Isabel Wünsche, "Homo Sovieticus: The Athletic Motif in the Design of the Dynamo Metro Station," Ibid., 65–90.

Stalin culture with the ostensibly remote regimes of ancient Egypt, Louis XIV, or Peter the Great is one way of providing a looser cultural context for discussion of the Socialist Realist style.

One point of entry to this topic is the poem "May There Always Be Sunshine," one of the most enticing ditties of the Stalin (ruled 1924–1953), Khrushchev (ruled 1958–1964), and Brezhnev (ruled 1964–1982) eras. The piece was written in 1928 by Konstantin Barannikov, a four-year-old boy; it then provided the lyrics for a Soviet hit song of the 1960s:

> May there always be sunshine,
> May there always be sky,
> May there always be Mama,
> May there always be me.[4]

The song is about illumination, fertility, life everlasting, and the yearning for divine or superhuman intervention — conditions that informed and defined Stalin culture in a very particular way. In Stalin's Russia, solar energy, aviation, abundance, and eternity were concepts that became especially manifest in both sociopolitical aspiration and visual and material culture. As a lyrical microcosm, therefore, "May There Always Be Sunshine" can be regarded as an apotheosis of and commentary on the spirit of Stalin's Russia. As Soviet life became more brutal in the 1930s, with rural catastrophes, famines, and mass arrests, the fine and applied arts became more florid, pictorial subjects more abundant, and construction projects more grandiose. There seems to be a diabolical logic in these disparities, and it is tempting to read the disengagement as the direct result of an emphatic propaganda that replaced complete information with half-truths, fables, and illusions. But this is only one of many components that must be

4. For the Russian and another English translation with the first and second lines reversed, see Vladimir Markov and Merrill Sparks, *Modern Russian Poetry* (New York: Bobbs-Merrill, 1967), 824–825.

remembered in understanding the genesis and evolution of the Stalin style.
Also critical are the imposition of ideology and the pressure of popular taste.
But the survival of alternative conventions and the weight of artistic legacy
still linked Socialist Realism of the late 1930s and the 1940s with the cultural pluralism of the preceding decade.

The late 1920s and early 1930s are an extremely complex period in
the history of Soviet culture, and any scholarly assessment must consider
many circumstances. Soviet art and design moved toward a more narrative,
more illustrative aesthetic — and, eventually, toward Socialist Realism
because of a variety of conditions, not just because the political elite,
the state bureaucracy, and the masses wanted it that way. It is important
to remember, for example, that more academic styles had continued to
flourish concurrently with the experimentation of the avant-garde just before
and after the October Revolution, reemerging by the late 1920s as a
formidable force. Artists such as Isaak Brodsky and Aleksandr Gerasimov,
court painters to Stalin during the 1930s, had received acclaim for their
proficient portraits and landscapes well before the revolution. Their
unswerving belief in the validity of figurative art and hallowed tradition —
whether that of the Italian Renaissance or of nineteenth-century Russian
realism — helped forge the principles of Socialist Realism. Conversely,
petty jealousies among the avant-garde artists had long threatened their
collective power (illusory or real), and key representatives of the artistic
left, such as Marc Chagall, Naum Gabo, Natalia Goncharova, Vasily
Kandinsky, Mikhail Larionov, Pavel Mansurov, and Ivan Puni (Jean Pougny),
had long forsaken the new Russia to develop their ideas abroad.

Still, a few artists of the avant-garde, such as El Lissitzky (1890–1941),
Aleksandr Rodchenko (1891–1956), and Varvara Stepanova (1894–1958),
began to create within the framework of Socialist Realism, accepting
major state design commissions and adjusting their style accordingly. The
propaganda magazine *USSR in Construction* relied substantially on
contributions by Lissitzky, Rodchenko, Stepanova, and Solomon Telingater
(1903–1969). Rodchenko and Stepanova were, likewise, responsible for
the photography and layout of several celebratory volumes of the 1930s —
applying bold ideas to photomontage, collage, foldouts, and typography.[5]
In some sense, the deluxe editions of the 1930s — promoting Soviet
triumphs in aviation, exploration, agriculture, and industry at the time of
Socialist Realism — such as the portfolio *Ot Moskvy kupecheskoi k Moskve
sotsialisticheskoi* (From Merchant Moscow to Socialist Moscow) (fig. 1),
were the ultimate receptacles of avant-garde experimentation. At the same

5. See *Raboche-krest'ianskaia Krasnaia armiia* (Moscow: Izogiz, 1934) (designed by Lissitzky);
   Krasnaia armiia (Moscow: Ogiz-Izogiz, 1938) (designed by Rodchenko and Stepanova);
   USSR. Red Army and Navy (Moscow: State Art Publishers, 1939) (designed by Rodchenko
   and Stepanova); and *Soviet Aviation* (Moscow-Leningrad: State Art Publishers, 1939)
   (designed by Rodchenko and Stepanova).

USSR AGRICULTURAL EXHIBITION

time, most citizens of the Soviet Union found the formal severity of the avant-garde alien, for they were operating, at best, with a nineteenth-century concept of art and design, one that favored narrative paintings, florid ornament, sentimental movies, and melodrama. In response to the will of the government and of the people, the Soviet fine and applied arts were, by the late 1920s, returning rapidly from abstraction to reality, from "construction" to "decoration."[6]

Socialist Realism was an artistic and literary style formulated in 1932 that was advanced as the aesthetic of the new Soviet state and of international communism. In 1934 the First Congress of Soviet Writers in Moscow advocated and ratified Socialist Realism as the only legitimate style for the new regime. A number of key politicians, writers, and artists spoke at that congress; and, although Stalin was absent, he surely agreed with the basic tenets promulgated by the writer Maksim Gor'ky (1868–1936) and by Andrei Zhdanov (1896–1948), secretary of the Central Committee of the Communist Party, who was largely responsible for Soviet cultural policy until his death:

> Socialist Realism is the basic method of Soviet creative literature and literary criticism, and this presupposes that revolutionary Romanticism must become an integral part of literary creativity, because the whole life of our working class and its struggle consists of combining the most severe, most sober practical work with supreme heroism and grand prospects.... Soviet literature must be able to show our heroes, must be able to catch a glimpse of tomorrow.[7]

Socialist Realism, therefore, emphasized certain orientations that distanced it from other "realisms," such as nineteenth-century Russian realism or twentieth-century American Social Realism, and also from representations of the past. As the Congress affirmed, Soviet Socialist Realism was to concern itself more with the future than with the present, with the golden land beyond the horizon, with eternal sunshine and eternal youth. Consequently, Soviet artists of the 1930s were guided by this forward-looking impulse as they strove to encapsulate the vision of the communist paradise. This helps to explain, for example, the iconography of confidence and strength in the poster for the *USSR Agricultural Exhibition* of 1939 (fig. 2) at a time of rural confusion and deficiency. A similar disjunction is identifiable in the government-sponsored exhibition *The Industry of Socialism*, held in Moscow in 1939. The publication accompanying this exhibition (with metal spine and edging designed by El Lissitzky) (fig. 3) suggests technological prowess, even though the pace of Soviet

6. A. Fevral'sky, "Detskaia bolezn' pravizny i konstruktivizma," *Zrelishcha* 34 (1923): 6.

7. From Andrei Zhdanov's speech at the First Congress of Soviet Writers, Moscow, August 1934. English translation in John E. Bowlt, ed., *Russian Art of the Avant-Garde. Theory and Criticism* (London: Thames and Hudson, 1988), 293–294.

fig. 3
El Lissitzky,
cover of *Industriia
sotsializma* (The
Industry of Socialism)
(Moscow: Stroim-Izogiz,
1935). The Mitchell
Wolfson Jr. Collection,
The Wolfsonian–Florida
International University,
Miami Beach, Florida.

industrialization was erratic at the time.[8] Similarly, the truth of environmental disaster and human loss associated with Soviet industry is belied by the pastel tones and serenity of the 1931 poster *Salt Mines in Central Asia* (fig. 4). Soviet paintings of the 1930s also expressed this imbalance between "today" and "tomorrow"— see, for example, the technological heights and conquest of nature implied in Serafima Riangina's *Higher, Ever Higher!* of 1934 (fig. 5).[9]

8. El Lissitzky, designer, *Industriia sotsializma* (Moscow: Stroim-Izogiz, 1935) (six fascicles and two maps in portfolio; includes the journal *Novoe litso SSSR* shown in figs. 9 and 23). The format of this publication was an apparent paraphrase of Fortunato Depero's *Depero Futurista* (Milan-Paris: Dinamo-Azari, 1927). Depero's album also was secured by metal nuts and bolts. A similar gesture to the genre of the industrial book is the account of how a group of Soviet Arctic explorers were saved, i.e., O. Yu. Shmidt, ed., *Kak my spasali cheliuskintsev* (Moscow: Pravda, 1934) (designed by Paula Freiberg, Fedor Reshetnikov, Nikolai Sedel'nikov, and Solomon Telingater). The covers and slipcase of this two-volume book are made of Bakelite.

9. Other examples include the sunshine and fertility of Sergei Gerasimov's *Collective Farm Harvest Festival* (1937, State Tretiakov Gallery, Moscow), and the benevolent and welcoming leader in Vasily Efanov's *A Memorable Meeting* (1938, State Tretiakov Gallery, Moscow).

ДОБЫЧА СОЛИ НА ОЗЕРЕ БАСКУНЧАК

ОГИЗ-ИЗОГИЗ
Москва 1931 Ленинград

Цена 60 коп.

fig. 4
(opposite page)
Artist unknown,
Salt Mines in Central Asia,
poster, 69 x 51 cm, 1931.
The Mitchell Wolfson Jr.
Collection, The
Wolfsonian–Florida
International University,
Miami Beach, Florida.

fig. 5
(above)
Serafima Riangina, *Higher,*
Ever Higher!, oil on canvas,
152 x 91 cm, 1934. State
Museum of Russian Art,
Kiev. Courtesy of Galart
Publishing, Moscow.

fig. 6
(above, far right)
Maquette, Palace of the
Soviets (not built), archi-
tects Boris Iofan, Vladimir
Geil'freikh, and Aleksei
Shchusev, 1934. Institute
of Modern Russian Culture,
Los Angeles.

The evocation and interpretation of certain themes, clearly illustrated in Soviet paintings, plates, posters, interior designs, and press photographs, contributed to the distinctiveness of Socialist Realism. One finds a concern with process and building rather than with completion, with youth rather than old age, with transition and rite of passage rather than arrival or departure, with warmth rather than cold. On the one hand, the art and literature of Socialist Realism were meant to portray the new and spectacular transformations of Stalin's Russia (electrification, collectivization, industri- alization), and on the other hand, they were meant to have universal and enduring appeal. That is one reason why Socialist Realism drew freely upon established symbols of prestige and power while applying them to the new social and political reality: simple workers could now be depicted enjoying the bourgeois pastimes of taking the waters, climbing mountains, and going to the seaside; architects included pastiches of Babylonian, Doric, and Corinthian columns in their proposals for the Palace of the Soviets (fig. 6); and a traditional Turkmenian rug maker saw fit to use the face of Stalin as the centerpiece of her handwoven, fringed woolen tapestry in 1936 (fig. 7).

As the tapestry indicates, universal applicability was an especially striking quality of Socialist Realism. With a predetermined syntax of images, attitudes, and captions, Socialist Realism was formulaic, "interdisciplinary,"

fig. 7
Artist unknown, *Tapestry with Portrait of Stalin*, wool and cotton, 160 x 112 cm, 1936. The Mitchell Wolfson Jr. Collection, The Wolfsonian–Florida International University, Miami Beach, Florida. Photograph by Silvia Ros.

and easily applied to any material surface and any national tradition.[10] Aviation, for example, was celebrated in statues, paintings, books, movies, posters, and plates (fig. 8). The fanatical campaign to conquer nature was reflected in books on the White Sea Canal of the mid-1930s and in the statistical data, maps, and photographic essays of the tundra and the deserts presented in *USSR in Construction*. Artists used photomontage to enhance their images of leadership, as in the elaborate transcript of the speech that Sergo Ordzhonikidze (1886–1937), the Communist Party official in charge of heavy industry, delivered to the Seventeenth Congress of the Soviets (fig. 9). The widespread picturing, packaging, and promotion of the Moscow metro in porcelain, books, and even textiles is especially enlightening in this regard. According to Karl Marx (1818–1883), culture is the superstructure (product) of an economic base. Since the Soviet Union was, allegedly, establishing a totally new economic system, Socialist Realism had to differ from any preceding feudal or capitalist artistic style. If Socialist Realism repeated or paraphrased previous forms of expression — especially late nineteenth-century imperial culture (the epic novel, the oil painting in the gilt frame, the symphony) — the thematic arsenal and emotional sensibility of the Stalin-era paintings, novels, decorative arts, and architecture did — or were meant to — contain proprietary elements less manifest in Hitler's and Mussolini's realisms. In the Soviet model is an evocation of lightness and buoyancy, of expanse and optimism, and of lavish excess — the denial of actuality in the invocation of the future. See, for example, *Higher, Ever Higher!* (fig. 5).

10. See Maksim Gor'ky and Lev Mekhlis, eds., *Tvorchestvo narodov SSSR* (Creativity of the Peoples of the USSR) (Moscow: Pravda, 1937). This deluxe edition celebrated the images of Lenin and Stalin in the various branches of folk art throughout the Soviet Union.

fig. 8
(right)
Plate commemorating
the first flight of the
Soviet North Line,
Dulevo porcelain factory,
porcelain and gilt,
33 cm diameter, c. 1935.
The Mitchell Wolfson Jr.
Collection, The
Wolfsonian–Florida
International University,
Miami Beach, Florida.
Photograph by Silvia Ros.

fig. 9
(below)
Artist unknown,
foldout printed
photomontage showing
Sergo Ordzhonikidze,
42 x 31 cm. From *Novoe
litso SSSR* (The New
Face of the USSR), 1935.
The Mitchell Wolfson Jr.
Collection, The
Wolfsonian–Florida
International University,
Miami Beach, Florida.

fig. 10
Solomon Telingater,
photograph illustrating
Stalin's statement,
"Life has improved,
comrades, life has
become more joyous."
From *USSR in
Construction*, no. 3,
1937. Institute of
Modern Russian Culture,
Los Angeles.

One result of this contradiction between present and future—between socialism and Socialist Realism—was the introduction of a romanticism or super-realism in artistic expression, replete with inconsistencies and non-sequiturs. For example, Telingater's photographic illustration of Stalin's maxim, "Life has improved, comrades, life has become more joyous," in the periodical *USSR in Construction* (1937) (fig. 10) presents a nude blond boy astride a dead sturgeon at the sunny seaside, a conglomeration of images that may be read didactically: the smiling child personifies the health of the young Soviet state—an analogue to the Hitler Youth—the sturgeon suggests an abundance of food for all, not just for survival, but for pleasure as well, and the sailboats indicate the desirable presence of outdoor recreation. Despite its message, this illustration is no less magical and perturbing than, say, Belgian artist René Magritte's *Collective Invention* of 1935 (fig. 11). Similar incongruences can be found in Aleksandr Gerasimov's celebrated icon of Socialist Realism, *Joseph Stalin and Kliment Voroshilov in the Kremlin Grounds* of 1938 (fig. 12), where everything seems logical and reasonable, except that Stalin—depicted as the taller man—was, in fact, shorter than Voroshilov (1881–1969), his right-hand man and head of the Red Army. At this point, Socialist Realism and Surrealism are almost one.

fig. 11
(right)
René Magritte, *Collective Invention*, oil on canvas, 73 x 116 cm, 1935. ©2002 C. Herscovici, Brussels/Artists Rights Society (ARS), New York.

fig. 12
(far right)
Aleksandr Gerasimov, *Joseph Stalin and Kliment Voroshilov in the Kremlin Grounds*, oil on canvas, 305 x 396 cm, 1938. State Tretiakov Gallery, Moscow. Courtesy of Galart Publishing, Moscow.

fig. 13
(below)
Boris Shvarts, frontispiece and title page of the book *Pod stalinskoi konstitutsiei* (Beneath the Sun of the Stalin Constitution) (Moscow: Iskusstvo, 1951). Institute of Modern Russian Culture, Los Angeles.

Sunshine and light are perhaps the motifs most recurrent in the representation of Stalin and his achievements, and the application of these motifs often expresses the disjunction between Socialist Realist representation and Soviet reality. In this respect, the previously mentioned song, "May There Always Be Sunshine," holds a key to understanding the cultural perspective of Stalin's time. In various aspects of cultural production one is led to surmise that Stalin is the sun, that the Stalin Constitution is the sun (fig. 13), and that, after Japan, the Soviet Union has emerged as another nation of the rising sun. This Stalinist sun would rise to the brilliance of midday after the Soviet victory in World War II, when the cult of light assumed an even more powerful meaning, real and metaphorical, with fireworks displays above the Kremlin and luminous pictures. The latter include Aleksandr Laktionov's *Letter from the Front*, a 1947 painting now housed at the State Tretiakov Gallery, Moscow, depicting a family group, bathed in sunlight, listening to a young boy read a letter, presumably from his father on active duty.

Such images evoke an immediate association with *La città del sole* (City of the Sun), the utopian novel written by Tommaso Campanella in 1602, in which a perfect race rejoices in health and freedom in a city of light and harmonious architecture and sculpture. Lenin, like many other

revolutionaries of his time, treasured this classic parable, and Campanella's concept of an ideal society had a formative effect on the so-called Plan of Monumental Propaganda that Lenin formulated in 1918. According to this plan, statues to social and political luminaries were to be erected in Moscow and Petrograd just as they were in *La città del sole*.[11] Also of particular relevance to *La città del sole* and the solar aesthetic was the

ПОД СОЛНЦЕМ
СТАЛИНСКОЙ
КОНСТИТУЦИИ

11. For information on Lenin's Plan of Monumental Propaganda, see John E. Bowlt, "Russian Sculpture and Lenin's Plan of Monumental Propaganda," in *Art and Architecture in the Service of Politics,* eds. Henry A. Millon and Linda Nochlin (Cambridge, Mass.: MIT Press, 1978), 182–193.

fig. 14
Ivan Leonidov,
design for *City of the*
***Sun*, mixed media,**
185 x 229 cm, 1944.
Courtesy of Professor
Misler, Italy.

Constructivist architect Ivan Leonidov (1902–1959), who elaborated an ambitious project called *City of the Sun* into a polyphony of images with radiant buildings, temples of light, pyramids of glass, and skyscrapers stretching toward the heavens (fig. 14).[12] Although the plans are not always identifiable with a particular city, they draw on Leonidov's recurrent combinations of the pyramid and the circle, transparency and opacity, the organic and the inorganic.[13] Leonidov envisioned a city of aerial forms and scintillating translucencies that coincided with the solar aesthetic of Stalin's hegemony. While he remained loyal to his own architectural credo of the avant-garde period, Leonidov nevertheless expressed the fundamental aspiration and symbology of Stalin's culture. Stalin then resurrected the sun after the avant-garde had vanquished it in their Dada opera

12. For information on Leonidov and his *City of the Sun*, see Andrei Gozak and Andrei Leonidov, *Ivan Leonidov* (London: Academy, 1988); Alesssandra Latour and Nicoletta Misler, *Ivan Leonidov: "The City of the Sun,"* catalogue of exhibition at the American Institute of Architects, New York, 1988; Hans-Peter Schwarz and Bernhardt Schneider, eds., *Leonidov. La città del sole*, catalogue of exhibition at the Istituto per gli Studi Filosofici, Naples, 1989.

13. The result, presumably, was to have been an ecologically sound environment protesting the super-city of Evgeny Zamiatin's novel *My* (We), in which the natural world, including the sun, survived only outside the hermetic glass dome of the socialist state. Written by Zamiatin in 1920, it was not published in its entirety until 1952 (New York: Chekhov Publishing House).

Victory Over the Sun of 1913, in which Kazimir Malevich and his friends had set about to capture and humiliate the sun. Stalin rendered preeminent the sanatorium and the sunroom and identified health, "fun," and economic power with the sunny south (Georgia)—"Let there be light!"

If solar power could not be adequately harnessed, then the implementation of Lenin's call for the rapid electrification of Russia would illuminate the new nation. One may hypothesize that Campanella also inspired Lenin's vision for a bright and iridescent Russia ablaze with electric lights. Lenin is even pictured on the frontispiece of a book about this subject, presumably lit from the front and behind by a glowing lamp (fig. 15). Symptomatic of this solar obsession is the fact that the light fixture became such an important part of Stalin interior design beginning in the 1930s. As Abram Damsky (1906–1992), Stalin's foremost lighting designer and engineer, wrote:

> The 1930s, 1940s and early 1950s were a period marked by the construction of major architectural projects in the Soviet Union.... In theaters, railroad and metro stations and high-rise public buildings, lamps and light fixtures occupied a special place and were often the most interesting features of the whole interior. Many of the outstanding architects who designed these major buildings paid close attention to the design and construction of light fixtures.... Some, like Shchusev [architect of the Lenin mausoleum], designed the chandeliers in their buildings.[14]

14. Abram Damsky, "Lamps and Architecture 1930–1950," *The Journal of Decorative and Propaganda Arts* 5 (1987): 91. Also see his *Osvetitel'naia armatura* (Moscow: Akademiia arkhitektury, 1947); Nikolai Gusev, *Arkhitekturnaia svetotekhnika* (Moscow-Leningrad: Gosudarstvennoe arkhitekturnoe izdatel'stvo, 1949); and Z. N. Bykov, *Osvetitel'naia armatura* (Moscow: Gosudarstvennoe izdatel'stvo arkhitektury i gradostroitel'stva, 1951).

fig. 16
Abram Damsky,
chandeliers of the
Taganskaia metro station,
Moscow, 1948.
Courtesy of Galart
Publishing, Moscow.

Damsky himself designed lamps and chandeliers for the Palace of the
Soviets and was responsible for some of the most complex illuminations
in theaters, hotels, office buildings, and the Moscow metro, including the
Oktiabr'skaia (formerly Kaluzhskaia) and Taganskaia stations (fig. 16).[15]
So resplendent were the metro stations that they were described as an
"artificial underground sun."[16] The identification of the Soviet Union
with the life-giving rays of the sun, and of her future with electrification,
are manifestations of the nation's extraordinary technological optimism
of the 1920s—the belief that everything was now possible.[17]

But, of course, Leonidov's *City of the Sun* and Stalin's metaphorical solar
power—both oriented toward the future—were at loggerheads with
the harsh realities of Soviet urban development. After all, in the 1930s
an increasing number of citizens were living, cramped and crowded, in
communal apartments. The outdoors represented the promise of fresh
air and sunshine, a release from collective living, and a chance to escape
the enforced intimacy of neighbors (many of whom were government
informants).[18] People took to the streets, and Socialist Realists, always

15. On the Moscow metro and its light fixtures, see A. Kosarev, ed., *Kak my stroili metro* (Moscow:
   Izdatel'stvo fabrik i zavodov, 1935), 614–625; Nikolai Kolli and S. M. Kravets, *Arkhitektura
   moskovskogo metro* (Moscow: Vsesoiuznaia Akademiia arkhitektury, 1936); S. M. Kravets et al.,
   Arkhitektura moskovskogo metropolitena (Moscow: Vsesoiuznaia Akademiia arkhitektury,
   1936); and *Moskovskii metropoliten* (Moscow: Izobrazitel'noe iskusstvo, 1953) (designed by
   Varvara Stepanova).

16. Kosarev, *Kak my stroili metro*, 624.

17. For many, this confidence included an interest in the conquest of space. The artist Kazimir
   Malevich contemplated spaceships that would be powered by Suprematist fuel, while Vladimir
   Tatlin planned his *Monument to the III International* to project the Earth's axis into outer space.

18. For information on the Soviet housing crisis in the 1930s, see William C. Brumfield and Blair
   A. Ruble, eds., *Russian Housing in the Modern Age. Design and Social History* (Cambridge:
   Cambridge University Press, 1993), especially chaps. 4 and 5; and Sheila Fitzpatrick, *Everyday
   Stalinism* (Oxford: Oxford University Press, 1999).

fig. 17
(above)
Petr Konchalovsky,
Spanish Pioneers at
Soviet Summer Camp,
oil on canvas, 208 x 330 cm,
1939. Moscow Section
of the Art Fund.
Courtesy of Galart
Publishing, Moscow.

fig. 18
(above, far right)
Embankment of Gor'ky
Park, photograph 1940.
Collection of Sonia
Brodsky, Moscow.
Institute of Modern
Russian Culture,
Los Angeles.

focused on capturing the optimistic side of Soviet culture, recurrently represented outdoor processions, amusement parks, gymnastic displays, and other forms of recreation—whenever possible bathing their subjects in sunlight (fig. 17). Not accidentally, the first line of the Moscow metro (1935) linked the two major parks of culture and rest—Sokol'niki and Gor'ky Park (fig. 18), and tourist information about Moscow tended to describe sunshine rather than snow as the city's dominant weather pattern. For example, the 1939 propaganda album *Moscow* contains approximately 180 photographs of Moscow outdoors, only four of which show snow, and the photographs of gymnastic displays by Aleksandr Rodchenko and others for the collection entitled *Pageant of Youth* also create the impression of perpetual sunlight.[19] As government control of personal destiny became ever sterner and the specter of Siberia ever more insistent, so Soviet art and photography grew ever more exuberant, focusing more and more on sunlight and creating a magic kingdom that had little to do with everyday life.

It is wrong to assume that Stalin was especially interested in the visual arts. His collected writings make no reference to painting, and it is rumored that he never set foot inside the Tretiakov Gallery, Moscow's principal museum of Russian art. But to understand the broader implications of the projects described above and why they appealed to the Soviet government, one must also consider Stalin's monumental architecture and urban planning projects. After all, Stalin was extremely interested in the physical and visual transformation of the Soviet Union and was instrumental in accepting or rejecting projects for the replanning of Moscow—like Hitler in Munich and Berlin and Mussolini in Rome. The sharp contrast between real and unreal, described above, extended to Stalin-era architecture, particularly the "wedding-cakes," in which the difference between outside (sunshine) and inside (darkness), between sacred and profane, was emphasized.[20]

DAPA 24

51

19. *Moscow* (Moscow-Leningrad: State Art Publishers, 1939) (photographer not indicated); a meteorological sequel to this is the English-language collection called *Pageant of Youth* (Moscow-Leningrad: State Art Publishers, 1939) (photographer not indicated, but presumably was Rodchenko).

20. Vladimir Paperny has discussed this issue in his examination of Stalin architecture and design, i.e., *Kul'tura dva*, chap. 1.

fig. 19
Cathedral of the Savior,
designed by Konstantin
Ton (destroyed 1929),
chromolithograph,
c. 1890. Institute of
Modern Russian Culture,
Los Angeles.

This is epitomized by Boris Iofan's fantastic winning entry for the Palace of the Soviets in 1933, a gigantic pile designed for the banks of the River Moscow, opposite the Kremlin, on the site of the dynamited Cathedral of the Savior (figs. 6 and 19).[21]

But the Palace of the Soviets project suggests links that extend far beyond Nazi Germany and Fascist Italy—historic links that provide a symbolic framework for interpreting Stalin culture. The Palace of the Soviets, never completed, represented a rigid demarcation between palatial and public spaces, a tension between indoors and outdoors, and the centralization of imperial power, all on a superhuman scale with a waterfront orientation. As encapsulated by this building, Stalin's new Russia of the twentieth century had much in common with Peter the Great's new Russia of the early eighteenth century. Peter, like Stalin, used canals as a major transportation system, and tried to turn Russia into a maritime power. Given the Soviet emphasis on solar symbolism discussed above, the Stalin-Peter analogy reaches a more graphic level when we recall that Peterhof, Peter's summer residence outside St. Petersburg, was modeled on Versailles, residence of Louis XIV, the Sun King—both featuring wondrous water artistries (figs. 20 and 21). Moreover, the projected Palace of the Soviets (intended to occupy an area of almost four million square feet and rise to 1,361 feet)[22] and Gor'ky Park elicited comparisons with Peterhof and Versailles. That Stalin countenanced such an association seems clear from the fact that the 1941 Stalin Prize was awarded to Aleksei Tolstoi for his novel *Peter the Great*.

21. On the Palace of the Soviets, see the bulletins issued by the Administration for the Construction of the Palace of the Soviets, Moscow, 1931 (edited by M. V. Kriukov); P. I. Antipov, ed., *Dvorets sovetov SSSR* (Moscow: Vsekokhudozhnik, 1933); and Isaak Eigel', *Boris Iofan* (Moscow: Stroiizdat, 1978), 80–125.

22. The project for the Palace of the Soviets was a component part of the general plan to reconstruct Moscow in the 1930s–1950s and vast resources—ideological, administrative, financial, technological, artistic—went into its elaboration. Although the foundations were laid, construction was interrupted by World War II and finally terminated. Under Khrushchev the site became a swimming pool, which, under Yeltsin, was then replaced by a reprise of the Cathedral of the Savior.

fig. 20
(above)
Peterhof, originally
designed by Peter the
Great in the early
eighteenth century,
photograph c. 1980.
Institute of Modern
Russian Culture,
Los Angeles.

fig. 21
(above, far right)
Versailles, originally
designed by
J. Hardouin-Mansart
in the late seventeenth
century, photograph
c. 1980. Institute
of Modern Russian
Culture, Los Angeles.

fig. 22
(right)
*Friendship of the
Peoples Fountain* at
the Exhibition of
Economic Achievements,
1954. Institute of
Modern Russian Culture,
Los Angeles.

The Exhibition of Economic Achievements in Moscow, planned in the late 1930s but completed only after World War II, with its gilt decorations, fountains, and promenades is a further extension of the analogy with Peter the Great and Louis XIV, and the eerie Rococo of its pavilions (now, unfortunately, in disrepair) echoes the gentler Rococo of the furnishings and plasterwork of Peterhof and Versailles (figs. 20, 21, and 22).[23] For Stalin, the Exhibition, first referred to as the Palace of Economic Achievements, propagandistically boasted of the new empire's wealth, fulfilling a function comparable to that of Versailles and Peterhof for their respective patrons. Via the palatial symbolism of gala celebrations, spectacular firework displays, and nocturnal illumination, the Exhibition of Economic Achievements invoked in the spectator the sense of historical legitimacy. The identification of Stalin with the Sun King via Peter the Great helps to explain the ostensible resplendence and iridescence of

23. For information on and photographs of the Exhibition (VDNKh-Vystavka dostizhenii narodnogo khoziastva), see I. A. Benediktov et al., *RSFSR na Vsesoiuznoi sel'skoi vystavke, 1939 goda* (Moscow: Goskinoizdat, 1940); P. Pospelov et al., eds., *Vsesoiuznaia sel'skaia vystavka* (Moscow: OGIZ, 1939); and *Vsesoiuznaia vystavka. Pavil'ony i sooruzheniia* (Moscow: Izobrazitel'noe iskusstvo, 1954).

his reign—the intricate façadism of his world of make-believe and the reflective surfaces in his public buildings (mirrors, crystal, marble, chandeliers). Such a direct appeal to aristocratic convention was of major importance to the welfare of both Peter the Great and Stalin. Given the scarcity of snow in depictions of the Soviet Union in the 1930s and Stalin's self-identification with Peter the Great, and by analogy with the Sun King, one may consider Moscow a veritable "City of the Sun."

In addition to the Soviet fixation with light, whether solar or artificial, there was a fixation with hydraulic culture, symbolized by the proposed placement of the Palace of the Soviets on the River Moscow, the inordinate attention given to the esplanades, embankments, and parapets of Gor'ky Park,[24] and, of course, to the canals and the hydroelectric dams.[25] This brings to mind the cities of the Nile and the pharaonic cult of Ra (the god of the sun) and Isis (the goddess of motherhood and fertility). In the 1930s and 1940s, Stalin was viewed as the life-giving sun, and the hymns and songs dedicated to him reiterate that "Like the sun, you have illumined the expanse,"[26] or "Glory to the golden sun, glory to the stars on the Kremlin, Glory to our native Stalin,"[27] or "Glory to our mother earth! Glory to the red sun in the Kremlin!"[28] The parallels are intriguing, but perhaps there is a more ominous historical precedent that can be invoked, one that brings a stronger logic to this interpretation of Stalin culture and to the song "May there always be sunshine," namely, the Egyptian divination of motherhood and fertility in the form of Isis and of the sun in the form of Ra. In other words, the Stalin culture of the 1930s and 1940s can be regarded as a pharaonic one, and the model upon which Stalin wished to construct his new state may well have been the dynastic territory of the Nile and its delta. But in order to reinforce the hypothesis, we should move back to the year 1933, just as the perimeters of Stalin culture were beginning to assume definition and focus. It is the year after the liquidation of artistic and literary organizations—whereby professional writers, artists, and musicians were to relinquish their memberships in local societies to join state-controlled trade unions[29]—and the year before

24. For a discussion of these and other embankments along Moscow's rivers, see P. I. Gol'denberg and L. S. Aksel'rod, *Naberehnye Moskvy. Arkhitektura i konstruktsiia* (Moscow: Gosudarstvennoe arkhitekturnoe izdatel'stvo Akademii arkhitektury SSSR, 1940).

25. On the hydroelectric dams, see M. A. Zakhar'evskaia, *Arkhitektura gorodotekhnicheskikh sooruzhenii. Plotiny* (Leningrad-Moscow: Gosudarstvennoe izdatel'stvo stroitel'noi literatury, 1939), especially chap. 5.

26. Aram Khachaturian, "Pesnia o Staline" (A Song About Stalin) (Moscow: Muzgiz, 1945), 2.

27. Aleksandr Prokof'ev, "Slava Stalinu" (Glory to Stalin), in *Pesni o Staline* (Songs About Stalin), eds. L. O. Belov et al. (Moscow: Gosudarstvennoe izdatel'stvo khudozhestvennoi literatury, 1950), 197.

28. Anatoly Sofronov, "Pesnia slavy" (A Song of Glory), Ibid., 196.

29. With the "Decree on the Reconstruction of Literary and Artistic Organizations" (1932), all official literature and art groups were dissolved and replaced by appropriate professional unions, e.g., the Union of Writers of the USSR.

fig. 23
Cover of the journal
Novoe litso SSSR
(The New Face of the
USSR), 1935, showing
the newly opened Dnepr
hydroelectric dam.
The Mitchell Wolfson Jr.
Collection, The
Wolfsonian–Florida
International University,
Miami Beach, Florida.
Photograph by Silvia Ros.

the formulation and universal superimposition of the doctrine of Socialist Realism.[30] It is the conclusive moment of the first Five Year Plan and the beginning of the second, and the year of the devastating results—or giddy successes—of enforced collectivization.

There were many urgent issues on the agenda in 1933, but a leitmotif that surfaced constantly in the press and public statements was water. On one hand, praise was showered upon the planners and engineers who were heeding Lenin's call for electrification and were harnessing the flow of Russia's rivers to create some of the world's most ambitious hydroelectric schemes. Perhaps the most famous of these projects was the dam on the River Dnepr (Dneproges), which, upon its completion in 1932, became the most powerful electrical generator in the Soviet Union (fig. 23). However, if water was plentiful in the lowlands and open spaces of Mother Russia, the situation was very different in Moscow and the Volga region. In 1933 Moscow faced a serious water shortage, for as the city increased its rapid growth and as the network of running water and hydraulic distribution continued to develop, so Moscow's water reservoirs proved to be grossly inadequate. It was calculated that, if urban expansion were to continue at the same rate, by 1935 the River Moscow, the main source of drinking and industrial water, would run dry. Therefore in 1933 Stalin entertained the extraordinary idea of exploiting the water of the River Volga, some ninety miles to the north of Moscow, by deviating part of that body of water south to Moscow via a canal. The resulting Moscow-Volga Canal represented Stalin's greatest act of geographical and topographical metamorphosis and victory over nature.[31]

Stalin and the engineers who undertook the planning and construction of the Mosow-Volga Canal argued that the system (opened in 1937) would provide an endless source of drinking water as well as a reliable industrial coolant. They also affirmed that it would raise the level of the River Moscow in central Moscow by six feet, turning local streets into canals and the city into a great international port, on the axis of a waterway joining Leningrad with the Black Sea and the Seven Seas (fig. 24). "Large ships alongside the Kremlin wall—does this sound too improbable?"—asked an

30. Zhdanov speech, in *Russian Art of the Avant-Garde*, ed. Bowlt, 293–294.

31. On the Moscow-Volga Canal, see V. F. Perlin et al., *Arkhitektura kanala Moskva-Volga* (Moscow: Vsesoiuznaia Akademiia arkhitektury, 1939).

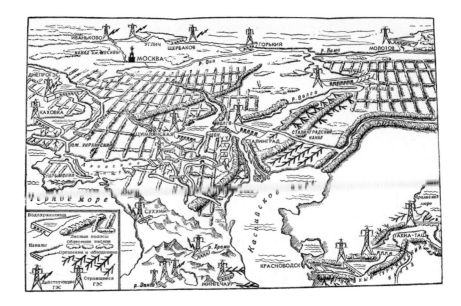

fig. 24
(right)
Map indicating how
Moscow would be turned
into an international port.
From *Velikie sooruzheniia
stalinskoi epokhi*
(Great Constructions
of the Stalin Epoch)
(Moscow: Molodaia
gvardiia, 1951). Institute
of Modern Russian
Culture, Los Angeles

fig. 25
(below)
Khimki River Station,
designed by Aleksei
Rukhliadev, now the
main station for tourist
trips on the River
Moscow, photograph
c. 1950. Institute of
Modern Russian
Culture, Los Angeles.

fig. 26
(opposite page)
Irakly Toidze, *Stalin at
the Ryon Hydro-Electric
Power Station,* oil on
canvas, 239 x 295 cm,
1935. Marx-Engels-Lenin
Institute, Tbilisi.
Courtesy of Galart
Publishing, Moscow.

English-language guidebook to Moscow in 1934.[32] The new accessibility
of water also would supply a constant source for irrigation projects to the
north of Moscow, creating temporary and permanent lagoons, beneficial
to agriculture and recreation alike.

The Moscow-Volga Canal was one link in a chain of canals that Stalin
developed in the 1930s, the most notorious being the White Sea Canal,

opened in 1934.[33] Neither the Moscow-
Volga Canal nor the White Sea Canal
was commercially viable inasmuch as the
locks did not function well, the water
level proved too shallow, the walls too
fragile, and the viaducts too narrow to
accommodate many barges and freight
ships. Moscow did not turn into the
great inland port that Stalin had imagined,
and although the Moscow-Volga Canal
now has some commercial value, its
real use has become the pleasurable
transportation of people from Khimki
River Station to points upstream
(fig. 25).[34] But practical success or
failure aside, the canals also carry a deep

32. M. I. Levidov, *Moscow. Past, Present, Future* (Moscow: Vneshtorgizdat, 1934), 140.

33. On the White Sea Canal, see the special issue of *USSR in Construction* 12 (1933). This carried
photographs that Rodchenko took of the canal as it was being constructed. Also see Maksim
Gor'ky, Leopol'd Averbakh, and S. Firin, eds., *Belomorsko-Baltiiskii kanal imeni Stalina. Istoriia
stroitel'stva* (Moscow: Istoriia fabrik i zavodov, 1934); and the English version, Leopold
Auerbach et al., eds., *Belomor* (New York: Smith and Haas, 1935).

34. See Roman Khiger, *Arkhitektura rechnykh vokzalov* (Moscow: Gosudarstvennoe arkhitekturnoe
izdatel'stvo Akademii arkhitektury SSSR, 1940).

fig. 27
Viktor Govorkov,
I zasukhu pobedim!
(We Will Overcome the
Drought, Too!), poster,
1949. Institute of
Modern Russian Culture,
Los Angeles.

symbolic value that, like the designation of Moscow as "City of the Sun," suggests an organic connection with Egypt. The Egyptians, like Stalin with his River Moscow, harnessed the power of the Nile for commercial and military purposes; the Nile quenched their thirst and irrigated their crops; and Isis and Ra, their gods of fertility and the sun, were associated directly with the life-giving force of the Nile, just as Stalin became the living symbol of Russia's hydraulic renaissance.

In addition, both pharaonic Egypt — with Memphis on the Nile Delta — and Soviet Russia — with Moscow on the Moscow-Volga Canal — were centralized, autocratic, pyramidal societies that depended on massive slave labor for their construction projects (slaves built the pyramids just as prisoners built the canals). Furthermore, as the pharaoh was perceived as a deity and credited with good harvests, Stalin was perceived as the sun and credited with the progress of Soviet agriculture and industry. Stalin culture also borrowed Egypt's dichotomous symbols of water and the desert so that paintings such as Irakly Toidze's *Stalin at the Ryon Hydro-Electric Power Station* of 1935 (fig. 26) assume a metaphorical significance, with Stalin clothed in white and bathed in sunlight as he pontificates to a group of heedful workmen in front of a new dam in a barren landscape.

A collection of essays on Stalin's transformations of nature, *Velikie sooruzheniia stalinskoi epokhi* (Great Constructions of the Stalin Epoch), published in Moscow in 1951, contains sections that could just as well have been written about Egypt: "Nastuplenie na peski" (Attacking the Sands), "Pokorenie pustyni" (Vanquishing the Desert), and "Bogatye urozhaia oroshaemykh polei" (The Rich Harvests of the Irrigated Fields).[35] Posters of the 1930s and 1940s also urged the viewer to "Overcome the Drought!" (fig. 27). Appropriately enough, camels are the beasts of burden in the *Salt Mines in Central Asia* poster referenced earlier (fig. 4).

The pharaonic metaphor is enticing, but in order to render it more credible the question as to why Stalin might have chosen to identify himself with the dynasties of Cheops, Ramses, or Tutankhamen must be answered. First, many regarded—and still regard—pharaonic Egypt as a highly successful society with advanced technology, effective law and order, and very efficient means of communication and transportation—a society that Stalin would have wished to emulate. Second, there was the precedent of Egyptian culture in Russian culture: from the authentically ancient sphinxes at the Academy of Arts Embankment on the River Neva in St. Petersburg in the late eighteenth century to Aleksandr Pushkin's fictional *Egyptian Nights* of the 1830s; from the importation of Napoleon's Egyptian taste into early nineteenth-century Russian architecture and furnishings to the cult of Cleopatra in Russia's *fin-de-siècle* poetry and dance; from the Egyptian motif on a pre-revolutionary elevator to the mummies displayed prominently in the main exhibition area of the Alexander III Museum in Moscow (now the Pushkin Museum of Fine Arts). This is not to say that Stalin was especially aware of Russia's Egyptomania, but the artistic, literary, and decorative sources were there, and their forceful presence helps to explain the continued fascination with Egypt during the Soviet period. This is reflected in the publication of several important art historical surveys, including Vladimir Pavlov's *The Sculptural Portrait in Ancient Egypt* and Moisei Ginzburg's *Egypt*[36]—although the passion for things Egyptian also ran high in other countries, such as Great Britain, France, and Germany, particularly when archaeological discoveries were made in the 1920s and 1930s.

The last line of "May There Always Be Sunshine," the song that unifies this essay, "May there always be me," expresses a simple desire that suggests the most solid bridge between Soviet and ancient Egyptian culture: the life everlasting, the immortality and superhumanity to which the healthy Soviet workers, ample peasants, and smiling children bear testimony in the sunlit photographs and paintings of the 1930s and 1940s. Surely the most obvious symbol of this aspiration is the Lenin mausoleum on Red Square

35. A. V. Topchiev et al., *Velikie sooruzheniia stalinskoi epokhi* (Moscow: Molodaia gvardiia, 1951).

36. Vladimir Pavlov, *Skul'pturnyi portret v Drevnem Egipete* (Moscow-Leningrad: Iskusstvo, 1937); Moisei Ginzburg, *Egipet* (Moscow: Akademiia arkhitektury, 1944).

fig. 28
Lenin lying in state. From
Arkhitektura mavzoleia Lenina (The Architecture of the Lenin Mausoleum) (Moscow: Gosudarstvennoe izdatel'stvo arkhitektury i gradostroitel'stva, 1950). Institute of Modern Russian Culture, Los Angeles.

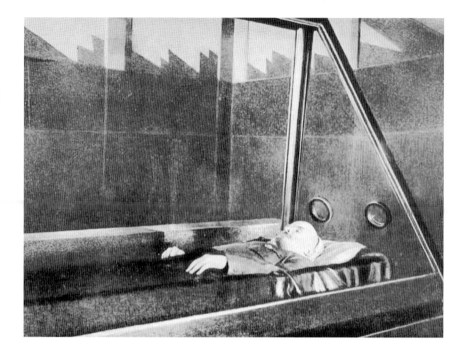

at the foot of the Kremlin wall, a stone's throw from the River Moscow, and inspired directly by the experience of ancient Egypt (fig. 28). There is evidence to suggest that Stalin, who supervised the plans for the granite mausoleum and followed the mummification of Lenin at all phases, was guided by the same arguments and rituals that inspired the Egyptians to create their pyramids, their sarcophagi, and their statuary.

The ancient Egyptians believed in life after death, and tried to preserve the human body as its container and vehicle for the journey of the spirit. Before they perfected the technique of mummification, the early Egyptians placed a sculptural likeness of the deceased within the tomb, so the effigy could assimilate the soul (a practice reminiscent of the multiplicity of statues to Lenin after his death). Since the pharaoh was God and his sepulcher the first abode of his soul, the structure of the sepulcher had to be durable and well appointed—which is why the pyramids were constructed to withstand time and were equipped with the appurtenances of the deceased for the voyage beyond. The alabaster sarcophagi, the texts and images (during the later dynasties), and, of course, the actual process of embalming were applied or interpreted in the entombment of Lenin.[37] Completed in October 1930 (corresponding with the thirteenth anniversary of the October Revolution), the permanent mausoleum betrayed a clear debt to pharaonic architecture (both Aleksei Shchusev, its architect, and Ignaty Nivinsky, its interior designer, were well versed in Egyptian antiquities). The polished surfaces of marble, granite, and porphyry, the mummy of Lenin under the plate-glass pyramid installed on the oxidized

37. For information on the embalming of Lenin, see Ilya Zbarsky and Samuel Hutchinson, *Lenin's Embalmers* (London: Harvill, 1998).

bronze base, the staircase leading to the room of mourning, the interior decorated in black and red, the diffused lighting, the proximity to the river of the capital — all remind us of the great pyramids of Saqqara and Giza.

Why was Stalin so enthusiastic about embalming Lenin, in spite of the adamant protests of Nadezhda Krupskaia, Lenin's widow?[38] Why did he undertake the extraordinary measure of placing the body on a catafalque in a mausoleum in order to observe an eternal lying-in-state, just as he was condoning the widespread destruction of saints' relics in the monasteries and churches? First, because a primary avenue of scientific inquiry in the early years of the Soviet state revolved around the quest for overcoming death; centers such as the Institute for Rejuvenation in Moscow conducted extensive medical research in this field.[39] The embalming of Lenin, therefore (and of Stalin later), held deep symbolic value and was a clear, though illusory, reference to the triumph over death. The Committee for the Embalming of Lenin, directed by V. N. Vorob'ev and Boris Zbarsky throughout the late 1920s, concluded:

> [The embalming] rests on solid scientific principles, which allow us to count on a state of preservation of Vladimir Il'ich's body for a long time — several decades; and can be viewed like this in a closed glass casket as long as the necessary humidity and temperature conditions are observed.[40]

38. See Ibid., especially chaps. 2 and 3.

39. The architect Konstantin Mel'nikov was especially interested in rejuvenation and immortality. See S. Frederick Starr, *Melnikov. Solo Architect in a Mass Society* (Princeton, N.J.: Princeton University Press, 1978), especially chap. 10.

40. Boris Zbarsky, *Mavzolei Lenina* (Moscow: OGIZ, 1946), 37.

For Stalin, there was also the appeal of the ancient ritual of the early dynasties, whereby the aged leader was killed in order to make room for his younger successor. The "ritual sacrifice" of Lenin countenanced the ascension of Stalin, so that Stalin, standing atop the mausoleum, now controlled the dynasty bequeathed to him (fig. 29). Nikolai Stoiarov's 1950 history of the mausoleum reinforces the message:

> The name of Lenin, written on the mausoleum, sounds as a call to battle, an appeal for victory. Lenin lives with us, he leads us. Stalin is Lenin today.[41]

This, of course, echoes the maxim that for decades graced the streets and squares of the Soviet Union: "Lenin lived, Lenin lives, Lenin will live."

Once again, Stalin's pharaonic connections—the solar power, the water-works, and the bid for eternity—bring us back to the images of aridity and fluidity. It is tempting to forge a relationship between the impending drought of 1933 and the imposition of Socialist Realism the following year—in broader terms, between the human desert of the "Great Terror" and the false waters of propaganda, bringing a plenitude of ideological irrigation. In the shifting sands of Stalin's Russia, people vanished, the gulags crisscrossed the Siberian tundra, and the regime of secrecy and reticence vied with the uniformity and silence of a natural desert. True, there were oases, real and metaphorical, restorative and invigorating, such as Gor'ky Park, genuine achievements in mass literacy and heavy industry, and enduring works of literature and art, which attracted unfailing optimism with their technical virtuosity. But as the Stalin era recedes ever further into the myth of history, the abiding danger becomes the temptation to see only the oases, not the desert, and to delight in the mirage of Socialist Realism while forgetting the cruelty of the unrelenting sun.

Stalin's dream of immortality did not come to pass, and the great visions and projects of his culture proved to be fragile illusions. The canals did not function, and the damming of the rivers and the irrigation of the deserts brought ecological disaster. The Palace of the Soviets was never built, the Exhibition of Economic Achievements continues to crumble, and the question still lingers whether Lenin's body will be buried and the mausoleum demolished. The brilliant sun high in the sky has been eclipsed, the gods cast down, nothing seems to remain from that grandiose legacy, and the little song "May There Always Be Sunshine" transposes into a lamentation. But perhaps not all is lost, for there is still the third and most uplifting line of the refrain, "May there always be Mama." Just one year before Stalin's death, the Socialist Realist Fedor Reshetnikov

41. Nikolai Stoiarov, *Arkhitektura mavzoleia Lenina* (Moscow: Gosudarstvennoe izdatel'stvo arkhitektury i gradostroitel'stva, 1950), 86.

fig. 30
Fedor Reshetnikov,
Bad Grades, Again!,
oil on canvas, 102 x 94 cm,
1952. State Tretiakov
Gallery, Moscow.
Courtesy of Galart
Publishing, Moscow.

painted his sentimental *Bad Grades, Again!*[42] (fig. 30), which now might read as a metaphor for Mother Russia chiding little Joseph: the school of life has treated him harshly and his dreams are in smithereens. So the happy note on which to finish this melancholy essay about a regime that proved to be so mortal is that there's always mother: Ra may fade, but Isis lives on. ✧

---

42. Reshetnikov also helped with the design of *Kak my spasali cheliuskintsev*. See note 8's reference to the industrial book designed by El Lissitzky, *Industriia sotsializma*.

Juliet Kinchin

Modernity and Tradition in Hungarian Furniture, 1900–1938: Three Generations

Juliet Kinchin is a lecturer in design history and honorary reader at the University of Glasgow where she established the graduate program in decorative arts in 1987. She headed a British team of scholars in a three-year collaboration with the Hungarian University of Design and the Hungarian Academy of Sciences, 1996–1999. Recent publications include essays in the anthologies *Art Nouveau 1890–1914* (2000), *E. W. Godwin Aesthetic Movement Architect and Designer* (1999), and *Charles Rennie Mackintosh* (1996). The research for this essay was initiated during her time as a Wolfsonian Fellow in 1997.

Using three case studies of furniture in The Wolfsonian's collection from 1905, 1923, and 1935, this article examines broad developments within a rich and fascinating phase of Hungarian design. Together, the studies reveal a creative dialectic between international and national tendencies, demonstrating how three generations negotiated issues of Hungarian identity, tradition, and modernity. The first third of the twentieth century was a period shaped by the devastating conflict of World War I, the subsequent dismemberment of the Austro-Hungarian Empire, and the rise of a conservative nationalist faction in the wake of the short-lived Bolshevik Council of Soviets in 1919. As one might expect, these larger political and socioeconomic changes were reflected in the shifting alignment of Hungarian design vis-à-vis the world at large, a process that can be traced through the successive stories of the three eminent designers featured in this article — Pál Horti (1865–1907), Lajos Kozma (1884–1948), and Ernö Goldfinger (1902–1987) — and the furniture they designed.

Horti, Kozma, and Goldfinger all participated in a cosmopolitan avant-garde, moving freely among artistic centers in Europe and America. In this sense their furniture was not produced in a closed world, with Horti spending significant time in the United States and dying in India, and Goldfinger residing for the majority of his life in London. Yet despite such a diaspora, these designers can also be linked to a distinctively Hungarian tradition, with Kozma's long and prolific career stylistically bridging Horti's National Romanticism and Goldfinger's fully fledged Modernism. The three men moved easily among furniture and interior design, architecture, and graphics, and were actively involved in disseminating their ideas through publications and exhibitions.

Detail of Lajos Kozma's preliminary artwork for a promotional design for the fashion house Antal and Hosszu, early 1920s.

fig. 1
Pál Horti, *Crafters Clock No. 331,* long-case clock, manufactured by Oscar Onken and Company for The Shop of the Crafters, oak with wood inlays, glass roundels, brass and beaten-copper panels, 208 x 55 x 36 cm, c. 1906. The Mitchell Wolfson Jr. Collection, The Wolfsonian–Florida International University, Miami Beach, Florida. Photograph by Silvia Ros.

The continuities between these designers have been obscured by the construction of design histories from a predominantly Western European or North American perspective. Although their work has been extensively published, exhibited, and represented in Hungarian collections, Horti and Kozma remain little known in a more international arena.[1] Goldfinger, on the other hand, like his compatriots Marcel Breuer (1902–1981) and László Moholy-Nagy (1895–1946), epitomizes the way in which émigrés have been absorbed into the history of more dominant cultures, often with little reference to their country of origin.[2]

Pál Horti in America

Pál Horti was born in Pest in 1865. He began his career as a fine artist, but following his appointment in 1890 as a lecturer at the Budapest School of Industrial Design (Iparrajiskola), Horti focused on an ever-increasing range of decorative arts. His international reputation was confirmed by medals received at the Paris Exposition Universelle in 1900—a gold for his carpets and furniture designs and a bronze for ornaments and decorative silverware. Subsequently Horti was charged with overseeing the Hungarian presence at the Louisiana Purchase International Exposition of 1904 in St. Louis, Missouri. Based on the strength of his participation at this event (for which he won a gold medal and a diploma of honor), Horti received commissions from two American furniture manufacturers. Reflecting on Horti's achievements, Hungarian critic István Dömötör commented in a 1908 article, "Anyone who is going to write about the early phases of Hungarian decorative art will come across the traces of Pál Horti's talent everywhere... He tried everything, and in everything he tried he achieved a European standard."[3]

The first item under consideration is a long-case clock designed by Pál Horti in 1905 and manufactured by Oscar Onken and Company of Cincinnati for their outlet in the same city, The Shop of the Crafters (fig. 1). The clock was part of a larger set of oak dining room furniture that was the firm's main product line for 1906.[4] Horti enlivened the strong, simple lines of Onken's Mission-style oak with colorful inlays of wood, glass roundels, and beaten-copper panels. Onken (1848–1948) felt that such pieces demonstrated Horti's far-reaching influence on the crafts

1. The Magyar Iparművészeti Múzeum has extensive holdings of both designers' work in a variety of media, which have featured in a sequence of exhibitions and monographs. The most important of these are Judit Koós, *Horti Pál élete és művészete 1865–1907* (Budapest: Akadémiai Kiadó, 1982); László Beke, Kozma Lajos (Budapest: Akadémiai Kiadó, 1975); Judit Koós, *Kozma Lajos Munkássága* (Budapest: Akadémiai Kiadó, 1975); Eva Kiss, *Kozma Lajos, az Iparművész (1884–1948)* (Budapest: Iparművészeti Múzeum, 1994).

2. Interestingly, the first study of Goldfinger was published in Hungary ten years before one appeared in Britain. See Máté Major, *Goldfinger Ernö* (Budapest, 1973), and James Dunnett and Gavin Stamp, *Ernö Goldfinger, Works* (London: Architectural Association, 1983).

3. Published in the magazine *Művészet* (Art) (1908); quoted in *Magyar Művészet 1890–1914* (Budapest: Akadémiai Kiadó, 1981), 1: 511.

4. Stephen Gray, ed., *Arts and Crafts Furniture. Shop of the Crafters at Cincinnati* (New York: Turn of the Century Editions, 1983). Includes reprint of the 1905 catalogue.

movement in America. Horti was producing comparable designs at the same time for Charles P. Limbert and Company of Grand Rapids, Michigan, another manufacturer of Arts and Crafts furniture.[5] Horti designed the clock at the culmination of his professional career and international reputation; it was one of the last pieces produced before his untimely death at age forty-two in 1907. Designed by a Hungarian and manufactured in the United States, the clock is a hybrid piece that relates to progressive tendencies in both nations. Furthermore, the commission, and the way it was promoted and reviewed in the press on both sides of the Atlantic, provides an unusually clear example of the impact of international exhibitions and the agendas behind them.

By the opening years of the twentieth century, Hungary had undergone a period of rapid industrialization and occupied a relatively privileged position within the Hapsburg Empire as a partner in the so-called Dual Monarchy that joined Austria and Hungary. Despite the economic advantages and political autonomy this afforded, however, it was a partnership very much dominated by Austria. In response to this imbalance, the Hungarian government increasingly sought to challenge Austrian hegemony by embarking on an international style offensive, which meant ambitious participation in world's fairs and other exhibitions abroad. On this international circuit, Horti proved to be a particularly effective ambassador of his country's brand of modern design. A contemporary described him as having

> a passion to show Hungary to outsiders as a place of culture, and the Hungarians as vigorous and capable of dealing with their own future rather than wallowing in turn-of-the-century angst. He longed to demonstrate that within a couple of decades they had shown themselves able to keep up with foreign peoples, while being Hungarian in all political, cultural and artistic matters.[6]

Horti had been prominently involved at the international expositions of Paris in 1900 and Turin, Italy, in 1902. At the latter he was hailed as "one of the most zealous advocates of the new trend in Hungary, a Proteus-like, many-sided artist."[7] This track record, combined with his experience as a teacher and entrepreneur in so many different areas of the decorative arts, made Horti ideally suited to coordinate the Hungarian installation at St. Louis in 1904. The Hungarian government commissioned Horti to design the architectural envelope for the nation's exhibit within the Manufactures Building and to curate the displays within, which included a dining room setting of his own design.

5. The earliest of the published Limbert designs is marked "St. Louis 1904," which implies that the armchair in question could have been designed for the exposition. The other documented designs for these firms seem to date to 1905, some designed in St. Louis and others in New York. See also the catalogue reprints in Robert Edwards, *The Arts and Crafts Furniture of Charles P. Limbert* (Watkins Glen, N.Y.: The American Life Foundation, 1982).

6. Gyula Schmidt, "Horti Utolsó Utjáról," *Magyar Iparművészet* 10 (1907): 173–176.

7. Letter accompanying the award of a Diploma of Honor quoted in *Magyar Iparművészet* (1903): 297.

fig. 2
Pál Horti, Hungarian
section in the
Manufactures Building
at the Louisiana Purchase
International Exposition,
St. Louis, 1904.
From *Magyar
Iparművészet*, 1904.
Collection OmvH Magyar
Epitészeti Múzeum,
Budapest, Hungary.

Not having participated at the Chicago World's Fair in 1893, the Hungarian government saw the St. Louis exposition as particularly important in establishing an identifiable and progressive image for Hungary in the United States.[8] Hungary was not, however, prepared to invest enough to erect a freestanding pavilion or to dispatch the kind of historical treasures that had been shown at Paris in 1900.[9] Given their budget, the Hungarians decided to focus on exhibiting saleable traditional crafts and their high-profile modern equivalents, as they were already trading in these types of goods with the United States. Some of the exhibits selected, such as the ceramics manufactured by Zsolnay and Herend, the colored glasswares, or the array of decorative wrought-iron products, were already familiar to American audiences. Indeed, Horti was able to identify various American imitations of the Zsolnay wares elsewhere in the exhibition. His own imposing wrought-iron gate at the entrance to the Hungarian section in the Manufactures Building had already sold for twelve hundred dollars before the start of the exhibition, with further orders indicating a healthy boost in exports of such decorative ironwork

8. The politician Count Apponyi remarked, "This display of decorative arts is extremely significant for our commercial connections, and shows the work in an international context. The development of a modern style that has been gaining momentum since Paris, is also of great importance to us nationally." Quoted in "St. Louis-i kiállitásunk," *Magyar Iparművészet* 7 (1904): 215.

9. Other than the decorative arts, Horti was frankly embarrassed by the Hungarian exhibits that were scattered around the various sections of the exposition. Having fought for the principle of independent representation, like many people, Horti felt that this was a missed opportunity, particularly as Austria was there in force.

fig. 3
Aladár Körösfői Kriesch,
*Kalotaszeg Peasants
on Their Way to Church*,
design for mural over
the gateway to the
Hungarian section in
the Manufactures
Building at the Louisiana
Purchase International
Exposition, St. Louis,
1904. From *Magyar
Iparművészet*, 1904.
Collection OmvH Magyar
Epitészeti Múzeum,
Budapest, Hungary.

to the United States.[10] Conversely, the whole exhibition and many of the American manufacturers were given tremendous coverage in the Hungarian design press. Louis Comfort Tiffany's products had already made a mark in Budapest and were a recognizable influence on the leading Hungarian stained glass artist, Miksa Róth (1865–1944).[11]

Following the precedent of the British Arts and Crafts movement, many countries, particularly Hungary, explored folk or vernacular sources in their 1904 exhibits. Horti's design for the Hungarian pavilion within the St. Louis Manufactures Building took the form of a modernized, wooden Transylvanian country house, with its characteristic towers, fence, and "Székely" gate—the latter referring to ethnic Hungarian peoples of the same name (fig. 2).[12] This was a brilliant piece of stage-set propaganda that illustrated both the survival of an ancient culture and its role as a source for modern art. For an Anglo-American audience there was the added frisson of Transylvania's bloodcurdling association with *Dracula*, Bram Stoker's bestseller published in 1897. In the period leading up to World War I, the search for a Hungarian cultural identity was very much tied to the ethnographic exploration and recording of folk arts in Transylvania. This geographically remote area in eastern Hungary was felt to be the country's cultural heartland, a place in which Hungarian traditions had survived in their most distinct form, relatively free from Hapsburg intervention. The artist-designer Aladár Körösfői Kriesch (1863–1920) celebrated Transylvania in a mural over the gateway to the Hungarian exhibit, depicting picturesquely clad peasants on their way to a church in the region of Kalotaszeg (fig. 3). Kriesch saw Transylvania as a "little

10. "St. Louis-i kiállitásunk," 215.

11. Béla Tákach worked for Tiffany's in 1902 and Géza Maróti was to employ both Tiffany and Miksa Róth in his design for the interior of the National Theatre in Mexico City, 1908.

12. In a similar vein, the Vajdahunyad Castle in Transylvania was re-created in Budapest as part of the Hungarian Millenary Exposition in 1896 and can still be seen in the city's Varosliget Park. The Székeley were the older of the two ethnic Hungarian peoples who settled in Transylvania. Their vernacular woodwork was much admired and collected around 1900.

Ruskinian land"—referencing English critic John Ruskin's (1819–1900) passion for the values and aesthetics of traditional society.[13]

Such an image of a spiritually driven, frictionless society, however, masked the ethnic tensions that were brought out in R. W. Seton-Watson's 1908 study, *The Racial Problems of Hungary*. Like America, Hungary was a melting pot for many different ethnic groups. This may be attributed to the nation's landlocked position at the crossroads between east and west. The rhetoric of the frontier and its pioneers, which pervaded the catalogue to the St. Louis world's fair and those of most other international expositions in the United States, would have struck a chord with anyone from Budapest, itself a relatively young capital. There were at least six culturally distinct minorities in Transylvania, and so it required a degree of manipulation to derive a clear-cut notion of "Hungarian" identity.

Horti's ability to move between the self-conscious folksiness of the exhibit's architecture and the more sophisticated urban aesthetic of the dining room he exhibited within clearly appealed to Onken and Limbert. While most of the furniture Horti designed for them was in an unpolished, vernacular style, his more glamorous Secessionist mode was played up in the graphics and photographs used for marketing purposes (fig. 4). Just as Hungary's modern, urban style only referenced some of the nation's myriad folk traditions, so The Shop of the Crafters—in a Horti-designed ad of 1905— aimed to pick up on "vibrations" from every state (fig. 5), transcending particular regional variations with an amalgam that would be nationally and internationally recognizable.

13. Aladár Körösfői Kriesch quoted in Akos Moravansky, *Competing Visions: Aesthetic Invention and Social Imagination in Central European Architecture, 1867–1918* (Cambridge, Mass.: MIT Press, 1998), 258. Kriesch had written a book on Ruskin and the Pre-Raphaelites.

fig. 6
(above)
Lajos Kozma, frontispiece for *A Ház* magazine, linocut, 1908. The Mitchell Wolfson Jr. Collection, The Wolfsonian–Florida International University, Miami Beach, Florida. Photograph by Silvia Ros.

fig. 7
(above, far right)
Deszö Zrumeczky, detail showing fenestration of a primary school, Budapest, Hungary, 1911–1912. Photograph by the author, 2000.

The aesthetic derived from Hungary's vernacular wooden architecture, which Horti pioneered at St. Louis, was subsequently adapted to both metropolitan architecture and furniture. The wooden spire in particular assumed iconic significance for the group known as A Fiátolok (The Young Ones), as demonstrated in the 1908 linocut by one of its members, Lajos Kozma (fig. 6). This image appeared as the frontispiece of the magazine *A Ház* (The House), a focal point for the group. In Horti's designs for Onken and Limbert of 1905, one can see traces of traditional carpenter detailing in the plank construction, the tulip cutouts, and the notched, chamfered, and pierced decoration. Particularly architectonic is the angled shape of the hood on the Onken clock, which is characteristic of eaves and openings in vernacular Hungarian architecture. It was a shape subsequently taken up in fenestration, doorways, and gables by other designers associated with The Young Ones, such as Károly Kós (1883–1977) and Deszö Zrumeczky (1884–1917) (fig. 7). One finds similar forms in contemporary architecture and furniture in Finland, a nation to which Hungary was closely related in this period, artistically and linguistically.[14]

Progressive Hungarian designers and critics of the time felt that folk ornament most clearly expressed both the eastern strain within Hungarian identity—which looked back to its mythic origins in Central Asia—and a connection to nature through stylized floral forms. Many folk embroidery patterns were stitched in strips, side-by-side, with a terminating line at their base, and one can see how these were readily transferable onto the often-vertical forms of Secessionist or Arts and Crafts furniture, like the long-case clock. For Horti, Native American and Aztec sources resonated with associations of ancient Hungarian folk traditions, and the incorporation of "Indian" decoration in his design for an Onken piano in 1905 was

14. Hungarian is a Finno-Ugric language.

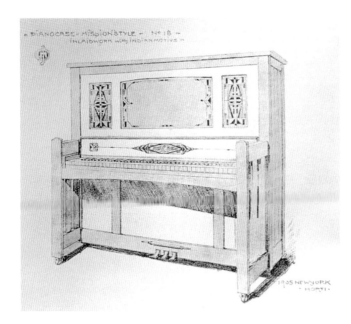

fig. 8
(above)
Pál Horti, *Pianocase –
Mission Style – No. 18
Inlaidwork with Indian
Motivs*, 1905. From
Magyar Iparművészet,
1907. Collection
OmvH Magyar
Epitészeti Múzeum,
Budapest, Hungary.

fig. 9
(above, far right)
Pál Dóczi, detail of
*Peruvian Reconstruction.
Yellow Peacock,* water-
color textile design for
the Manus Weaving
Workshop, Budapest,
Hungary, 1912. Arte
Galéria és Aukciós Iroda,
Budapest, Hungary.

about awakening the "vibrations" of a common ancient culture (fig. 8).[15] In this sense Horti's journey to the New World was part of a process of self-exploration, an examination of origins, "which would bring about a revolution not only in all their ideas about art but also about their [Hungarians'] ancient original history." At the St. Louis world's fair he had the chance to observe directly the arts of Japan and China, and the next year he traveled to Mexico and then San Francisco, all the while avidly sketching, collecting, and photographing with a view to holding an exhibition at the Museum of Decorative Arts on his return to Hungary. In Mexico, he actually took part in the excavation of Aztec remains.[16] Horti's pioneering interest in American indigenous culture would later emerge in other Hungarian work, such as the 1908 National Theater in Mexico City by Géza Maróti (1875–1941), the famous Aztec-mask logo designed in 1924 for the electronics firm Orion by József Bottlik (1897–1984), and a 1912 "Peruvian" rug design by Pál Dóczi (fig. 9).

Apart from looking to the Americas for further resolution of Hungarian style and history, Horti was on an economic mission. He was to report to the Hungarian government on decorative art manufacturing in the United States, in particular the furniture industry.[17] There was help from Hungarian contacts, such as Arnold Somlyó, managing director of the Baldwin Piano factory in Cincinatti. Horti also looked at some of the large commercial firms in Grand Rapids, Michigan, which produced rocking chairs or what he described as "practical and inventive" office furniture. Hungarians felt that they had much to learn from America about

15. Schmidt, "Horti Utolsó Utjáról," 73.

16. Ibid., 74.

17. His extended tour was supported by two grants of 6,000 krona from the Ministries of Commerce and Foreign Affairs. *Magyar Iparművészet* 8 (1905): 222.

business practices and workshop organization. A growing number of young designers had been attracted to the United States by the kind of working conditions described in a glowing account published in *Magyar Iparművészet* (Hungarian Decorative Art) in 1903 by József Galánszky, a decorative artist who had moved to New York the previous year. Among the advantages Galánszky described were better living conditions, union-established minimum wages, and the lack of army conscription.[18]

A central problem for many designers in this period was how to reconcile the social and aesthetic ideals of the Arts and Crafts movement with the economic and technological conditions of modern life. While many in Europe and America looked to Britain for ideological leadership on this issue, others increasingly saw the actual products of the British Arts and Crafts movement as exclusive and irrelevant. Writing in 1902 about British arts and crafts on display in Budapest, the Hungarian socialist József Diner-Dénes warned, "We are not rich enough, we are not aesthetic enough to encourage this art," and urged Hungarian designers to turn instead to Germany and America, noting of the latter:

> The Americans are adapting to modern developments in their arts and crafts. Their purpose is to abandon handcraft and to work only with machinery... This is the realization of democracy in art. The same kind of idea, the same kind of forms for everyone, only the price varies.[19]

This orientation away from Britain was consistent with Horti's conclusions about the St. Louis exposition, where he found the German pavilion to be the most modern, homogenous, and well organized.[20] He saw designers like Peter Behrens, Hans Olbrich, and Bernard Pankok as representing "the modern style of the future," although he found their aesthetic "too dry, too bulky, too forced and too cold," and felt they needed to inject a little Italianate color and a touch of French refinement.[21] Arguably this was the sort of blend that Horti himself was attempting in his designs for Onken and Limbert. Particularly in Horti's graphics for these firms—the advertisements, stationery, and greeting cards—the swirling, organic lines of the frames that evince traces of his earlier, more Francophile style are balanced by a new, more rectilinear sense of restraint and symmetry (figs. 4 and 5). These American manufacturers appealed to the entrepreneur in Horti. Both Onken and Limbert purported to operate their businesses in the manner of William Morris, promoting values of craftsmanship, "truth to materials," and improved working conditions for artisans, all

18. József Galánszky, "Levél Amerikáböl," *Magyar Iparművészet* 6 (1903): 90–91. Designers and artisans there, he felt, dressed better and had more of a sense of self-worth. On the whole the unions seemed to have set fair minimum wages, compared to the dire position of apprentices in Hungary. Another plus was the absence of taxation for the majority of tradesmen.

19. József Diner-Dénes, "A Brit Művészet Kiállítás," *Művészet* (1902): 324.

20. His extensive report was fully published as "A St. Louis-i Világkiállítás," *Magyar Iparművészet* 7 (November 1904): 249–313.

21. Ibid., 268.

combined with mechanized production methods and a modern approach to marketing and distribution. Horti's 1905 design for what he labeled a "Morris chair"—a type of plain oak, leather-upholstered armchair—paid tribute to the intellectual influence of the British Arts and Crafts movement in both America and Hungary.[22]

The time seemed ripe for the introduction of a Secession style that had been tried and tested on the European market, particularly as most Hungarian commentators felt that America had no modern design to speak of.[23] "The Americans are waiting for designers with real talent, and the better ones are offered fairytale wages," claimed one writer in *Magyar Iparművészet*.[24] Yet many expressed ambivalence about the frantic speed and naked commercialism of the New World:

> The slogan of the American people is "business." The Yankee businessman does not feel the need to consider art, unless it be something to trade with, in which case he imports it from wherever it is available in the best quality and quantity.... There is nothing in Europe, in terms of forms or materials, which cannot be copied. They simply do not have time for art.[25]

This was fundamentally at odds with the lifestyle and art espoused by such purists as Sándor Nagy (1868–1950) and Aladár Körösfői Kriesch in their colony at Gödöllő.[26]

Horti's continuing American adventures were tracked in the Hungarian news.[27] On his way home he intended to make a personal study of bronze casting, patination, and enameling, and the domestic crafts of Japan, China, and India, but the trip proved fatal. He arrived in San Francisco just after the earthquake and fire in 1906. There he contracted malaria, which took its toll during his visit to Japan. Finally, in May 1907, Horti was finished off by yellow fever in sweltering Bombay (today's Mumbai).

There is a certain self-fulfilling symbolism in the last years of Horti's life-journey. He was one of the first prominent Hungarian designers to head west from the Old World, presaging the veritable flood of émigrés that was to follow. While on his homebound journey he delved backward into Hungary's spiritual and ethnographic origins in Asia. In this sense there could hardly have been a more fitting place to die than India. Like the

22. The design for the "Morris chair, library suit [*sic*]" was illustrated in *Magyar Iparművészet* 10 (1907): 182. Onken, Limbert, and Stickley all produced plain oak "Morris" chairs, often with an adjustable back and upholstered in leather.

23. Horti reported: "America lacks modern decorative art. There are a few pieces, but these tend to be copies after English and Scottish models." *Magyar Iparművészet* 7 (November 1904): 257.

24. Loránd Ballogh, "Takách Béla. Egy Amerikában élő Epítő-művész," *Magyar Iparművészet* 10 (1907): 197–198.

25. Ibid.

26. In 1929 Sandor Nagy was still lamenting the threat posed by "German genre stylization and industrially made products." Sandor Nagy, "Múlt, Jelen, Jövő," *Magyar Iparművészet* 32 (1929): 1–3.

27. *Magyar Iparművészet* 8 (1905): 67; *Magyar Iparművészet* 10 (1907): 182–183.

fig. 10
Pál Horti's grave marker
in the Kerepési cemetery,
Budapest, Hungary,
designed by Ede Telcs
with mosaics by Miksa
Róth, 1907. Photograph
by the author.

fig. 10
Pál Horti's grave marker
in the Kerepési cemetery,
Budapest, Hungary,
designed by Ede Telcs
with mosaics by Miksa
Róth, 1907. Photograph
by the author.

architects Ödön Lechner (1845–1914) before him and István Medgyaszay (1877–1959) after, Horti was fascinated by the view that, of all eastern cultures, India was perhaps the most important for "Magyar" (Hungarian) identity. For several decades, ethnographers and philologists had sought the origins of the Hungarian peoples among the tribes and language groups of northern India and Tibet. This was part of a larger search for national identity and of the move toward political self-determination in Hungary.[28] Horti's remains were transported home, where his friends Ede Telcs and Miksa Róth designed a suitably affectionate gravestone to him in Budapest's famous Kerepési cemetery. The larger-than-life bust of Horti tops a marker inlaid with stylized gold tulips (a symbol of Hungarian identity) such as he himself might have designed (fig. 10).

Furniture to Dream by: Lajos Kozma and the Neo-Baroque

Lajos Kozma was born in 1884 to a family of German extraction in Somogy county, southwest of Budapest. He qualified as an architect in 1906, but it was as a graphic designer that he first came to public attention. Throughout his working life, Kozma was closely associated with numerous literary and artistic figures, including Hungarian poet Endre Ady and French painter Henri Matisse, having studied with the latter in Paris from 1909 to 1910. Over the course of a career spanning two world wars, Kozma worked in a succession of styles that reflected Hungary's changing political and economic situation, emerging as one of the most prominent Hungarian designers of his generation. In the 1920s his name was synonymous with the development of a neo-Baroque manner that was applied to architecture, interiors, furniture, textiles, and graphic design. As its second case study this article focuses on a 1923 bedroom cabinet designed by Kozma that exemplifies this style (fig. 11).

Kozma has been described as picking up Hungarian design at the place where Horti left off,[29] but at first sight Kozma's neo-Baroque cabinet appears to have little in common with the austere clock designed by Horti (fig. 1). And yet, the two are not the polar opposites one might expect.

28. The search for linguistic and ethnic roots of the Magyar has been a constantly recurring theme in Hungarian cultural and scientific journals from the mid-nineteenth century to the present day.

29. *Magyar Művészet 1890–1914,* 1: 516.

fig. 11
(opposite page)
Lajos Kozma, bedroom
cabinet, ebonized walnut,
made by József Krausz,
70 x 63 x 35 cm, 1923.
The Mitchell Wolfson Jr.
Collection, The
Wolfsonian–Florida
International University,
Miami Beach, Florida.
Photograph by Silvia Ros.

fig. 12
(above)
Attributed to Gyula Kaesz
or a student at the
Magyar Iparművészeti
Főiskola, drawing room
cabinet, ebonized
wood and gilt, c. 1925.
Collection OmvH Magyar
Epitészeti Múzeum,
Budapest, Hungary.

Both addressed the expression of Hungarian identity in design. Symptomatic of the connection between Horti and Kozma is the fact that in 1898 both men dropped their Germanic-sounding names (Hirth and Fuchs) in favor of more Hungarian alternatives.[30] The continuity is also clear in Kozma's powerful graphic stylizations of Hungarian folk motifs and Symbolist literary themes during the period of his association with The Young Ones in the years leading up to World War I (fig. 6). Like Horti, this group was intent on establishing a distinctively Hungarian identity rooted in folk traditions. Kozma's personal commitment to the ideal of Hungarian nationhood was underlined by his active service as an artillery officer throughout World War I and his subsequent appointment at the Budapest Technical University under the short-lived Bolshevik government of 1919.

Kozma never lost his fascination with folk culture and Hungarian mythology, but increasingly he also looked to historical precedent to express national identity and the blend of eastern and western influences that was such an integral part of Hungarian design. As early as 1911 he was designing furniture that referred not only to folk arts, but also to the materials, construction, and styling associated with Hungarian and English cabinet-making traditions of the eighteenth century. By the early to mid-1920s, Kozma successfully developed this tendency into a full-blown "folk baroque" manner, and through his teaching he inspired a generation of students and colleagues to work in a similar vein (fig. 12). Although referencing a historically specific style, such designers viewed the experimental and dynamic forms of the Baroque as potentially progressive. Moreover, it was associated with the time of Rákóczi (1676–1735), a Transylvanian prince who had sought Hungary's political independence.

The evolution in Kozma's work from National Romanticism to neo-Baroque was theoretically informed by his understanding of how German art historians Alois Riegl (1858–1905) and Heinrich Wölfflin (1864–1945) sought to explain stylistic change.[31] In developing broad conceptual tools to present the visual culture of all eras, these scholars deliberately looked

30. Béla Lajto, a Jewish architect with whom Kozma collaborated, changed his name from Leitesdorfer. Aladár Kreisch added the prefix "Körösfői" to his surname, just as Ede Wigand interpolated "Thoroczkai."

31. See draft of the lecture series he planned to deliver at the Budapest Technical University in the autumn of 1919, reprinted in *Lapis Angularis* 1 (Budapest: OmvH Magyar Epitészeti Múzeum, 1995): 131. He was drawing on Riegl's *Spätrömische Kunstindustrie* and Wölfflin's recently published *Kunstgeschichtliche Grundbegriffe*. Béla Kuhn's government fell and the lectures were not delivered.

at what were then unfashionable periods, such as the late Roman (Riegl) and Baroque (Wölfflin). In doing so they challenged the dominant, morally inflected perception that such styles reflected the decline and decay of the cultures that produced them. John Ruskin, for example, the critic who was so influential on Horti's generation, had abhorred the Catholic Baroque as socially and aesthetically degenerate. This changing historiography of the Baroque indicates how the intellectual context in which Kozma was operating differed with that of the preceding generation. Both Riegl and Wölfflin suggested that styles have an inherent tendency to change. For Wölfflin this process comprised a fluctuation between polarities, whereas for Riegl ornament was one of the elements in an endless sequence of transformation, whereby what started as a classical statue, for example, might end up as a carpet pattern.

Like the original Baroque style, its revival in the 1920s and 1930s had an international dimension.[32] Kozma's friend Imre Kner, a publisher, described how the designer had been looking for "the big style" that would reflect all cultural tendencies in an epoch.[33] In the context of Hungary, the neo-Baroque certainly expressed the political and cultural identity crisis triggered by World War I and its aftermath. Austro-Hungarian forces had been brought into direct and bloody combat with the Allied powers of Britain and France. Although Kozma had lived in Paris from 1909 to 1910, the Hungarian designer found himself in active service as an artillery officer for nearly four years, much of it on the front in Transylvania. As demonstrated so vividly at St. Louis and in the work of The Young Ones, the folk arts of this eastern part of Hungary had been central to the development of a Hungarian style. But under the terms of the 1920 Treaty of Trianon, this whole region was ceded to Romania, resulting in another layer of complication for designers trying to evoke a genuinely "Magyar" identity. This was particularly problematic for those with family connections to Transylvania or those who had invested heavily in ethnographic studies of that region. The transition was perhaps slightly less painful for Kozma in that the region of Somogy, where he had grown up, remained within the nation's newly contracted borders.[34]

Transylvania was not the only loss. Altogether Hungary ceded about seventy percent of its territory and sixty percent of its population, and was made to pay reparations. The dismemberment of the Hapsburg Empire meant that Hungarian producers no longer had straightforward access to a large and secure domestic market, and the country retained only a fraction of

32. Stephen Calloway, *Baroque Baroque, the Culture of Excess* (Oxford: Phaidon, 1994), provides a study of the neo-Baroque as an international style.

33. Emerich [Imre] Kner, "Introduction," in Ludwig [Lajos] Kozma, *Das Signetbuch* (Gyoma: Kner, 1925), xiv.

34. Together with artist friends he had organized a couple of exhibitions at Kaposvár, juxtaposing local traditional crafts with modern designs. Gyula Mihalik, "A Kaposvári kiállítás," *Magyar Iparművészet* 8 (September 1905): 245, 249–252.

fig. 13
Lajos Kozma, stock
woodcut borders and
vignettes for Imre
Kner's publishing house,
Gyoma, Hungary,
c. 1925. From Lajos
Kozma, *Tipografiai*
Diszetmények **(Gyoma:**
Kner, 1927). Magyar
Iparművészeti Múzeum,
Budapest, Hungary.

its iron production, forests, and railroad network.[35] Nearly all industrial machinery and raw materials now had to be imported. In the furniture industry this resulted in a delayed adoption of the mass-manufacturing techniques in which Pál Horti and the prewar government had shown such interest. Kozma was far from averse to mass production. Indeed, his collaboration with the publisher Imre Kner, for whom he developed a corporate design policy in the early 1920s, yielded stock patterns, typefaces, and layouts (fig. 13).[36] Together with Kner, Kozma also became a founding member of the Hungarian Werkbund (Magyar Műhely Szövetszeg), revamped in 1932; by that time he was designing tubular steel furniture for manufacturers like Thonet.

Mass production and large-scale public commissions, however, were not options for the Budapesti Műhely (Budapest Workshops) that Kozma had established in 1913.[37] Like their counterparts in Vienna and Prague, proponents of the Műhely intended to create an intimate contact between the client, the designer, and the craftsman, and there was clearly still a small but sufficiently affluent bourgeois clientele to support such an enterprise. This meant Kozma could continue working in different media, maintaining the quality control, craft ethic, and collaborative practices that he valued. Closely related pieces of furniture were produced in small runs or as part of individual commissions. A drawing for The Wolfsonian's cabinet, and another version made of chestnut in the collections of the Hungarian Museum of Decorative Arts, were produced by craftsman József Krausz.[38] Similar pieces were made by another Műhely craftsman, Károly Kozma (no relation), who wrote a small booklet in 1925 on cabinetmaking.[39] Many of Karoly Kozma's views hark back to English designer Charles Ashbee's 1908 pamphlet, *Craftmanship in Competitive Industry,* showing the extent to which a British Arts and Crafts mentality still prevailed in Hungarian design circles.

Lajos Kozma was part of Hungary's successful, affluent, and well-assimilated Jewish community of the early twentieth century. Many of his clients and associates in the design professions and building trades belonged to this

35. For an historical account of this period, see Peter Sugar, ed., *A History of Hungary* (London: Tauris and Co., 1990).

36. See György Haiman, "Imre Kner and the Revival of Hungarian Printing," in *Design History,* ed. Dennis Doordan (Cambridge, Mass.: MIT Press, 1995), 53–63.

37. He was also still closely associated with the Budapest Textile Workshop (Budapesti Textilművészeti Műhely).

38. Inventory numbers: MAA 62.1558.1; MAA KRTF 1846. See Kiss, *Kozma Lajos, az Iparművész (1884–1948),* 40, 47.

39. Károly Kozma, *Az Asztalos-mesterségröl* (Gyoma: Kner, 1925). A related cabinet is illustrated on page 9.

community as well, which represented a distinctive facet of Budapest's intellectual and cultural life. Like Kozma, many Jewish architects and designers in the opening decades of the twentieth century were passionately committed to the nationhood of Hungary. As a result, the National Romantic style these designers had helped to forge, in particular its oriental streak, became associated with their ethnic identity. The style may be seen as emblematic of the assimilation of the Jewish community in the multiethnic Hungarian nation. By the 1920s, however, the institutional-ization of anti-Semitism had begun.[40] In a climate newly dominated by the Christian right, Kozma's Baroque was more acceptable than his earlier National Romantic mode, on account of the style's historical associations with the Catholic church and bourgeois culture.

Progressive tendencies were automatically held suspect under Admiral Miklós Horthy's regime (1920–1944), to the extent that more radical Constructivist designers like Lajos Kassák (1887–1967) and László Moholy-Nagy chose to operate in exile. The Communist Party, to which Kozma had belonged, was banned in 1920. Correspondingly, there was a relatively large market for more conservative culture, such as neo-Baroque design, that would express stability, prosperity, respect for authority, and identification with Europe as a whole. The projection of such values through international exhibitions and cultural exchange was seen by the government as an important means of improving diplomatic and, ulti-mately, economic relations with the outside world. In its shrunken form Hungary could not afford to be isolated.[41]

To give the neo-Baroque more explicit national connotations, many Hun-garian commentators played up the association of the original style with the freedom fighter and national hero Rákóczi, the Transylvanian prince. The style was, however, unquestionably oriented toward Austria and Germany. It had taken root in the northern and western parts of Hungary during the early phase of Hapsburg domination in the early eighteenth century.[42] From that time there had been a steady buildup of resentment in Hungary against Austrian cultural hegemony. Hungary had enjoyed immense political and economic advantages following the Ausgleich (Compromise) in 1867, which established the Dual Monarchy of Austria-Hungary. Nonetheless the nation's need to assert a distinct cultural identity was undiminished—an outlook that fueled the development of Hungary's National Romantic style. Separationist politics and culture

40. From 1920 to 1928, this occurred through the legislation entitled Numerus Clausus, which restricted the number of Jews entering higher education.

41. Hungary's cultural sophistication was also one of the arguments mobilized by Admiral Horthy in support of regaining the lost territory of Transylvania from the Romanians.

42. Kozma would have been familiar with important German studies of Baroque furniture being published around this time, such as Hermann Schnitz, *Deutsche Möbel des Barock und Rococo* (Stuttgart: Julius Hoffman, 1922); and Marianne Zweig, *Wiener Bürgermöbel aus Theresianischer und Josephinischer Zeit 1740–1790* (Vienna: n.p., 1922).

fig. 14
Lajos Kozma, view
of a bedroom suite
for a lady, Budapest,
Hungary, 1924.
From *Möbel und*
Raumkunst von Ludwig
***Kozma* (Leipzig and**
Vienna: Friedrich Ernst
Hübsch Verlag, 1926).
Courtesy of
Iparművészeti Főiskola.

were no longer an issue, however, following the dismantling of the Hapsburg Empire in 1920. In other words, the Austrian, and also the Germanic, associations with the Baroque were not problematic following Trianon. Austria had been cut down to size, and German investment proved crucial to the Hungarian economy in the 1920s and 1930s.

Even earlier than this, Kozma enjoyed a close relationship with several German publishers, including Alexander Koch in Darmstadt, who since 1914 had been publishing his work regularly in the magazine *Innen-Dekoration* (Interior Decoration). It is in such German publications that we find more details about the commission of the "dreamlike and yet unassumingly matter-of-fact" bedroom suite for a wealthy lady, of which The Wolfsonian cabinet was part (fig. 14). The scheme demonstrates how Kozma intended individual items to function within a larger architectural or interior conception (perhaps more neo-Rococo than neo-Baroque in this instance). Deemed "as unified as a rococo salon," according to designer and critic Ernö Kallai, the suite was an exercise in the orchestration of varied shapes, scales, colors, and textures, which together exuded an impression of restfulness. Observers noted the playfully contrasted elements of excess and restraint, of imposingly dramatic and diminutive features, of white walls and bursts of concentrated decorative detail or strong color. The bedroom suite also exhibited the air of intimate sensuality combined

fig. 15
Lajos Kozma, view of
the alcove with drawn
curtains in a bedroom
suite for a lady, Budapest,
Hungary, 1924. From
*Möbel und Raumkunst
von Ludwig Kozma*
(Leipzig and Vienna:
Friedrich Ernst Hübsch
Verlag, 1926). Courtesy of
Iparművészeti Főiskola.

with airy practicality.[43] There were two Kozmas, noted Kallai, "one inclining to preciousness and extravagance, a bourgeois aesthete of the modern metropolis, and another, who takes pure pleasure in a playful, popular naïveté full of crackling color."[44]

The small, gleaming black cabinet was one of a pair symmetrically placed beneath gilt mirrors to either side of a platformed recess facing the entrance to the suite (figs. 11 and 14). A general sense of dynamism was implicit in the "musculature" of the legs and the rhythmic undulation of the front doors over which shadow and light played. Kozma located the piece within a network of visual connections rippling back and forth within the room, making it an integral part of this *Gesamtkunstwerk,* or unified work of art. Its overall form picked up on the perfume cabinet in the alcove, while its shaped top echoed the profile of the raised platform emerging from the recess. The ornament on the cabinet doors was related to other tiny details on the wall paneling and the door and mirror frames. The plasticity of the ornament and its subtle application to so many different forms and materials required phenomenal academic discipline and attention to detail. "You do not stop to think about whether it is a constructional element or a piece of ornament," wrote Pál Nádai, "Each detail clings to the body of the furniture, merges with the definition of its forms, and with its function in the room."[45]

Through their animal or anthropomorphic qualities such pieces of furniture were seen as having "peopled" the space. In describing such a room, one critic employed metaphors that drew on notions of family values and individualism prevalent in much contemporary writing on domestic interiors. "In the apartment are distinctively shaped pieces of furniture, in different colors, which look to us like animated figures…. Just as close relatives bring fresh life into the family circle with their individual quirks of character, so the differences [in the furniture] introduce an elegant vitality into the unity of the room." A red sofa was grouped together with its "younger brother," a blue armchair.[46]

Kozma clearly reveled in the theatrical nature of the commission (he had produced various set designs), and its links with the world of female fashion. The concept of "dressing up" as a type of spectacle or playful masquerade

43. Jenö Mohácsi, "Das Schlafgemach einer Dame," *Innen-Dekoration* (January 1924): 4–8.

44. Ernst [Ernö] Kallai, *Möbel und Raumkunst von Ludwig Kozma* (Leipzig and Vienna: Hübsch Verlag, 1926), 13.

45. Pál Nádai, "Landhäuser und Räume in Ungarn," *Innen-Dekoration* 38 (May 1927): 181.

46. Mohácsi, "Das Schlafgemach einer Dame," 6.

fig. 16
(right)
Lajos Kozma,
preliminary artwork for a
promotional design for
the fashion house Antal
and Hosszu, Budapest,
Hungary, colored pencil
and ink, early 1920s.
Arte Galéria és Aukciós
Iroda, Budapest, Hungary.

fig. 17
(far right)
Lajos Kozma, illustration
from a series of drawings
for the fairy tale
Zsuzsa Bergengóciában
(Susie in Fairyland), 1917.
(Budapest: Sacelláry
Kiadó, 1921). Arte Galéria
és Aukciós Iroda,
Budapest, Hungary.

was captured in the form of the dramatic, elevated alcove, accented by red curtains—drawn closed in another photograph from the earlier mentioned German publication (fig. 15). Kozma repeated the curtain motif in his early 1920s design for the Budapest fashion shop Antal and Hosszu (fig. 16). While the curtained stage encouraged a voyeuristic gaze, that "look" in fact bounced back at the spectator via mirrors on either side of the alcove and at the center of the inner sanctum. This play on spectator and performer, illusion and reality, inner and outer was heightened by the abundance of reflective surfaces and themes in the fantastical plaster decoration. Above the recess, for example, an exotic nude reclined dreamily beneath a palm tree. The idea of the alcove as a shrine to the revelation of female beauty also was suggested by another plasterwork detail of a miniature cabinet with doors opened to reveal the figure of an Indian goddess.

In many ways, Kozma gave tangible expression to ideas he had already elaborated in a sequence of fairy tale illustrations, which were published as *Zsuzsa Bergengóciában* (Susie in Fairyland) with text by Frigyes Karinthy in 1921 (fig. 17).[47] Kozma had drawn the pictures for Susan, one of his daughters, during his military service on the Transylvanian front in World War I. Accessing this fantastical dream world that he so playfully filled with light, color, and familiar furnishings must have helped him cope with the wartime situation. Kozma tended to work things out on paper, developing ideas quickly and giving full rein to his imagination. Like Horti, he had been trained in a system of design education, closely related to British models, which encouraged the development of proficiency in different branches of the decorative arts and architecture. Furniture design was only one of the areas in which both of them excelled. In Kozma's case,

---

47. In 1924 the book appeared in German, and an additional limited edition was produced by Imre Kner for his friends and family.

fig. 18
(top, right)
Lajos Kozma, printed monogram for his personal use, 1925. From *Das Signetbuch* (Gyoma: Kner, 1925). The Mitchell Wolfson Jr. Collection, The Wolfsonian–Florida International University, Miami Beach, Florida.

fig. 19
(center, right)
Lajos Kozma, printed monogram for his personal use, 1930. From *A Magyar Könyv és Relámművészek Tarsaságának Kiállitása* (The Exhibition of the Hungarian Book and Advertising Association) (Budapest: The Hungarian Book and Advertising Association, 1930). The Mitchell Wolfson Jr. Collection, The Wolfsonian–Florida International University, Miami Beach, Florida.

fig. 20
(bottom, right)
Lajos Kozma, corner of a living room, Budapest, Hungary, 1930. From *Modern Interiors* (London: Studio Publications, 1930).

this link with his graphic work was particularly strong, both stylistically and in terms of working method. His collaboration with Imre Kner, previously described, was most intense during the period 1918 to 1925. Some of the woodcut details Kozma designed for Kner bear comparison stylistically with the painted decoration on the doors of the bedroom cabinet (fig. 13). In 1925 Kner published a book of emblems designed by Kozma for close friends, associates, and the artist himself, many of them featuring representations of typically neo-Baroque furniture (fig. 18).

Kozma never lost his fascination with folk culture or with the East, but as the arguments around national style became increasingly racial and conservative, so the focus of his interests shifted away from the neo-Baroque. The exuberant and richly ornamental style, of which the little cabinet is typical, had by 1930 mutated into a form of domesticated, antidogmatic Modernism. Compare, for example, Kozma's personal logo or his design for a living room, both of 1930 (figs. 19 and 20), with earlier counterparts. Given the rapidity and fundamental nature of change in Central European life at this time, it is not surprising that Kozma expressed himself with such complexity and apparent contradiction. "Poet and artist, romantic and materialist, revolutionary and conservative, but remaining a true individual in response to many influences—such a man is Lajos Kozma," wrote his friend Pál Nádai.[48]

Kozma continued to operate at the forefront of his profession until his death in 1948, shortly after he became the director of the Hungarian School of Applied Arts. Unlike many, he did not emigrate in the 1930s when the political situation became increasingly ugly for Jewish Hungarians. He avoided deportation by going into hiding during World War II.

48. Pál Nádai, *Az Iparművészet Magyarországon* (Budapest: Miklos Biro, 1920), 58.

fig. 21
(right)
Exterior of Ernö Goldfinger's house at 2 Willow Road, London, photographed shortly after its completion in 1939. Collection of Dr. Gavin Stamp.

fig. 22
(below, right)
Ernö Goldfinger, sideboard for a house in Hendon, London, green marble with mahogany carcass and cast iron base supports, c. 1935.
The Mitchell Wolfson Jr. Collection, The Wolfsonian–Florida International University, Miami Beach, Florida. Photograph by Silvia Ros.

His close friend Gyula Kaesz described how, even in these circumstances, with bombs falling around him, "Kozma puffed on a cigar and without fear read and wrote about the methods of designing space in baroque and medieval architecture."[49]

Ernö Goldfinger in London

Ernö Goldfinger and his family were among those to leave Budapest in 1920, following the Romanian government's annexation of their property in Transylvania. Later in his life, Goldfinger reflected back upon his experience as a teenager, writing: "One student left Pest to find his fortune, somewhere."[50] While retaining strong Central European contacts, like many other peripatetic Hungarians at the time, Goldfinger merged, chameleon-like, into avant-garde circles—first in Paris, then in London, having moved to the latter in 1934. He was to "find his fortune" in London, becoming best known for his postwar architecture. Following the public opening in 1996 of his home in Willow Road, designed 1936 to 1939, Goldfinger has gained prominence for his furniture and interiors of the 1930s (fig. 21).[51] This was the period in which he designed the third highlighted object of this study, a sideboard, as part of an interior modernization for the north London home of a couple named the Benroys (fig. 22). Goldfinger designed new furniture for several rooms, and the sideboard was one of three made for the dining room. One of the other sideboards from the Benroy residence is in the collection of London's Victoria and Albert Museum.[52]

Goldfinger was the least self-consciously Hungarian of the three designers featured in this article, which was, in part, a reflection of his commitment to International Modernism. Nevertheless, it is possible to demonstrate that Hungarian culture and contacts remained important to him. In addition, Goldfinger's work was known in Hungary, and he shared preoccupations with designers who continued to work there. In many ways there were direct parallels between the reception and development of Modernism in Britain and Hungary. There was an essential conservatism in both countries, and initially Modernism often found expression in domestic commissions for individual clients.

Before moving to Budapest, Goldfinger had spent much of his childhood in Transylvania, where his family owned forests and sawmills. Like Horti and Kozma before him, Goldfinger was drawn to record the country's folk culture. Among his papers from the 1920s are sketches of traditional

---

49. *Uj Epitészet* 2–3 (1949): 44.

50. Ernö Goldfinger, "Juvenalia," The Goldfinger Archive, RIBA Drawings Collection, the National Archive of Art and Design, London.

51. This was listed in 1970 and subsequently taken over by The National Trust, which opened the house to the public in 1996.

52. Inventory number W4-1988. The whereabouts of the third and largest sideboard featured in contemporary photographs taken by Ursula Goldfinger is not known.

fig. 23
Ernö Goldfinger, interior
of a beauty salon for
Helena Rubinstein,
Grafton Street, London,
England, designed in
1926. From *Ter és Forma*,
December 1929.

Hungarian houses, dress, and ceramics.[53] In a drawing of 1925, Goldfinger juxtaposed a Hungarian and a Mexican peasant, alluding to the internationalism of folk culture in a way that is reminiscent of Horti's two decades earlier. At the time, however, Goldfinger was studying in Paris, where the architect Le Corbusier was expounding a more radical view relative to the appropriation of vernacular culture. In the same year as Goldfinger's drawing, Le Corbusier wrote:

> We grow certain that the folklore of today is in the process of formation, indeed already exists, born of unanimous collaboration.

> But the idle and the sterile plagiarize the folk cultures of the past, fill the air with the deafening cries of crickets, and sing out of tune with the songs and the poetry of others.[54]

This critique would not have been lost on Goldfinger, who had interviewed Le Corbusier for a Hungarian newspaper and, together with other students dissatisfied with the conservative teaching of the École des Beaux-Arts, had approached him to set up a breakaway atelier. Instead, they ended

53. Goldfinger, "Juvenalia." Like Horti and Kozma, Goldfinger designed several ex libris plates (bookplates), a form of graphic art that had maintained its popularity at all levels in Central Europe while declining to something of a curiosity in the West.

54. Le Corbusier, *L'Art décoratif d'aujourd'hui* (Paris: Editions G. Crès, 1925), 25.

up working with Le Corbusier's associate, Auguste Perret. The young Goldfinger also was influenced by the Viennese designer Adolf Loos (1870–1933), with whom he had visited the 1925 Exposition Internationale des Arts Décoratifs et Industriels Modernes (International Exposition of Modern Decorative and Industrial Arts). For Loos, the suppression of ornament was a sign of intellect, and sensuality was implicit in materials themselves.

In Paris, Goldfinger set up a small practice with fellow Hungarian András Szivessy (1901–1958).[55] Elements of the furniture they designed together in the late 1920s would reemerge in the later Benroy sideboard. Among these were the cast iron supports and tambour doors, the latter an elegant and traditional feature of French cabinetmaking. They also worked on a range of shops and exhibition stands, including Goldfinger's first London commission, a salon in Grafton Street for cosmetician Helena Rubinstein (fig. 23). The design was streamlined and austere, but suggested opulence in its combination of Bakelite, chrome, and stainless steel furniture. Apparently, Rubinstein thought it had "just a slight appearance of an operating theatre." Goldfinger's response, delivered in his somewhat rudimentary English of the time, indicates an approach that would also inform the design of the 1935 sideboard:

> We don't believe in a decoration applicated [sic] arbitrary… The stuff we are doing is simple and plain and gets all its value of the balance of its proportions of the perfect satisfaction it gives in fonction [sic], of the materials in their right place.[56]

A contributor to the journal Ter és Forma (Space and Form) felt that the design concepts of Goldfinger and Szivessy's shop furnishings were familiar to a Hungarian audience, but what gave the partnership an edge was their ability to work with a higher quality of materials and craftsmanship in Paris than in Budapest.[57] At this stage they were still referred to as "Hungarians working abroad." It was noted, however, that "these two Hungarian architects have soaked up a lot of Gallic culture,"[58] consistent with a decisive orientation in Hungarian architectural circles toward French and German models by the late 1920s. Such intellectual currents were familiar not least through the prominent involvement of Hungarians in both the Bauhaus (Marcel Breuer, Farkas Molnár, József Fischer) and the Hungarian chapter of CIAM (Congrès Internationaux d'Architecture Moderne), the association promoting International Modernism that included Le Corbusier and was established in 1928.[59] In 1927 Goldfinger

55. Possibly related to Kozma's friend, the architect Tibor Szivessy (1884–1963).

56. Quoted in Robert Elwall, *Ernö Goldfinger* (London: Academy Editions, 1996), 33.

57. "Üzlethelyiségek berendezése," *Ter és Forma* 2 (December 1929): 526.

58. "E. Goldfinger és a A. G. Szivessy Munkái," *Ter és Forma* 3 (October 1930): 447.

59. See Eszter Gabor, *A CIAM Magyar Csoportja (1928–1938)* (Budapest: Akadémiai Kiadó, 1972).

fig. 24
Gordon Russell Limited's
showrooms at 40
Wigmore Street,
London, 1935.
The Gordon Russell
Trust, Broadway,
Worcestershire, England.

and Szivessy entered a competition run by the Austrian furniture manufacturer Thonet. They submitted designs for a wardrobe, which had a
space at the top for filing clean shirts and a ventilated bin below for dirty
laundry. Admired by Le Corbusier, the firm of Thonet had factories and
showrooms in Budapest and manufactured many furniture designs by
Hungarians, such as Kozma and Breuer. Goldfinger began his furniture
design process by analyzing function and user needs. This was most
apparent in his solutions to clothes storage, but in a similar vein the drawers
both of his own and of the largest Benroy sideboard were custom fitted
with felt-lined trays for each piece of the family's silver cutlery.[60]

Following Goldfinger's relocation to London in 1934 with his wife, Ursula,
he became one of several Continental architects who helped establish
the Modern movement in England. Other famous Hungarians who spent
time in London in the mid-1930s before moving on to reinvent themselves
in the United States were the Korda brothers, Marcel Breuer, and László
Moholy-Nagy. The market was still slack for major architectural projects,
with the result that Breuer and Moholy-Nagy were chasing the same
sorts of design work as Goldfinger, predominantly for furniture, shops,

60. Letter from the clients' daughter, 19 May 1988, Department of Furniture and Interiors Object
File, Victoria and Albert Museum, London, England. Jack Pritchard, who had founded the
Isokon furniture company and worked with Breuer, felt this was not going far enough. In his
view the sideboard was a redundant piece of furniture symbolizing all that was wrong with the
middle classes: "What would I want with a sideboard? I wouldn't have one in the house," from
an interview quoted in Rosamund Allwood and Kedrun Laurie, *R. D. Russell and Marian Pepler*
(London: Geffrye Museum, 1983), 8.

exhibition stands, and even toys. The Benroy commission was typical of such work.

In Gordon Russell Ltd., Goldfinger found a sympathetic furniture company with which to work.[61] Their new showrooms at 40 Wigmore Street, London, had opened in October 1935, and contract sales like the Benroy commission were now the lifeblood of the firm rather than the moderately priced modular furniture they had introduced with limited success (fig. 24). The parent company in the town of Broadway, Worcestershire, a site close in place and spirit to Chipping Camden, where Charles Ashbee had set up his Arts and Crafts movement Guild of Handicraft, still concentrated on the production of rather staid natural-oak furniture in a traditional but modern style. The London branch projected a more cosmopolitan and unequivocally Modernist aesthetic, introducing German wallpapers and Thonet furniture alongside the firm's own productions. Gordon Russell's new London buyer was none other than Nikolaus Pevsner (1902–1983), who was on the point of publishing his seminal study, *Pioneers of Modern Design*. Wigmore Street, in the West End of London, attracted a reasonably affluent avant-garde clientele, consisting in part of the Central European (often Jewish) émigrés who lived in the area. In 1936 Goldfinger designed a shop down the road from Gordon Russell for the toymakers Paul and Marjorie Abatt, who, like Gordon Russell, also sold products by émigré Modernist designers.

In his book *British Furniture To-day,* published in 1951, Goldfinger talked about mass production as the "basic feature of modern furniture." He also described machines as having utterly changed everyday life. This did not really tally with his experience. While Goldfinger viewed all his furniture designs as prototypes, few were put into wider production. The modular units he designed for Easiwork, a London firm of furniture manufacturers specializing in hygienic and laborsaving products, however, were an exception. At the 1937 *Ideal Homes Exhibition* in London, for example, Goldfinger designed the firm's stand in the form of an "All-In" Bungalow containing standardized modular cupboards with rolling shutter fronts (like those in the Benroy sideboards), which functioned both as storage units and wall dividers. It is questionable whether the Benroy sideboard would have been suitable for replication. The piece evoked the *idea* of functionality and reproducibility in its rigorous geometry, but the combination of materials meant that it was never a very practical design. The marble slabs cladding the cupboard are incredibly heavy, and are attached to the wooden carcass by the flimsiest of means, making the item extremely difficult, if not dangerous, to move.[62] In both The Wolfsonian

61. See Allwood and Laurie. They were the only British furniture makers to be illustrated in *Tér és Forma* at this time, incidentally in an article by Kozma.

62. On each side of the smaller cabinets, a comparable patch is missing, suggesting that in their original location they might have been fixed to the walls.

and the Victoria and Albert examples, pieces of the marble have become detached. Furthermore, the alignment of the metal legs flush with the extreme edges of the sideboard gives only minimal support to the main span of the structure, and adds to the strain at the juncture between the legs and carcass. In the Victoria and Albert example, this inadequate support has been addressed by adding two bars across the width of the piece, joining the two legs. The iron has not aged well, having corroded in places, and its silver paint has flaked off. Given such flaws in the design of this custom-made sideboard, there is a certain irony in Goldfinger's comment that, owing to mechanized production, "Exquisite craftsmanship is no longer required, nor obtainable in the old sense."[63] It was certainly not a piece designed with cabinetmaking skills or the sort of sensitivity to materials and construction that Kozma had demonstrated.

Perhaps part of the problem was that Goldfinger's design was so overwhelmingly architectural. With its compact and controlled geometry, its low, broad proportions, and its main volume hovering on slim supports, the sideboard may be compared to the exterior of Goldfinger's residence on Willow Road (figs. 21 and 22). The slats of the sideboard's tambour doors can be read in tandem with the vertical wood cladding on the ground floor bays of the building. Also comparable is the sensual appeal arising from the juxtaposition of the contrasting temperatures, colors, and textures in the different components. In Willow Road, the natural qualities of the wood and brick are played off against the cooler, modern associations of the shuttered concrete columns and steel window frames, while in the sideboard the marble and mahogany (natural materials associated with luxury and a tradition of high-class cabinetmaking) are contrasted with the mass produced and industrially resonant cast iron base supports. Goldfinger delighted in such juxtapositions of traditional and less-familiar materials, with their opposing tactile and cultural connotations. This was, in his view, what raised furniture design beyond the search for meeting physiological needs. The English artist Paul Nash (1889–1946) also saw this as characteristic of the modern room, writing in 1932:

> In the differing surfaces of metal and wood, glass and paper, stuff and stone, we derive pleasure, not only from actual contact, but by the sensation, which perception supplies through sight. To sit idly, in a well-proportioned room, furnished even economically, from the immense store of different materials available to-day; to feel through the eyes, the subtle contrasts of texture and temperature; is surely something of a new pleasure.[64]

Goldfinger felt Willow Road had an affinity to the Georgian and Regency architecture of London, which had impressed him from the time of his

63. Ernö Goldfinger, *British Furniture To-day* (London: Alec Tiranti, 1951), 6.
64. Paul Nash, *Room and Book* (London, 1932), 53.

first visit in 1927, perhaps influenced by Adolf Loos's admiration of the same. Paul Nash believed, too, that furniture and interiors should pick up where the Regency had left off, expressing corresponding values without imitation. It is interesting, therefore, that, in a Hungarian article entitled "The old and new objectivity," the early nineteenth-century, Regency-era furniture of Johann Wolfgang Goethe's sparse Weimar study was seen as the stylistic precedent to furniture by Goldfinger and Szivessy.[65] In the Benroy sideboards the combination of mahogany and green marble — which Goldfinger also used in the living room hearth at his Willow Road home — would not have been out of place in a Regency interior.

Signs of Goldfinger's Hungarian origins were still to be found within the startling Modernism of Willow Road. Once Goldfinger's children moved out of the nursery, his mother, Regine, moved to the top floor of the house. She remained there until her death at the age of 101, resolutely speaking Hungarian, and surrounded by the swelling forms of eighteenth-century

65. *Ter és Forma* 3 (June 1930): 296–297.

Austro-Hungarian furniture of the kind that had inspired Kozma (fig. 25). Yet by 1937, Goldfinger had become so identified with London that he was asked to design the children's section in the British Pavilion at the international exhibition in Paris.[66]

Horti, Kozma, and Goldfinger were connected by a web of biographical and aesthetic factors. All three demonstrated extraordinary flexibility in working with different genres and media, and were influential as theorists and educators. They responded sensitively to the sociopolitical and economic circumstances of their times. Their furniture clearly resonated with broad orientations in the visual culture of the period. Horti and Goldfinger are representative of the role of Central European designers in the formation of a Modern idiom in both America and Britain. Kozma worked with the folk aesthetic of Horti and the Modern aesthetic of Goldfinger, but gained broadest recognition for his resurrection of the Baroque. It would be easy to construct a linear narrative extending from the rational simplicity of the Onken clock to the standardized geometry of the Benroy sideboard, in which Kozma's cabinet appears as a temporary diversion or disruption. On the other hand, the latter can be taken to highlight another constant strand in the development of a Modern sensibility in its celebration of more feminine, sensual, and theatrical values. ✧

Acknowledgments
Apart from the patience and generosity of colleagues at The Wolfsonian, this article would not have been possible without the help of many people in both Scotland and Hungary. Without being able to name everyone, I extend extra special thanks to Gustav Fenyö, András Ferkai, András Hadik, Eva Kiss, László Kiss-Horváth, Tom Markus, Ibolya Plank-Csengel, Pal Ritóok, Erika Sinka, Paul Stirton, and Zsuzsa Vámos-Lovay.

66. Goldfinger's design, with its cutout clouds and rather sinister planes in the sky, is reminiscent of Kozma's surrealistic response to World War I through his illustrations for a children's fairy tale.

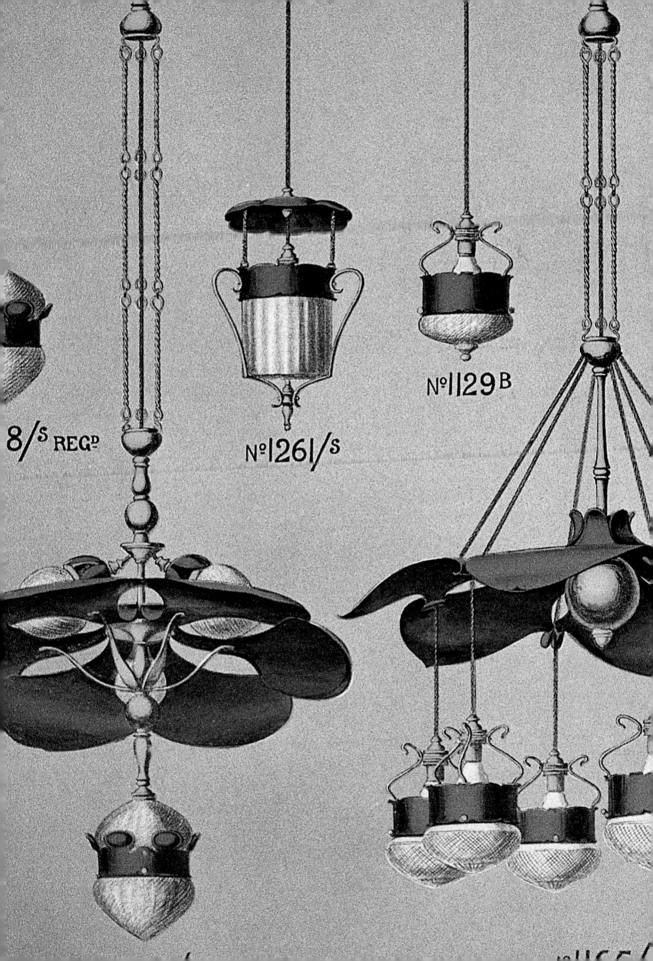

8/S REGᴰ

Nº 1261/S

Nº 1129 B

Alan Crawford

W. A. S. Benson, Machinery, and the Arts and Crafts Movement in Britain

Alan Crawford is an independent scholar living in London who specializes in the history of British architecture and decorative art around 1900. He is currently working on a history of the Arts and Crafts movement in Britain for Yale University Press. He conducted research toward this book as a Wolfsonian Fellow in 1996.

The Wolfsonian–Florida International University holds about one hundred objects relating to the Arts and Crafts movement in Britain, and they exemplify the interest and idiosyncrasies of Mitchell Wolfson Jr.'s collecting.[1] This essay is an account of the life and work of an important figure in that movement: metalworker, furniture designer, and architect W. A. S. Benson (1854–1924). I chose to write about Benson partly because there is no recent account that deals with his life and work as a whole, and partly because his career raises interesting questions about the Arts and Crafts movement in Britain.[2] I learned about the diaries of his wife, Venetia (1864–1946), during my research, and these have strengthened the biographical character of this article.[3] These diaries cover almost the whole of Benson's married life and throw a side-long but valuable light on an otherwise poorly documented personality.

Benson's career progression was typical of the Arts and Crafts movement. He was trained as an architect, but took up metalwork at the suggestion of Edward Burne-Jones (1833–1898) and William Morris (1834–1896), leading figures of the movement. He was a founding, active, and lifelong member of its three principal organizations: the Art Workers' Guild, the Home Arts and Industries Association, and the Arts and Crafts Exhibition Society. The light fittings and hollowware that he designed became a

1. See Wendy Kaplan, *Leading "The Simple Life": The Arts and Crafts Movement in Britain, 1880–1910* (Miami Beach: The Wolfsonian–Florida International University, 1999).

2. The fullest account is William Napier Bruce's "Memoir," published in W. A. S. Benson, *Drawing: Its History and Uses* (Oxford: Oxford University Press, 1925), vii–xxxi. This is still the principal source of information until the time of Benson's marriage. Recent literature includes Shirley Bury, "A Craftsman Who Used the Machine," *Country Life* (18 March 1965): 624, 627; Michael Whiteway and Paul Reeves, *W. A. S. Benson: Metalwork* (London: Haslam and Whiteway, 1981); Peter Rose, "W. A. S. Benson: A Pioneer Designer of Light Fittings," *Journal of the Decorative Arts Society, 1850 to the Present*, 9 (1985): 50–57; and Peter Rose, "W. A. S. Benson: A Pioneer of Modern Design Rediscovered," *The Magazine Antiques* (June 2001): 934–941.

3. Diaries of Venetia Benson *née* Hunt, 1882–1887, 1891–1937, in the possession of her family. In later references, "Diaries."

Detail of W. A. S. Benson & Company's *Price List of Fittings for Electric Light*, c. 1901.

model for other Arts and Crafts metalwork. He fits snugly into the main-stream of the Arts and Crafts movement in Britain—all but for one thing: both his production methods and designs demonstrate a fascination with machinery.

Unlike their counterparts in the United States, most Arts and Crafts practitioners in Britain had strong, slightly incoherent, negative feelings about machinery. They thought of "the craftsman" as free, creative, and working with his hands, "the machine" as soulless, repetitive, and inhuman. These contrasting images derive in part from John Ruskin's (1819–1900) *The Stones of Venice*, an architectural history of Venice that contains a powerful denunciation of modern industrialism to which Arts and Crafts designers returned again and again. Distrust for the machine lay behind the many little workshops that turned their backs on the industrial world around 1900, using preindustrial techniques to create what they called "crafts." It is reflected in the liking among Arts and Crafts practitioners for roughness, "the avoidance of machine finish." We are not dealing with careful thought here; these were motivating symbols. The definition of "the machine" was slippery, however, sometimes referring to this or that loom or stamping press, sometimes to the whole culture of industrialism, and the power of its symbolism lay partly in this ambiguity.

If machinery was an object of taboo in the context of the British Arts and Crafts, how can we understand Benson's enthusiasm for it? In the first scholarly article on Benson, "A Craftsman Who Used the Machine" (1965), Shirley Bury wrote that he "designed his metalwork almost entirely for machine production" and so ran "counter to the accepted canons of the Arts and Crafts movement."[4] Most subsequent writing has followed this line, stressing Benson's apartness from other individuals associated with the Arts and Crafts movement.[5] This essay gives a rounded account of Benson's life and work. It shows, first, that Benson's strong and lasting interest in machinery was as much that of a gentleman-amateur or hobbyist as of an industrialist, and, second, that he was an active member of the Arts and Crafts movement all his life. From these reflections comes a third: that we should not try to define the Arts and Crafts movement and its allegiances too precisely if we hope to understand Benson's place in it. Shirley Bury assumed a clear-cut opposition between Benson's "machine production" and the "accepted canons of the Arts and Crafts movement." But this essay shows that Benson's experience was not polarized in this way.

William Arthur Smith Benson was born in London in 1854 (fig. 1). The Benson family was of the upper class, with interests in banking, but Benson's father, also named William, was a barrister who retired early because of illness. The designer and his brothers and sisters grew up at Langtons, a country

4. Shirley Bury, "A Craftsman Who Used the Machine," 624.

5. For example, Gillian Naylor, *The Arts and Crafts Movement: A Study of Its Sources, Ideals and Influence on Design Theory* (London: Studio Vista, 1971), 159–160.

fig. 1
W. A. S. Benson in the
roof garden of his
home, 39 Montagu
Square, London,
c. 1897. Courtesy of
Haslam and Whiteway.
Photograph by
Alfred Ellis.

house outside Alresford in Hampshire, southwest of London.[6] Benson's interests were shaped partly by his mother, Elizabeth, a gracious, unworldly woman who read Ruskin and admired Pre-Raphaelite paintings, and partly by her brother, William Arthur Smith, who lived at Colebrook Park in Kent. According to William Napier Bruce in his 1925 "Memoir" of Benson:

> This uncle, to whom he was much attached, was himself a great worker with his hands and addicted to scientific pursuits; he introduced his nephew to the use of lathes and the mysteries and delights of elementary mechanics.[7]

The beginnings of Benson's interest in art and in machines lay in these childhood experiences. At preparatory school in Brighton, he was fascinated by ships and engineering. At Winchester College, where Benson studied from 1868 to 1872, he dreamed of becoming an architect. As a student at Oxford from 1874 to 1877, according to Bruce's "Memoir," Benson found that academic work made him ill and he had some kind of breakdown. He wavered between having a career in law and becoming an artist.[8] Eventually, in 1876, he decided on architecture and was accepted as a pupil by Basil Champneys (1842–1935), a rising London architect. Writing to his father to tell him of this decision, he acknowledged:

> The fact is that neither in talking nor in writing, except under the influence of excitement of some sort, do I at all know how to express what I feel in the least degree.[9]

6. Jehanne Wake, *Kleinwort Benson: The History of Two Families in Banking* (Oxford: Oxford University Press, 1997).

7. Bruce, "Memoir," ix–x.

8. Ibid., x, xvi–xvii, xxxi.

9. Ibid., xvii.

Benson was apprenticed to Champneys from 1877 to 1880, but it was soon clear that he would not make architecture his career. In 1877 Benson met Edward Burne-Jones, and they developed a lasting friendship. Benson helped Burne-Jones with the design of a piano and thought seriously about furniture and metalwork.[10] Through Burne-Jones he met William Morris, and both encouraged Benson to start a workshop near theirs in west London. In January 1880 Benson wrote to his mother, "The long and the short of it is I must make something or be miserable."[11] Much of the struggle of his early career is implied in this emotional phrase. He was happy making things, and the odd, practical, artistic world of Arts and Crafts suited him. But, in the upper-middle-class codes of late Victorian England, his decision to set up a workshop and "make something" represented a fall from grace. In spring 1880, he opened a small workshop in North End Road, Fulham, near Burne-Jones's house. For some of his acquaintances, this amounted to "a social misdemeanour."[12]

The workshop got off to a slow start. Metalwork was Benson's real passion, but he could not find skilled workmen, and in his first year only produced simple furniture. In 1881 he hired the brass- and copper-worker John Lovegrove, on whose skill and experience he would rely for many years, and metalwork production got under way.[13] Benson's metalwork remained strikingly consistent over the years, and though he produced thousands of designs, they seem to have been generated from ideas about materials and lighting methods developed at this early, experimental stage.

By 1882 the workshop was too small and he moved a mile and a half to Eyot Gardens, a short street running down to the Thames at Hammersmith in west London.[14] At this time Benson himself was living in Kensington, a more fashionable district.[15] In 1882 or 1883 he opened a studio and showroom there.[16] Shortly after, he found a good bookkeeper, and from this point was able to concentrate his attention on design.[17] That Benson chose to distance himself from his workshop was odd, but consistent with his version of Arts and Crafts, which was more dilettante than has been supposed.

Arts and Crafts became an organized movement in London in the 1880s. In January 1884, Benson was one of a small group of architects and artists who met to discuss ways of bringing progressive artists, architects, designers, and craftsmen together. This led to the foundation of the Art Workers' Guild, which served as the most important meeting place for those associated

10. Michael Wilson, "Burne-Jones and Piano Reform," *Apollo* 192 (1975): 344.

11. Bruce, "Memoir," xxii.

12. Ibid., xxiii.

13. A. H. Church, "Benson's Lamps," *Portfolio* 21 (1890): 19.

14. Ibid., 20; Bruce, "Memoir," xxiv.

15. Membership list in Society for the Protection of Ancient Buildings, *Sixth Annual... Report... 1883.*

16. W. A. S. Benson, *Notes on Some of the Minor Arts* (London: W. A. S. Benson, 1883), 6.

17. Church, "Benson's Lamps," 20.

with the Arts and Crafts movement in London, though it was simply a male talking club.[18] Later in 1884 he was involved in the establishment of the Home Arts and Industries Association, set up to promote craft classes among the poor. Benson said at the first council meeting

> that he had long recognized the necessity for some organisation of the kind. He had himself had the idea of establishing workshops for the teaching of the smaller decorative arts.[19]

In 1886 Benson married Venetia Hunt (fig. 2), daughter of the landscape painter Alfred William Hunt.[20] They both moved in the artistic circles of Kensington and Holland Park and met through Burne-Jones's daughter, Margaret, in 1882.[21] Venetia, ten years younger than her husband, was spirited and sociable; she loved clothes and shopping. One of her diary entries reads: "To Harrods, & then to every shop in town!"[22] They were a handsome couple, and though Benson had his silences, Venetia was a

18. H. J. L. J. Massé, *The Art-Workers' Guild, 1884–1934* (Oxford: Shakespeare Head Press, 1935), 133.

19. Minutes book of the Home Arts and Industries Association, 20 November 1884. British Architectural Library, Archives and Manuscripts Collection, HAIA/1.

20. Marriage certificate; for A. W. Hunt, see Allen Staley, *The Pre-Raphaelite Landscape* (Oxford: Clarendon Press, 1973), 144–147.

21. "Diaries," 4 January 1882.

22. "Diaries," 12 March 1914.

brilliant talker. They had no children, but one can sense grown-up lives fitting together behind the matter-of-factness of her diaries. W. N. Bruce wrote that Benson

> was not specially gifted to look after himself, and on that account, as well as for other more spiritual and incalculable blessings, it was a crowning mercy when in 1886 he married Venetia...[23]

At first they lived at 2 Gordon Place, a stone's throw from his showroom and from her parents' house.

During 1887 Benson worked to create an organization that would exhibit decorative art. The Royal Academy did not exhibit decorative art, and the Art Workers' Guild did not see itself as an exhibiting body. A provisional committee was formed, and artist Walter Crane (1845–1915), best known for his book illustrations, was elected as its chairman and Benson as its secretary. After much fundraising and searching for premises, the newly established Arts and Crafts Exhibition Society held its first show in the New Gallery, Regent Street, from October through November 1888. It was a success in terms of attendance and sales, and the Society's exhibitions became the public face of the Arts and Crafts movement in Britain.[24] Benson was involved in the Society's work for much of his life, as he was in the Art Workers' Guild and the Home Arts and Industries Association.[25]

23. Bruce, "Memoir," xxvii.

24. Peter Stansky, *Redesigning the World: William Morris, the 1880s and the Arts and Crafts* (Princeton, N.J.: Princeton University Press, 1985), chap. 4.

25. Arts and Crafts Exhibition Society: "Diaries," 6 July 1920; Home Arts and Industries Association, 19 March 1924; Art Workers' Guild, 22 May 1924.

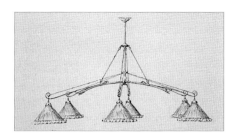

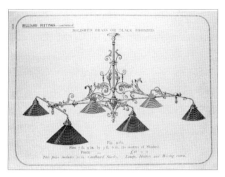

fig. 4
(above, top)
W. A. S. Benson, billiard-table pendant. From W. A. S. Benson & Company, *Price List of Fittings for Electric Light*, c. 1901. The Mitchell Wolfson Jr. Collection, The Wolfsonian–Florida International University, Miami Beach, Florida.

fig. 5
(above)
Artist unknown, billiard-table pendant. From Swan–Edison Company catalogue, c. 1900. Courtesy of Denton Antiques, London.

In the mid-1880s, production at Benson's Hammersmith workshop increased steadily and the number of patterns used in production could be counted not by the dozens but in the hundreds.[26] In the autumn of 1887, Benson moved his showroom from Kensington to 82 New Bond Street in the heart of London's West End.[27] New Bond Street was then an upper-middle-class shopping thoroughfare, with many fashionable tailors, hatters, dressmakers, jewelers, perfumers, and art galleries at its south end, including the prestigious Grosvenor Gallery, which was associated with the Aesthetic movement. Benson's showroom was at the north, less fashionable end, and the designer took a bold step in trusting that his lamps and light fittings, so stripped and simple compared with those of other manufacturers, would appeal to Bond Street shoppers.[28] Most lighting showrooms were in less fashionable areas: Clerkenwell or the edges of the City of London. There were only four other lighting shops on New Bond Street, three of them "By Appointment" to the Queen, which suggested their exclusiveness.[29] But business was good, and a year or two later Benson enlarged his premises to include the shop next door, rebuilding the façade to his own design.[30]

A visitor to Benson's New Bond Street shop would have been struck by the glow of copper and brass coming from the dishes, teapots, and standard lamps, and the lights hanging from the ceiling (fig. 3). Most of Benson's wares combined copper and brass, and critic A. H. Church, writing in 1890, thought that Benson "practically reintroduced and extended" the combination.[31] William Morris called him "Mr. Brass Benson."[32] According to Church, Benson used brass for rigidity and copper for a range of other purposes, though he sometimes used both for the same purpose, relishing the visual contrast.[33] Much of the appeal of his designs, then as now, depended on smooth, unornamented surfaces of copper. The visitor would have been struck also by the plainness of Benson's designs. They were less ornate than comparable products from other manufacturers. Compare, for example, Benson's lamp for a billiard table to that by the Swan-Edison Company (figs. 4 and 5). Not that other manufacturers did not make plain designs,

26. Church, "Benson's Lamps," 20.

27. "Diaries," 19 August 1887 records the acceptance of his offer for the premises on that date.

28. *The Times*, 9 July 1924, 16.

29. *Post Office Directory of London for 1889* (London: Kelly & Company, 1889).

30. Church, "Benson's Lamps," 20; *Post Office Directory... 1889* and *1890*. The ground-floor showroom of 82 New Bond Street was given up in 1908, see "Diaries," 25 December 1908.

31. Church, "Benson's Lamps," 21.

32. Norman Kelvin, ed., *The Collected Letters of William Morris* (Princeton, N.J.: Princeton University Press, 1984–1996), 2:141.

33. Church, "Benson's Lamps," 21. Church illustrates the knob of a curtain pole where brass and copper are used for the same decorative purpose.

fig. 6
W. A. S. Benson, electric
light sconce (one of a
pair), copper, brass, glass,
c. 1902. The Mitchell
Wolfson Jr. Collection,
The Wolfsonian–Florida
International University,
Miami Beach, Florida.

but they did so for their less prestigious ranges. Benson stands out because he offered plainness — for a high price — to affluent customers in New Bond Street.

Benson's lamps are light and open, and their character derives from their structural role. They express the functions of hanging from a ceiling, projecting from a wall, and standing upright. Such natural ornament as they have reinforces this character. In a Benson-designed wall lamp, for example, the leaf at the base, the tendril-like arm, and the snowdrop-like pendant underline the tasks of projecting and hanging (fig. 6). There is almost no reference in these designs to the styles of the past — Gothic, Classical, Renaissance, and so on — and on the whole Benson's designs may be described as "styleless" — a most unusual trait in the late nineteenth century. They were very frankly constructed. In one example, the foot and upper stem of the lamp have soldered joints (figs. 7 and 8). But there are obvious screws where they join the curving arms; the joint is the focus of the design. Benson's lamps also were made precisely. As A. H. Church wrote of his work: "Stopcocks are accurately ground; truth of gauge is everywhere maintained."[34] In *The Nature and Art of Workmanship*, David Pye drew a valuable distinction between the workmanship of risk that goes with handwork, and the workmanship of certainty, in which skill ensures mechanical, predetermined results.[35] Benson's lamps belonged to

34. Ibid.

35. David Pye, *The Nature and Art of Workmanship* (Cambridge: Cambridge University Press, 1968), chap. 2.

fig. 7
(right)
W. A. S. Benson, table lamp, copper and brass, n.d. At Standen, East Grinstead, England, a property of The National Trust. Photograph by the author.

fig. 8
(far right)
W. A. S. Benson, detail of table lamp, copper and brass, n.d. At Standen, East Grinstead, England, a property of The National Trust. Photograph by the author.

fig. 9
(below)
W. A. S. Benson & Company, *Price List of Fittings for Electric Light,* c. 1901. The Mitchell Wolfson Jr. Collection, The Wolfsonian–Florida International University, Miami Beach, Florida.

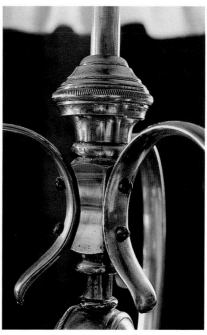

the second category, whereas the anti-mechanistic philosophy of Arts and Crafts celebrated the first. In fact, Benson's designs were an assembly of standard parts that could be used in different combinations. The pages of his catalogues, such as that from 1901 to 1902, show this (fig. 9). If prospective customers at Benson's shop had seen the designer's fire screen of c. 1891 (fig. 10), would they have thought that it looked like a propeller? It is hard to say. This gadget-like quality of Benson's designs derived from his lifelong interest in machine tools and may have struck an odd note in New Bond Street.

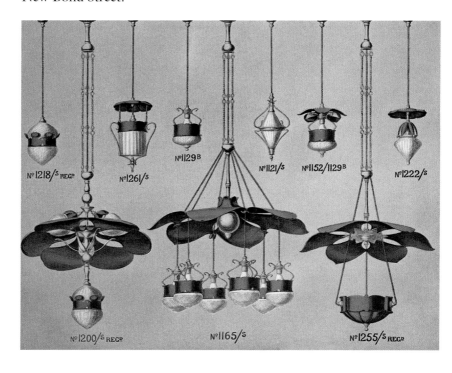

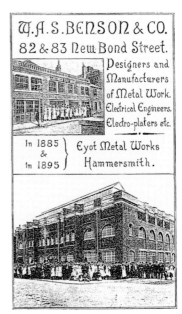

fig. 10
(opposite page)
W. A. S. Benson,
fire screen, copper and
brass, 1891. The Mitchell
Wolfson Jr. Collection,
The Wolfsonian–Florida
International University,
Miami Beach, Florida.

fig. 11
(above)
Morris & Company,
decoration and furnishing
of the drawing room,
The Swan House,
Chelsea Embankment,
London. Photographed
by Bedford Lemere in
1884. Courtesy of
National Monuments
Record, London. © Crown
copyright. NMR.

fig. 12
(above, far right)
Advertisement for W. A. S.
Benson & Company
showing earlier and later
workshops in Eyot
Gardens, Hammersmith,
c. 1895. Courtesy of
Peter D. Rose. Probably
from a catalogue; original
now untraceable.

Benson's lamps quickly found a place in the Arts and Crafts movement. T. J. Cobden-Sanderson, the pioneer of Arts and Crafts bookbinding, was given a Benson table lamp when he married in 1882, and wrote in his diary:

> The lamp...which is our ever-increasing delight, is on the table... I sit and think, and look at the books, and at Chérie, and at the lamp, and at the lovely light upon its copper shade...[36]

With time, Benson's light fittings came to typify the Arts and Crafts movement, like Morris's textiles and Ernest Gimson's furniture. From the mid-1880s, Morris & Company regularly used Benson lamps in their interior decoration projects, and we should imagine these simple designs, not in the spare white interiors of modern taste, but among the dark furniture and sumptuous wallcoverings of Morris interiors (fig. 11).[37] In the 1890s metalworkers like C. R. Ashbee and Arthur Dixon followed Benson's lead when designing in brass and copper. And A. H. Church noted, as uncomfortable evidence of Benson's success, the many flimsy imitations of his wares, which appeared in shops as early as 1890.[38]

As a result of this success, Benson's metalwork business continued to expand. From 1889 to 1890 Benson built larger premises on the corner of Eyot Gardens and Hughenden Road, next to his existing workshop, calling them the Eyot Metal Works as shown in an advertisement of c. 1895 (fig. 12).[39] These premises have been demolished, and all that remains is a smudgy

36. *The Journals of Thomas James Cobden-Sanderson, 1879–1922* (London: Richard Cobden-Sanderson, 1926), 1: 178.

37. Charles Harvey and Jon Press, *William Morris: Design and Enterprise in Victorian Britain* (Manchester: Manchester University Press, 1991), 177.

38. Church, "Benson's Lamps," 22.

39. Hammersmith and Fulham Archives and Local History Centre: Drainage plans, envelope no. 8051A; Church, "Benson's Lamps," 21.

fig. 13
Ground plan of the Eyot
Works as proposed, 1889.
Hammersmith and
Fulham Archives and
Local History Centre,
London. Photograph by
the author. This
image has been digitally
manipulated to remove
drainage details.

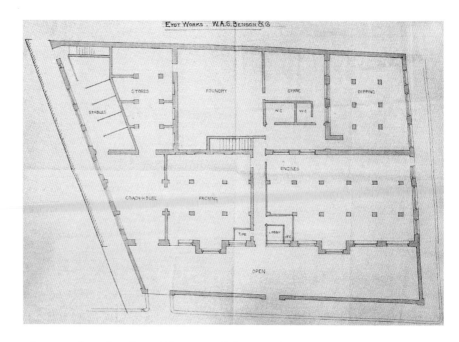

photograph and a plan of the ground floor made when the building was first proposed (fig. 13). This plan shows the foundry for casting, a dipping room—presumably for plating and lacquering—and the engine room, which supplied power to machinery elsewhere. Had the building survived, it might have told us something about Benson's methods of production. As it is, we must rely on the evidence of the objects he produced and on written documentation. Among the latter, the most substantial reference to his process appears in his obituary in *The Times:*

> He preferred to approach his subject as an engineer rather than as a hand-worker, to produce beautiful forms by machinery on a commercial scale, rather than single works of art. Thus his lamps, vases, entrée dishes &c. were all the outcome of profound study of the capabilities of heavy stamping plant, spinning lathes, and shaping tools which he was able to put down in the large Hammersmith works. Visitors to the works, who knew him as a rather dreamy artist...were amazed and almost aghast to find themselves in what appeared to be an engineering workshop full of large machines, with endless rows of turning and polishing lathes, a casting shop capable of the largest work, plating vats, screw-cutting and turret-lathes, and a lacquering department which had benefited so much from his inventive genius that constant efforts were made by trade rivals to penetrate his secrets.[40]

This passage is the source behind much modern interpretation of Benson as "a craftsman who used the machine." The author of the obituary was right to emphasize Benson's use of machinery, for it was unusual in the Arts and Crafts movement. But his description was selective. The lathes

40. *The Times,* 9 July 1924, 16.

fig. 14
W. A. S. Benson, chimney-
piece and decorations in
the dining room, 39
Montagu Square, London,
c. 1891. Courtesy of
Haslam and Whiteway.

and presses were only part of the production process. We must remember that lathes and presses had to be *handled,* and that many shaping processes, much finishing, and all assembly of the wares would have been done by hand. Benson's workshop, therefore, like much British industry at the time, combined hand- and machine-production.[41]

In November 1890, the Bensons moved to 39 Montagu Square in Maryle-bone, an 1820s house in a socially prominent square, near the New Bond Street shop. They redecorated the interior of their home with Benson-designed furnishings (including fireplaces, cupboards, and, of course, light fittings) and Morris wallpapers and textiles (fig. 14).[42] The result was rich and eclectic, like a Morris & Company interior, though lighter.

Looking back over the 1880s, we see that Benson went about creating a career for himself. In 1880 he had taken a chance when he followed his instincts and set up a workshop in North End Road, risking the disapproval of his peers. But he succeeded in his chosen work and became a figure of some consequence in the Arts and Crafts movement. Marriage to the sociable Venetia, the opening of the West End shop, and the move to Montagu Square all confirmed his recovered social status; he had found a hybrid identity as architect and gentleman, artist and engineer.

If we look forward to the 1890s, on the other hand, we find a blank in the accounts of Benson's life, for there were no great changes to record in these years. He was thirty-six in 1890 and had reached a plateau.

41. See Raphael Samuel, "The Workshop of the World: Steam Power and Hand Technology in mid-Victorian Britain," *History Workshop Journal* 3 (1977): 6–72.

42. The interiors are illustrated in W. Shaw Sparrow, ed., *Flats, Urban Houses and Cottage Homes* (London: Hodder & Stoughton, n.d. [c. 1906]), 61, 72–73, 75. Work on the interiors was done in 1891–1892, but the diaries show much more work in 1901–1902, including installation of Benson's patent windows.

Here Venetia's diaries come into their own, for they tell us what Benson was doing almost every day. "Willie to the works" appears often in the diaries. But he did not need to go every day because the Eyot Works was run by senior employees: the long-serving Lovegrove and metalworkers Elie Hinton and C. J. Scott.[43] (Later, Scott told him not to bother coming in more than twice a week.[44]) His days were peripatetic. He might work at home in the morning, go to the shop, have lunch at the South Kensington Museum (now the Victoria and Albert), see a client about a lighting scheme in the afternoon, and in the evening, if he were not going to the Art Workers' Guild or a committee meeting, he would "play," as the diary puts it, in his lathe room.

Architectural work was woven in and out of Benson's other activities. From 1897 to 1899 he was often at Gerrards Cross in Buckinghamshire, northwest of London, where he enlarged an existing farmhouse for his brother-in-law, the banker A. H. Drummond (fig. 15).[45] But Benson never had a large practice, and most of his architecture work was for family and friends.[46] There is published evidence of eight buildings by Benson, and the diaries document about fourteen more jobs. Benson was an ingenious architect, best perhaps at solving small problems and handling details. Using only paint, paving, and trelliswork, he could transform the grim backyard of a London townhouse into somewhere pleasant and private to sit.[47] But, judging by the published examples of Benson's work, he was more accomplished in detail than in massing or proportion.

Venetia Benson's diary also records her husband's visits associated with installing electric lights in public buildings, the houses of the wealthy, and churches. Notably, he installed lighting in Saint Paul's Cathedral, London, in 1899 and 1900.[48] Benson designed fixtures for all the common light sources of his day: candles, oil, gas, and electricity, but he specialized in electric light. W. A. S. Benson & Company, in fact, offered their services as electrical engineers (fig. 12), and when Benson designed individual

fig. 15
(above)
View of Maltman's Green, Maltman's Lane, Gerrards Cross, Buckinghamshire, England, c. 1897–1899. Courtesy of Haslam and Whiteway.

fig. 16
(opposite page)
W. A. S. Benson, chandelier, brass, copper, cord, c. 1909. The Mitchell Wolfson Jr. Collection, The Wolfsonian–Florida International University, Miami Beach, Florida.

43. Lovegrove and Hinton were both made directors of the limited company Benson formed in 1900, see memorandum and articles of association, 22 December 1900 in Public Record Office, London, BT31, Box 16564, Company file no. 68597 (in later references, "Company file no. 68597"). According to Bruce, "Memoir," vii, Scott was employed by Benson c. 1881; he was appointed assistant manager in 1907, see "Diaries," 1 May 1907.

44. "Diaries," 12 October 1911.

45. The house, Maltman's Green, Maltmans Lane, is now a school.

46. Bruce, "Memoir," xix.

47. See W. A. S. Benson, "Back-window prospects in London," *Art Journal* (1903): 1–4, which documents work on 88 Portland Place, a residence in Wilton Place, and 39 Montagu Square.

48. "Diaries," 18 February, 23 June, and 26 October 1899; 7 March 1900.

lamps and fittings, he was sensitive to the special requirements of electricity—flexible wire and a hanging bulb. In a fan-like ceiling light, for example, he incorporated the electrical cords into the structure (fig. 16).

We can see his interest in electricity as a form of technological modernism, the progressive artist using the light source of the future. But social and personal contexts also were important in shaping Benson's involvement with electricity. The story of lighting in Britain around 1900 was not that of gaslight vanquished by electricity. The use of gas lighting in Britain peaked between 1880 and 1914 and was only seriously challenged by electricity toward the end of this period. Electric lighting was cleaner, but it was more expensive to install and to operate, and it remained a luxury throughout Benson's career.[49] In working with electricity, Benson was, thus, not only aligned with modernity but also with wealth, which explains perhaps why he opened a showroom on New Bond Street. His family was also involved with the fledgling utility. In the late 1880s, his cousin Robin Benson, a successful investment banker, and Sir Coutts Lindsay, proprietor of the Grosvenor Gallery, formed the London Electric Supply Corporation Limited, with the ambitious plan of supplying London's electric light and power from one large station at Deptford, southeast of the city center. This company was refinanced in the 1890s by Lord Wantage.[50] I do not know of specific connections between London Electric and Benson's company, but it is hard to imagine that Benson worked independently of his cousin, given their shared interests. In May 1897, an entry in Venetia's diary hints at the possibilities, noting: "Willie... met Lord Wantage, Lady Wantage, & Lady Jane Lindsay & manager of the London Electric Lighting Co. at Charing Cross & went to the works at Deptford."[51]

Sometimes, according to the diaries, it was windows, not lighting, that Benson fitted. "Willie to the Manuels to measure for their new window," reads an entry of February 1897.[52] Like many late Victorians, Benson preferred the intimacy of small casement windows to those with large panes of plate glass. But he thought leaded lights or wooden glazing bars were difficult to maintain. So, probably in the mid-1890s, he designed a window with two layers in each opening: a pane of glass on the outside, for ease of maintenance; and an ornamental screen or frame of metal on the inside—a quarter inch from the glass—to ensure intimacy.[53] He installed such windows in his own house and in several others in London; two good examples, both for the Manuel family, survive at 5 Aubrey Road,

49. Helen Long, *The Edwardian House: The Middle-Class Home in Britain, 1880–1914* (Manchester: Manchester University Press, 1993), 89–92.

50. Wake, *Kleinwort Benson*, 192–194.

51. "Diaries," 20 May 1897.

52. "Diaries," 18 February 1897.

53. Benson took out patents for casements in 1896–1897; see property agreement of 1 January 1901 in Company file no. 68597.

fig. 17
W. A. S. Benson, bay
window at 63 Bayswater
Road, London, showing
Benson's patent decorative
glazing, 1900. Photograph
by the author, 2001.

Holland Park (1897), and at 63 Bayswater Road, overlooking Hyde Park, (fig. 17).[54] However, no other architect adopted this idea. Benson the architect and designer here merged with Benson the inventor, the man who produced a metal-reinforced building system called "Texyll," patents for jacketed vessels, galvanized iron roofing, and a teapot designed for use in trains.[55]

On 30 August 1887, Venetia wrote, "Little wardrobe for my room... came from the works"; and on 10 January 1900, "Willie... to Henry's to see chair making for the Paris Exhibition." These two entries mark the transition in Benson's work as a furniture designer. In his first year on North End Road he produced simple furniture, and his workshop seems to have continued making furniture for several years.[56] At some stage he began designing elaborate pieces that were probably beyond the capacity of his workshop; Morris & Company or the London cabinetmaker J. S. Henry produced most known examples of these Benson designs. Often elaborately decorated, either with inlays or metalwork, these furniture pieces sometimes fail, like Benson's buildings, to integrate details with overall design. Even on The

54. See "New Decorative Windows," *Architectural Review* 9 (1901): 43–46.

55. For galvanized iron roofing, "Diaries," 3 May 1898; jacketed vessels, property agreement of 1 January 1901, Company file no. 68597; "Texyll," "Diaries," 26 February and 25 November 1903, and 7 March 1905; teapot, "Diaries," 4 March 1905.

56. The "joiner-made" designs by Benson in Morris & Company Decorators, Limited, *Specimens of Furniture Upholstery and Interior Decoration* (c. 1912) may be of this early date. Photocopy in the Department of Furniture and Woodwork, Victoria and Albert Museum, London.

Wolfsonian's simple mahogany table, which stands somewhere in the middle of these two classes of work, the cast metalwork between the legs seems extraneous (fig. 18).

On 28 October 1891, the diary reads: "The English Illustrated with Willie's article on 'The Use of the Lathe' came. Contains a not flattering portrait of the author at his lathe" (fig. 19). *The English Illustrated Magazine* was a monthly periodical for middle-class readers, and Benson's article was written for hobbyists like himself. The illustration shows him in his lathe room at 39 Montagu Square, where he was most at home with machinery. In the article, Benson stressed the satisfactions to be derived from making simple turned-wood objects with a lathe.[57] His other published writings also deal with traditional handwork and reflect mainstream Arts and Crafts values.[58] They do not make a case for "the machine" and against handwork. On the contrary, as this article and its illustration demonstrate, Benson thought of his lathe, a simple machine and his favorite piece of equipment, as a normal part of Arts and Crafts making. Venetia's diary for 19 January 1901 reads: "Willie and Mr. Marillier to lunch. They played in the workshop all the afternoon." We can understand Benson's relationship to machinery better if we see it more in this spirit of play and less in the abstract and polarized terms of "the hand versus the machine."

During the 1890s Benson enjoyed a growing reputation on the Continent. When Siegfried Bing opened his Salon de l'Art Nouveau in Paris in 1895, giving a name to the style the world had just begun to recognize, Benson's lamps flanked the entrance to the gallery. In 1896 the Kunstindustrimuseum

57. *The English Illustrated Magazine* (1891–1892): 121–126.

58. Though Benson did lecture to the Art Workers' Guild on "Mechanical Aids to Production," see "Diaries," 15 March 1895. I do not know whether this lecture was published.

fig. 19
W. A. S. Benson in his lathe room. From *The English Illustrated Magazine,* November 1891. By permission of The British Library.

in Trondheim, Norway, bought his metalwork for their collections.[59] And, in 1897, the new Munich-based magazine *Dekorative Kunst* (Decorative Art) declared that Benson's work had all the pared-down elegance of "a good American bicycle."[60] But Venetia's diaries record none of these developments, apart from a meeting in November 1902 between Benson, Morris & Company, retailer Ambrose Heal, and glassmaker Harry Powell to consider a joint shop in Paris, which they ultimately decided against. It may be that, like some other English Arts and Crafts designers, Benson was not interested in developing a Continental reputation.

In the spring of 1898, the Bensons went for a holiday at Tenby, in Pembrokeshire, on the Atlantic coast in Wales. Perhaps they did not realize it at the time, but this holiday marked the beginning for them of a much looser relationship to London, and to the metalworking business. In their explorations they came to the village of Manorbier, with its ruined twelfth-century castle and grassy valley sloping down to the sea. They arranged to rent a house there for the summer,[61] returning in August and remaining through October. (The diaries record that, on 16 August, Benson went to Pembroke and "had an orgie in a tool shop."[62]) From this date Manorbier and Castle Corner—the house they stayed in and ultimately purchased in 1909—played a bigger and bigger part in their lives.[63] The Bensons went to Pembrokeshire two or three times each year and stayed for several months in the summer; Benson traveled to London or elsewhere when necessary. For Venetia, Manorbier brought the pleasures of country life, and for her husband it meant a respite from business. At the end of 1903, Venetia noted that they had spent 151 days at Manorbier, sixty-nine in "other country," twenty-seven abroad, and eighty-nine in London.[64]

On 22 December 1900, W. A. S. Benson & Company was registered as a limited company.[65] It is not clear why Benson took this step, but perhaps it was the result of a letter he received the previous February from Henry Currie Marillier (1865–1951), expressing his interest in being a manager and eventually a partner in Benson's business.[66] Marillier started work as

59. Gabriel P. Weisberg, *Art Nouveau Bing: Paris Style 1900* (New York: Abrams, 1986), 60, 73; *Nordenfjeldske Kunstindustrimuseum Årbok* (1961–1962): 93–101.

60. *Dekorative Kunst* 1 (1897–1898): 7.

61. "Diaries," 9 April 1898.

62. "Diaries," 16 August 1898.

63. "Diaries," 13 October 1909.

64. She left twenty-nine days unaccounted for.

65. Company file no. 68597, certificate, 22 December 1900.

66. "Diaries," 15 February 1900.

company secretary in April 1900, and became a shareholder and director in the newly formed limited company.[67] Benson had always run the company himself, with the help principally of Lovegrove and Hinton. Now he seemed glad to offload some responsibility. Marillier was of Benson's class—he is described as "gentleman" in the company files—and he had had an eclectic career, working as a laborer in a turbine factory, editing a new electrical weekly, *Lighting,* writing books about the artists Aubrey Beardsley and Dante Gabriel Rossetti. This combination of art, industry, and journalism would have intrigued Benson.[68] For the next few years the diaries are full of references to their joint activities: "Willie and Mr. Marillier to lunch," "Willie and Mr. Marillier to the works." The two men were hardly out of each other's company.

But the partnership was not a happy one for long. In December 1904, Frank and Robert Smith, who had managed Morris & Company since William Morris's death, approached Benson and Marillier with an offer to sell them their firm. Benson and Marillier accepted, and for some years they were content to run both companies. But their accounts of these events differ. According to Marillier, he raised the money, set up the new company (Morris & Company Decorators, Limited), and involved Benson as a favor, writing, "As I could not leave Benson in the lurch with a failing business, after the way he had treated me, I brought him in as a director as well..."[69] Marillier perhaps gives himself too much credit. The diaries show that Benson and Marillier worked together to raise the money, and Benson was not only a director of the new company, but also the first chairman of its board.[70] What is more, when W. A. S. Benson & Company did face difficulties in 1907, an external audit revealed that the root of the problem lay in Marillier's divided allegiance, since he was managing two companies at once.[71] From this time, Marillier remained as a director and secretary of Benson's company, but virtually disappeared from the diaries.[72]

In 1904 the Bensons sold 39 Montagu Square, and for a few years lived nomadically, much of the time at Manorbier. Then from 1906 to 1908 Benson designed and built a house for himself and Venetia in southeast England, at Withyham in East Sussex (fig. 20).[73] The Bensons called their substantial house Windleshaw and probably chose the site for its proximity

67. "Diaries," 6 March 1900; Company file no. 68597, memorandum and articles of association, 22 December 1900.

68. E. T. Williams and Helen Palmer, eds., *Dictionary of National Biography, 1951–1960* (London: Oxford University Press, 1971); notes by Linda Parry on Marillier's typescript memoirs, "Those Jollier Days."

69. Henry Currie Marillier, "Those Jollier Days," n.p.; see also Linda Parry, "Morris & Company in the Twentieth Century," *Journal of the William Morris Society* 6 (Winter 1985–1986): 11–16; and Harvey and Press, *William Morris,* 222.

70. "Diaries," 29 December 1904 and first half of 1905; for Benson as chairman, 8 August 1905.

71. "Diaries," 29 January, 18 February, and 19 April 1907.

72. For Venetia's dislike of Marillier, see "Diaries," 7 February 1908.

73. See "Diaries," 28 December 1906 and 2 October 1908.

to their cousin Robin Benson's much larger mansion, Buckhurst, which had been enlarged by Edwin Lutyens. There one could meet aristocrats, financiers, and society artists. Willie and Venetia Benson appear to have seen themselves as a cadet branch of the Benson family, living alongside "the big house."[74] The building of Windleshaw, like the long holidays in Manorbier and the alliance with Marillier, marks Benson's further withdrawal from his business.

There was a good railway connection to London, and Benson went to town often. In 1908 he served on a committee advising on the installation of collections in the Victoria and Albert Museum's new buildings.[75] In 1915 he became a founding member of the Design and Industries Association, established to bring a sense of good design—so powerfully developed in the Arts and Crafts movement—to bear on modern industry.[76] Benson was well qualified to comment, and had some initial discussions with leading figures of the Association, but they did not go far.[77] World War I directed Benson's inventive enthusiasm into munitions, and the diary for 1915 is peppered with remarks like "W worked at a bomb."[78] From 1916 his company produced shells for the Ministry of Munitions and equipment for launching torpedoes for the Admiralty.[79]

After the war Benson decided to close down his company, for he was reaching retirement age, and in 1920 he sold it to a manufacturer of

74. "Diaries," 12 January 1908.

75. Bruce, "Memoir," 31.

76. Nikolaus Pevsner, "Patient Progress Three: The DIA," in *Studies in Art, Architecture and Design: Victorian and After* (London: Thames and Hudson, 1968), 229.

77. "Diaries," 5 May and 2 June 1915.

78. "Diaries," 29 June 1915.

79. Company file no. 68597, Particulars of a mortgage, 19 February 1916; Bruce, "Memoir," xxxii.

oxyacetylene equipment.[80] In 1922 he also sold Windleshaw, and much of his time in retirement was spent at Manorbier, writing for the *Times Literary Supplement,* tinkering in his lathe room, and swimming in the glorious waters of a nearby bay, Skrinkle Haven.[81] He died at Manorbier on 5 July 1924, after a short illness.[82] Venetia lived until 1946, mostly at Manorbier.

Having considered the details of Benson's life, we may revisit the quandary of his relationship with machinery. It is obvious that Benson was part of the Arts and Crafts movement, and equally obvious that the means of production at the Eyot Works were at odds with the anti mei haniletic mii in iduii ot the movement. The problem can be solved partly by revising our understanding of Benson, and partly by adopting a looser sense of the Arts and Crafts movement. In the modern literature on Benson, he has always been identified with the Eyot Works; he is "a craftsman who used the machine."[83] We have seen that though Benson started the metal-work shop, he quickly distanced himself from it. He owned the business, had appropriate control of it, and supplied designs; but he had little to do with the machines to which his reputation is linked. Indeed, in 1916, Cecil Brewer, then secretary of the Design and Industries Association, told his friend Harry Peach that Benson was "a most unbusinesslike dreamer and... the real managers only pray for his absence from the works or board room."[84]

If Benson was "a craftsman who used the machine," the machine was perhaps a presence as much in his lathe room at 39 Montagu Square as it was in his workshop at Hammersmith. We should see him not simply as a manufacturer who used particular technologies but as a hobbyist, a man who made his own furniture, studied astronomy, and built small boats.[85] The lathe room connected with Benson's childhood experiences at Cole-brook Park, his inventing, his writing about craft, his involvement with the Home Arts and Industries Association, and his gadget-like designs for metalwork. Even his social life was connected with that room, for working at home, at a hobby, would not have compromised him socially in the way that manufacturing in a workshop did.

And then we need to see the Arts and Crafts movement for the loosely defined phenomenon it was, and in particular to accept that its practices were not determined by its beliefs. The anti-mechanistic rhetoric was there, but it coexisted with a practical and positive attitude toward

80. Company file no. 68579, "Minutes of an extraordinary general meeting," 26 May 1920; John Culme, *The Directory of Gold and Silversmiths, Jewellers and Allied Traders, 1838–1914* (Woodbridge, Suffolk: Antique Collectors' Club, 1987) 1:42.

81. "Diaries," 11 July 1922.

82. "Diaries," 5 July 1924.

83. Bury, "Craftsman," 624.

84. Letter of 22 November 1916, Peach Papers, British Architectural Library, Manuscripts and Archives collection.

85. Furniture referenced in "Diaries," note at end of 1892; astronomy referenced in Bruce, "Memoir," xxx–xxxi; small boats referenced in "Diaries," 27 August 1901.

machinery. William Morris was the most powerful critic of the industrial process in the Arts and Crafts movement, but it was Morris who started the Arts and Crafts revival of printing at his Kelmscott Press, and a printing press, even when it is powered by hand, is unquestionably a machine. The Arts and Crafts movement was large enough — perhaps vague enough — to embrace Morris and his presses, Benson and his lathes.

If Benson's use of machinery had been seriously at odds with the Arts and Crafts movement, people within the movement would have raised objections to his way of working. I do not know that anyone did. I know of only one commentator during Benson's lifetime who addressed the issue of his working method: German critic Hermann Muthesius, who was not affiliated with the movement. Writing about "Benson's electric light fittings" in *Dekorative Kunst,* Muthesius noted positively that Benson had

> really separated himself from the "Arts and Crafts" group by his manufacturing project. For it contradicts the basic principle of hand work that is cherished in that camp. The Morris group still clings to the Ruskin-Morris doctrine of hand work...[86]

Muthesis thought in terms of a crude polarity between "hand" and "machine," and could not understand the complex reality of the Arts and Crafts, and the way its anti-mechanist rhetoric could coexist with the use of particular machines.[87] He thought that British Arts and Crafts design could serve as a model for German industrial production if only it could be separated from romantic ideas about "craft" and handwork. He wrote, "Everyday economic circumstances point us in the direction of the machine."[88] From this point of view, of course, Benson stood out from his Arts and Crafts colleagues as the only one who seemed to be aligned with the machine, on Muthesius's side, so to speak. But Muthesius's was not an Arts and Crafts point of view, and it misconstrued Benson, his work, and his place in the movement. The whole weight of this essay has been to show that Benson and his work were part of the Arts and Crafts movement, and we should accept that complexity. ✧

Acknowledgments

I would like to thank members of the Benson family, Susie Barson, Avril and Michael Denton, Jane and Kurt Hellman, Linda Parry, Peter Rose, and Michael Whiteway for their help with this article.

86. Hermann Muthesius, *Dekorative Kunst* 9 (1901–1902): 105.

87. Ibid.

88. Ibid.

Alston W. Purvis

Feast of Dutch Diversity: Nieuwe Kunst Book Design

Alston Purvis is director of the School of Visual Arts at Boston University. He is author of the book *Dutch Graphic Design, 1918–1945* (1992) and numerous articles on related subjects. From 1971 to 1981, he served on the faculty at the Royal Academy of Fine Arts in The Hague. Purvis holds an MFA in graphic design from Yale University. He was a Wolfsonian Fellow in 1999 and continued his research in 2000.

The Wolfsonian's collection of Dutch Art Nouveau (Nieuwe Kunst) books is unrivaled in the United States, and even in the Netherlands few equal or surpass it. When I mentioned to a rare book dealer in Amsterdam that she might contact The Wolfsonian to suggest the possibility of expanding its collection of Dutch Art Nouveau books, she replied: "There is nothing they need. This collection is already complete." Amassed by the Amsterdam collector Dick Veeze during a twenty-year period, it consists of approximately three thousand rare books, periodicals, and ephemeral items from the 1890s through the 1920s. The Veeze holdings are made up primarily of books, but also include original artwork (such as sketches and design drawings) and publishing house revision notes. During my memorable summers at The Wolfsonian in 1999 and 2000, I had the privilege of helping to catalogue the collection. Each day as we explored another stack of books, more wonderful discoveries would appear. My experience there engendered a fervent enthusiasm for this vital segment of graphic design history.

This article explores the formal qualities of Nieuwe Kunst books and bindings and looks closely at the illustrious bindings produced by one particular publisher, Lambertus Jacobus Veen (1863–1919).[1] It is the first to look exclusively at The Wolfsonian's collection of Dutch books and

1. The most complete study of Nieuwe Kunst as a whole is Ernst Braches, *Het boek als Nieuwe Kunst, 1892–1903, Een studie in Art Nouveau* (Utrecht: A. Oosthoek's, Uitgeversmaatschappij N.V., 1973). Braches, the preeminent scholar of the Nieuwe Kunst book, was curator at the library of the University of Leiden, specializing in Western printed works. He later became director of the Museum of the Book in The Hague and finally a librarian at the University of Amsterdam Library, where he was foremost a book historian. A definitive source on the Nieuwe Kunst movement as a whole is L. Gans, *Nieuwe Kunst, De Nederlandse bijdrage tot de Art Nouveau* (Utrecht: A. Oosthoek's, Uitgeversmaatschappij N.V., 1966). More recently, H. T. M. van Vliet, *Versierde verhalen, De oorspronkelijke boekbinden van Louis Couperus' werk* (Amsterdam/Antwerpen: L. J. Veen, 2000), explores the noteworthy Dutch writer Louis Couperus and his books published by L. J. Veen.

Detail of book cover design for *Een boek van verbeelding* by Jan Theodoor Toorop, 1892.

bindings, but includes only a fraction of the objects and artists in that collection; making the selection was a difficult and sometimes painful task.[2] The final product focuses on those pivotal figures whose contribution I considered the most consequential in Dutch book design during the Art Nouveau period. Of particular interest are the younger artists who led the Nieuwe Kunst avant-garde. Not intending to provide a comprehensive overview of the subject, I hope this essay will inspire others to delve more deeply into this fascinating area of study.

Art Nouveau was not only an art movement, it was a social movement as well, representing the lifestyle of a prosperous and broadminded bourgeoisie that emerged around the end of the nineteenth century.[3] The movement had various names: in Germany it was called Jugendstil, based on the title of the new magazine *Jugend,* which was dedicated to the integration of art and society and first published in Munich in 1896. Though some minor and now largely forgotten publications branded the movement with derogatory labels such as "Vermicelli Style," by 1900 Nieuwe Kunst had become the accepted term in the Netherlands (a literal translation of Art Nouveau or "new art," and the term used in this article to refer solely to the Dutch contribution). When a particular period in art history begins and ends is always disputable, but it is generally accepted that Nieuwe Kunst spanned the fourteen years between 1892 and 1906. This was a vital period in architecture and the applied arts, especially in the Netherlands, since it represented a decisive break from the extravagant embellishment and historicism of the past. Although expressions of this new style varied from country to country, they were all part of the same family.[4] Through Nieuwe Kunst many young Dutch artists sought new vistas with energy and enthusiasm, encouraged by fresh, optimistic, and progressive ideals. By invigorating the arts in the Netherlands, they provided the seeds for future movements such as De Stijl, Art Deco, and what is now known as the Wendingen Style — an architecture-based typography promoted roughly between 1918 and 1932 by the Dutch architect Hendricus Theodorus Wijdeveld (1885–1987) and the Amsterdam art society Architectura et Amicitia (Architecture and Friendship).

The term Art Nouveau originated in the Paris art dealership of Siegfried Bing (1875–1920), which opened in 1895 as the Salon de l'Art Nouveau. Bing's gallery exhibited Japanese art and the so-called new art, and it became an international meeting place where many important artists were

2. See also Ellinoor Bergvelt, "The Decorative Arts in Amsterdam, 1890–1918," in *Designing Modernity: The Arts of Reform and Persuasion, 1885–1945,* ed. Wendy Kaplan (New York: Thames and Hudson, 1995), 79–109. Bergvelt provides a brief overview of The Wolfsonian's holdings of Dutch book decoration, referencing some of the items that appear in this essay.

3. Alston W. Purvis, *Dutch Graphic Design, 1918–1945* (New York: Van Nostrand Reinhold, 1992), 11. This book investigates the history of all Dutch graphic design from the latter half of the nineteenth century until the end of World War II.

4. Purvis, *Dutch Graphic Design, 1918–1945,* 11.

introduced to European audiences. Among them was the American glass artist Louis Comfort Tiffany (1848–1933), who had a sizable influence on the Continent.[5] Those who worked in the Art Nouveau style soon embraced all areas of the visual arts: architecture, painting, arts and crafts, posters, vases, furniture, ornament, and book design. Nikolaus Pevsner's 1936 book, *Pioneers of Modern Design,* was one of the first studies to grant Art Nouveau a significant role in the development of twentieth-century modern art and architecture. He saw the movement's principal characteristics as

> the long sensitive curve, reminiscent of the lily's stem, an insect's feeler, the filament of a blossom or occasionally a slender flame, the curve undulating, flowing and interplaying with others, sprouting from corners and covering asymmetrically all available surfaces.[6]

These were indeed aspects of Art Nouveau, but the Dutch Nieuwe Kunst contribution, notably in book design, was far richer than Pevsner's description.

Bookbinding was one of the principal expressive media of Nieuwe Kunst. It had a direct effect on other design forms, and more diverse and significant artists worked in this medium than in any other connected with the movement. In contrast to Art Nouveau book design in other European countries, the Netherlands's version was far more playful and provocative, reflecting the complexity and diversity of Dutch society. Especially in the early 1890s, natural forms—mainly floral decorative devices—were recurring motifs, representing, to some extent, the influence of design themes from the Middle Ages. Although they ignored the actual relationship of plant and flower forms to the picture plane, some artists were faithful to nature in their depictions of flora. These included Theodoor (Theo) van Hoytema (1863–1917) and Ludwig Willem Reijmert (L. W. R.) Wenckebach (1860–1937). Others, such as Gerrit Willem Dijsselhof (1866–1924), took this idea a step further by simplifying natural forms into stylized motifs. In both cases, however, artistic considerations prevailed over adherence to nature. Eventually there emerged an abstract approach, where undulating and swerving lines were united into intricate patterns. Reality was no longer a factor, and line and color assumed autonomous functions. After 1895, mathematics—always a Dutch passion—was seen as a creative source, with symmetry and rationalism each playing a part. This design development is seen in the bindings of Theodorus Johannes Josephus (T. J. J.) Neuhuys (1878–1921), Joris Johannes Christiaan (Chris) Lebeau (1878–1945), the early work of Sjoerd Hendrik (S. H.) de Roos (1878–1962), and the later work of Hendrik Petrus (H. P.) Berlage (1856–1934).

5. Gans, *Nieuwe Kunst,* 21.

6. Nikolaus Pevsner, *Pioneers of Modern Design: From William Morris to Walter Gropius* (London: Penguin Group, 1984), 68.

fig. 1
J. H. and Jacoba M.
de Groot, book cover,
designed c. 1896.
From *Driehoeken bij
ontwerpen van ornament*
(Triangles in the Design of
Ornament) (Amsterdam:
Joh. G. Stemler, 1896).

Some Nieuwe Kunst book designers were interested in the style primarily for its decorative qualities.[7] Other artists were dissatisfied with the use of modern ornament simply as an end in itself. Instead they sought to use physical materials in a rational and systematic manner and did not limit themselves to the repetition and assimilation of accepted forms and motifs. Such artists constantly addressed technical issues and new media. Through experimentation they acquired considerable knowledge about the materials with which books were made and used these materials as the foundations for decorative elements. They sought solutions that brought harmony and unity to the overall design and construction of books. Unlike much of the Art Nouveau in other countries, experiments in the Netherlands were not merely a passing fashion.

Nieuwe Kunst artists consistently voiced their ideas in journals and in debates at art societies such as Architectura et Amicitia. They cautioned against reactionary influences and delineated, explained, and defended their work, reflecting on its role in the broader context of modern art. Passion, defiance, and self-confidence were distinguishing characteristics of the Nieuwe Kunst artists. None of them hesitated to broach new disciplines: architects, painters, and ceramists were active in book design, and because of this heterogeneous approach, improvisation and experimentation became a dominant part of the creative process. The importance of nature as an element in Nieuwe Kunst engendered a number of books on how to adapt natural forms to stylized decoration. These books are at once sources for and examples of Nieuwe Kunst design. One of the most popular books was *Driehoeken bij ontwerpen van ornament* (Triangles in the Design of Ornament) by J. H. de Groot, a teacher at the Quellinus arts and crafts school in Amsterdam, and his sister Jacoba M. de Groot (fig. 1). Published in a large edition in 1896, it reached a broad audience and exerted much influence. The book had fifty plates accompanied by descriptive texts, providing artists with vivid instructions about the construction of abstract forms based on nature. As suggested by the cover, it demonstrated that almost any imaginable figure could be created from variations of thirty- and forty-five-degree triangles.[8] The system was based on combinations of basic forms as espoused by the English artist and writer Walter Crane (1845–1915) in his book *Claims of Decorative Art* (1892). In addition to this summary of recently developed decorative and artistic ideals in England, Crane presented his aesthetic

7. Gans, *Nieuwe Kunst*, 26.

8. J. H. and J. M. de Groot, *Driehoeken bij Ontwerpen van Ornament* (Amsterdam: Joh. G. Stemler, 1896).

fig. 2
J. D. Ros, book pages,
designed c. 1905. From
*Het ontwerpen van
vlakornament* (The
Design of Flat Ornament)
(Rotterdam: W. L. en
J. Brusse, c. 1905).

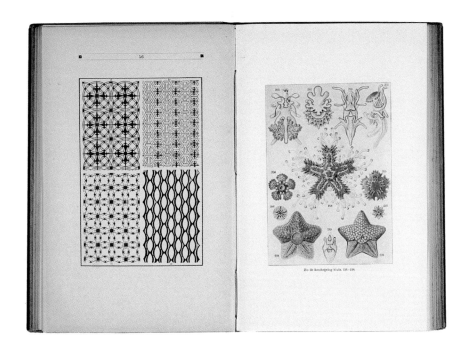

theories in books such as *The Bases of Design* (1898) and *Line and Form* (1900). He also produced a large body of illustrated work, ranging from children's books to limited-edition publications for William Morris's Kelmscott Press. Crane was immensely popular in the Netherlands.

A number of other theoretical design books were published in the Netherlands around 1905. These include *Ornament ontwerpen voor iedereen* (Ornament Design for Everyone) by Herman Hana and *Het ontwerpen van vlakornament* (The Design of Flat Ornament) by J. D. Ros, instructor at The Hague Academy of Fine Arts (fig. 2). The latter was a meticulously written handbook revealing ways in which stylized ornaments could be derived from plant and animal sources. *Het ontwerpen van ornamenten op systeem en naar natuurvormen* (The Design of Ornaments According to a System and After Natural Forms) by W. Bogtmans also was published in 1905. Many of the two hundred decorative motifs in Bogtmans's treatise refer to earlier English sources, such as James Ward's *The Principles of Ornament* and Owen Jones's *The Grammar of Ornament*.[9]

Among the artists working with motifs inspired by nature was Johan Thorn Prikker (1868–1932). Born at The Hague, Thorn Prikker received his artistic training at The Hague Art Academy, now the Koninklijke Academie van Beeldende Kunsten (Royal Academy of Fine Arts), and spent most of his career as a teacher in Germany. His 1896 cover for *Souvenir de La Haye et Schéveningue* (Souvenir of The Hague and Scheveningen) suggests some of the later covers of Jan Theodoor Toorop (1858–1928), as the lettering and surrounding decoration blend together to form a single

9. Gans, *Nieuwe Kunst*, 37.

fig. 3
(right)
Johann Thorn Prikker,
book cover, designed
1896. From *Souvenir de La
Haye et Schéveningue*
(Souvenir of The Hague
and Scheveningen)
(Haarlem: H. Kleinmann
et Cie, c. 1896).

fig. 4
(below)
Ludwig Willem Reijmert
Wenckebach, book
cover, designed 1894.
From *In de muizenwereld:
Een nieuwe vertelling
aan 't klavier* (In the
World of Mice: A New
Tale on the Piano)
(Amsterdam: H. J. W.
Becht, 1911). Photograph
by Francis X. Luca.

fig. 5
Theodoor van Hoytema,
book cover, designed
1892. From *Hoe de vogels
aan een koning kwamen*
(How the Birds Came to
Have a King) (Amsterdam:
C. M. van Gogh, 1892).

entity (fig. 3). In this asymmetrical composition, an austere framework surrounds the word "souvenir," and the decorative lines emerge from the letterforms themselves rather than being an independent floral motif.

Also interested in natural forms were Wenckebach and Van Hoytema, whose careers and styles show many similarities. Both artists were born in The Hague, studied at The Hague Art Academy, and remained in their native city for the rest of their lives. Wenckebach's graceful linear illustrations are among the most lyrically beautiful of his generation of Nieuwe Kunst designers. A highly prolific artist, he produced an immense amount of work, consisting mainly of simple and charming drawings for children's books, so-called women's novels, and print books. His 1894 design for *In de muizenwereld: Een nieuwe vertelling aan 't klavier* (In the World of Mice: A New Tale on the Piano) by Agatha Snellen and Catharina van Rennes shows familiar characteristics of Art Nouveau as the vines intertwine to create a somewhat symmetrical pattern (fig. 4).

Van Hoytema's 1892 enchanting cover design and illustrations for *Hoe de vogels aan een koning kwamen* (How the Birds Came to Have a King) is generally considered by bibliophiles to be the first modern Dutch print book, an initial attempt to break with the nineteenth-century tradition of crowded and elaborate illustrations (fig. 5). Many of the books with which Van Hoytema is associated as a designer or illustrator are about animals, which he not only loved but also saw as characters. In contrast to earlier picture books, here Van Hoytema exercised a greater decorative freedom using whimsical contours. This simple children's book would not have been possible without the influence of English illustrators such as Walter Crane; but it was of great importance to the decorative arts in the Netherlands.[10] Through its clear break with the Victorian past, it opened new vistas for Dutch children's book illustration and influenced an entire generation.

Van Hoytema steadily refined his use of line toward integrating natural forms into an overall decorative pattern. Although he never deviated from a close observation of nature, his designs gradually became more stylized, approaching what we generally associate with Art Nouveau. Beginning in 1896, his decorative work took on new dimensions as his compositions became more playful and less con- fined within the borders of the rectangle. One example

10. Ibid., 47.

MAANDSCHRIFT voor VERCIERINGSKUNST

SEPTEMBER en OCTOBER 1896

HOOFDREDACTEUR: F.H.BOERSMA UITGAVE EN LICHTDRUK VAN
H.KLEINMANN&Cᵒ HAARLEM

DE TUIN

UITGAVE van H.KLEINMANN & Cᵒ
HAARLEM
1ᵉ JAARGANG
AFLEVERING III

fig. 6
(opposite page, top)
Theodoor van Hoytema,
magazine cover, designed
1896. From *Maandschrift
voor vercieringskunst*
(Monthly Magazine
for the Decorative Arts),
September 1896.

fig. 7
(opposite page, bottom)
Theodoor van Hoytema,
magazine cover, 1899.
From *De Tuin,
Geïllustreerd maandschrift.
Kunst, letterkunde,
tooneel, muziek,
politiek, sociologische
wetenschappen en
maatschappelijk werk*
(The Garden, Illustrated
Monthly Magazine.
Art, Literature, Theater,
Music, Politics, Social
Sciences, and Social
Work), August 1899.

fig. 8
(below, right)
Gerrit Willem Dijsselhof,
book cover, designed
c. 1894. From *Kunst en
samenleving* (Art and
Society) (Amsterdam:
Scheltema en Holkema's
Boekhandel, second
revised printing 1903).

is his 1896 cover for *Maandschrift voor vercieringskunst* (Monthly Magazine for the Decorative Arts), which shows the influence of Japanese prints (fig. 6). His use of naturalistic space is partially retained, but the composition is devoid of most illusion. Instead, the pattern of stalks and leaves seems almost arbitrary.[11] Van Hoytema demonstrates similar formal characteristics in his ebullient cover of 1899 for *De Tuin, Geïllustreerd maandschrift. Kunst, letterkunde, tooneel, muziek, politiek, sociologische wetenschappen en maatschappelijk werk* (The Garden, Illustrated Monthly Magazine. Art, Literature, Theater, Music, Politics, Social Sciences, and Social Work) (fig. 7). Here, the effusion of energy and exuberance of line seem to suggest the physicality and fragrance of flowers. Van Hoytema's covers demonstrate an asymmetrical arrangement of natural forms and extravagant lines. His illustrations never evolve into silhouettes or two-dimensional compositions.

The same may not be said of G. W. Dijsselhof, primarily a painter of aquariums, whose work did become more simplified.[12] In 1892 Dijsselhof was selected to design the diploma for the Vereeniging ter Bevordering van de Belangen des Boekhandels (Society for the Promotion of the Interests of Booksellers), the result of his winning a contest in conjunction with the Internationale Tentoonstelling voor Boekhandel en Aanverwante Vakken (International Exhibition for the Book Trade and Related Professions). Theodoor Willem (T. W.) Nieuwenhuis (1866–1951) and Carol Adolph Lion Cachet (1864–1945) also participated in the competition, with all three designers producing their entries by woodcut, a clear break with past tradition. In 1893 Klaas Groesbeek, director of the Amsterdam based publishing house Scheltema en Holkema's Boekhandel in Amsterdam, commissioned Dijsselhof to design *Kunst en samenleving* (Art and Society).

This was one of the masterpieces of Nieuwe Kunst book design and Dijsselhof's most significant contribution to the movement (fig. 8). *Kunst en samenleving* was the artist and critic Jan Pieter Veth's (1864–1925) retitled adaptation and translation into Dutch of Walter Crane's 1892 book, *The Claims of Decorative Art*. The volume presented a unified approach to Nieuwe Kunst book design and became a paradigm for the new generation of designers. It took Dijsselhof a

11. Braches, *Het boek als Nieuwe Kunst*, 305.
12. Gans, *Nieuwe Kunst*, 48.

INLEIDING.

year to complete the distinct, yet related, woodcut designs for the binding and jacket. These, with the vignettes inside the book, are of special beauty and importance, for Dijsselhof was the first in the Netherlands to successfully combine typography with a refined woodcut technique (fig. 9). Reducing flora and fauna motifs to ornamental compositions, he kept naturalistic illusion to a minimum.

As a result of Dijsselhof's diploma design and *Kunst en samenleving*, the woodcut technique experienced a modest revival in the Netherlands but failed to generate much interest as an illustrative medium for future publications. Inspired by folk art, Dijsselhof's decorative designs for *Kunst en samenleving* are based largely on natural forms found in the Dutch countryside and coastal areas.[13] These include trees, flowers, dragonflies, beetles, spiders, frogs, tendrils, fish, crustaceans, and peacock feathers. Dijsselhof's stylized illustrations represent a departure from the past, especially in the way that naturalistic space is replaced by the manipulation of black and white two-dimensional designs. Also, in spite of the fact that the book is about Western art, *Kunst en samenleving* is one of the most successful examples of the Dutch enchantment with Javanese ornament. It displays the geometric and organic design that was used in all applied arts in the Dutch East Indies (now Indonesia), including mats, baskets, woven fabrics, batik, woodcarving, metal, pottery, sculpture, musical instruments, and architecture.

As with many Nieuwe Kunst books, the materials for *Kunst en samenleving* were carefully selected. The leather and paper were of the highest quality, contributing to the book's strength and durability, and real gold was used for stamping the binding.[14] In addition, the years 1892 and 1893 showed a surge in symbolic decoration, in which the binding design implied the content of the book. Then, during the next eight years, the creation of the book as an object in itself played an increasingly important role, and sometimes the design suggested the actual binding technique. In fact, Dijsselhof later stated that the brown background and white line images of *Kunst en samenleving* represented the wood cover and the linen yarn with which a book is sewn. In this way the design was intended to give a feeling of strength and to suggest the functional objectives of bookbinding—to protect the book and hold it together. On the spine background

13. Braches, *Het boek als Nieuwe Kunst,* 290; see also Bergvelt, "The Decorative Arts in Amsterdam," 88.

14. Braches, *Het boek als Nieuwe Kunst,* 291.

fig. 10
(right)
Gerrit Willem Dijsselhof,
book cover, designed
1892. From *Een pic-nic in
proza* (A Picnic in Prose)
(Amsterdam: S. L. van
Looy, H. Gerlings, 1893).

fig. 11
(far right)
Sjoerd Hendrik de Roos,
book cover, designed
1902. From *De
vrouwenkwestie,
haar historische
ontwikkeling en
haar ekonomische
kant* (The Woman
Question, Her Historical
Development and
Her Economical Side)
(Amsterdam: A. B. Soep,
1902).

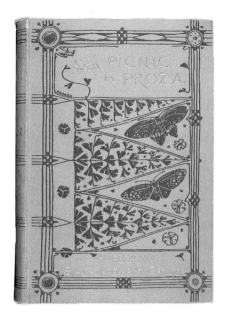 

of *Kunst en samenleving,* five gatherings of lines represent binding threads; as the lines move over the fold they become the tails of lobsters. On the front, the two-dimensional forms of the lobsters are realistically depicted (fig. 8), and on the spine and back the drawing is reduced to abstract outlines.[15] In 1892, a year before the publication of *Kunst en samenleving,* Dijsselhof designed the binding for *Een pic-nic in proza* (A Picnic in Prose) for the Amsterdam publisher S. L. van Looy & H. Geerlings (fig. 10). There are similarities between the two designs, and the binding strings are clearly depicted in the earlier book.

Despite *Kunst en samenleving's* popularity in the Netherlands, Crane was not satisfied with what he considered an overly elaborate edition of his book. The publisher Klaas Groesbeek, though, extolled Dijsselhof's design and published a second edition in 1903. In addition, his firm, Scheltema en Holkema's Boekhandel, reused the vignettes for numerous later publications.

In stark contrast to the majority of designers who were interested primarily in nature, there were some who found refuge in the familiar solidity of geometry. They derived decorative ornaments predominantly from a mathematical basis, and books such as *Driehoeken bij ontwerpen van orna-ment* were sources of inspiration. An outstanding example is the cover for Lily Braun's *De vrouwenkwestie, haar historische ontwikkeling en haar ekonomische kant* (The Woman Question, Her Historical Development and Her Economical Side), designed in 1902 by S. H. de Roos (fig. 11).[16] Here, the type is enclosed in a geometric frame composed of circles and

15. Ibid.; referenced also in Bergvelt, "The Decorative Arts in Amsterdam," 90.

16. De Roos would later play a major role in the reformation of Dutch book design, and he was the first important modern Dutch typographer and type designer. His typeface "Hollandsche Mediaeval" (Dutch Medieval) in 1912 had a major impact on the renewal of Dutch typography.

fig. 12
(right)
Theodoor Willem Nieuwenhuis, book cover, designed 1897. From *Gedichten* (Poems) (Amsterdam: S. L. van Looy, second printing 1897).

fig. 13
(far right)
Theodoor Willem Nieuwenhuis, book cover, designed 1898. From *Hilda van Suylenburg* (Amsterdam: Scheltema en Holkema's Boekhandel, seventh printing c. 1910).

straight lines. It is no coincidence that the religion of Theosophy, in which geometry is seen as an ordering principle of the cosmos, was popular in the Netherlands during this period.

After nature, of particular importance to the Nieuwe Kunst movement were influences from the Dutch East Indies. The Dutch had a special bond with their overseas colonies that was quite different from that of other colonial powers, drawing artistic inspiration from the Javanese rather than imposing Dutch culture upon them. Dutch artists readily absorbed East Indian motifs and techniques and assimilated them into a new, modern idiom. The establishment in Haarlem of the Colonial Museum in 1863 and in Rotterdam of the Museum for Geography and Ethnography in 1878 manifested the growing interest in the culture of the East Indies and provided an additional stimulus for using Javanese design motifs as sources of inspiration for new decorative forms.

In this context, the introduction of batik as a contemporary design medium was one of the important contributions of the Netherlands to the international Art Nouveau movement. Batik-making had long been a traditional craft for women in the Dutch East Indies. At the 1883 Internationale Koloniale en Uitvoer Tentoonstelling (International Colonial and Export Exhibition) in Amsterdam, an entire section was devoted to batik. This technique quickly caught on in the Netherlands and soon spread throughout Europe. Batik is produced by first making a drawing on cloth with a liquid wash and then tracing the pattern by dripping wax through a pointed metal tool. The cloth is then dyed, but the waxed design remains impervious to the coloring. As the wax is melted away, an image of the drawing remains in the original color of the fabric. The technique can be repeated many times, and it is possible to produce an intricate pattern of layers in a seemingly infinite number of colors.

fig. 14
Jan Theodoor Toorop,
book cover, designed
1892. From *Een boek van
verbeelding* (A Book of
Imagination) (Amsterdam:
Elsevier, 1892).

The lush and organic designs of Javanese batik greatly inspired artists such as Chris Lebeau and Jan Toorop, and their adaptation of these flat patterns soon evolved into a distinctive Dutch national style. Chris Lebeau produced some of the most striking and complex designs in batik and was successful in assimilating traditional patterns and colors of the East Indies into his own work. Most of his pieces were produced in Haarlem and distributed through the Amsterdam shop, 't Binnenhuis. However, the first and most prominent center for batik was the Arts and Crafts workshop in The Hague, owned by John Uiterwijk from Apeldoorn. Here thirty women worked under the supervision of Agathe Wegerif-Gravestein, who had studied the technique in Java. Through her efforts and those of Uiterwijk the business expanded and became the largest in the Netherlands. In Apeldoorn they set up studios for the design of furniture, copper work, and batik. In addition to cloth for bookbinding, they made batiks for the decoration of household items such as tablecloths, curtains, and cushions.

T. W. Nieuwenhuis's most important contribution to Nieuwe Kunst book design is his highly acclaimed 1897 batik binding and accompanying illustrations for the second edition of *Gedichten* (Poems) by Jacques Perk (fig. 12). This was a monumental project that took him two years to complete. The dark gray background and brown lines of the binding give a subdued appearance, and the symmetry of the design is broken only by the right and left borders. In 1898 his binding design for the romantic novel *Hilda van Suylenburg*, by C. Goekoop-de Jong van Beek en Donk, indicated a refinement in his approach (fig. 13). Here the use of floral decoration is completely symmetrical as the delicate, almost geometrically inspired lines flow inward from the border ornaments to converge in the center of the design.

The Javanese influence is also clear in Jan Toorop's binding design for *Een boek van verbeelding* (A Book of Imagination), fairy tales and stories by Louise Ahn-de Jongh, published in 1892 (fig. 14). Toorop was born on the East Indies island of Java and died at The Hague. At the age of thirteen he left Java to study in the Netherlands and attended the Polytechnic School at Delft, the Amsterdam Academy, and the École des Arts Décoratifs in Brussels. For Toorop, Javanese culture was a natural source of inspiration. His use of the silhouette, his linear style, and the forms, expressions, and hairstyles of his female figures are clearly derived from Javanese shadow puppets. Toorop's design showed a new

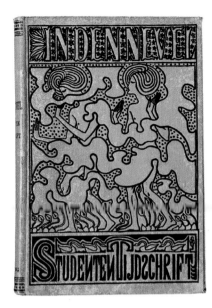

fig. 15
(right)
Jan Theodoor Toorop, yearbook cover, designed 1896. From *In den nevel, Delftsche studenten tijdschrift* (In the Mist, Delft Student Magazine) (Delft: J. Waltman Jr., 1897). Photograph by Francis X. Luca.

fig. 16
(far right)
Gustaaf Frederik van de Wall Perné, book cover, designed 1903. From *Donkere dagen* (Dark Days) (Amsterdam: Van Holkema & Warendorf, c. 1903).

direction in bookbinding illustration, with its free approach far removed from traditional illustrations contained within rectangles. In this publication, Toorop sought a decorative solution by giving his lines an important ornamental function in the composition, but the result is still more illustrative than decorative.[17] All in all, this is a strange and abstruse binding indeed. The hair of three of the four women is depicted in the stylized and helical manner associated with Art Nouveau, while the smoky exhalations of all four take a similar form. Three are clothed in garments of white, black, and brown with dark spots. One woman is nude, however, and the smoke emanating from her mouth resembles an oily black substance that might suggest something sinister, such as opium. The title and author are interwoven among these ethereal specters, but the unity of letters and line patterns so familiar in Toorop's later work has yet to materialize. His 1896 design for *In den nevel, Delftsche studenten tijdschrift* (In the Mist, Delft Student Magazine), like the design of *Een boek van verbeelding,* also shows thin figures, in this case two of them with similarly expressive hairstyles, walking through a tulip bed discreetly covered by cloud forms (fig. 15).[18]

Gustaaf (Gust) Frederik van de Wall Perné (1877–1911), who died at the age of thirty-seven, was a maverick designer totally enraptured by visual themes from the East Indies, and his bindings display a Javanese directness. In many of his works, such as the 1903 binding for the Italian literary work *Donkere dagen* (Dark Days) by Antonio Fogazzaro, the only aspect that bespeaks the West is the lettering (fig. 16). Although Van de Wall Perné was often criticized by his peers for having poor knowledge of book production technology, he brought to his work an expressive and uninhibited

17. Braches, *Het boek als Nieuwe Kunst,* 168.

18. Ibid., 172. In 1895 Toorop's design for the Delftsche Slaolie (Delft Salad Oil) poster, dominated by two enigmatic female figures, brought him acclaim in decorative arts circles.

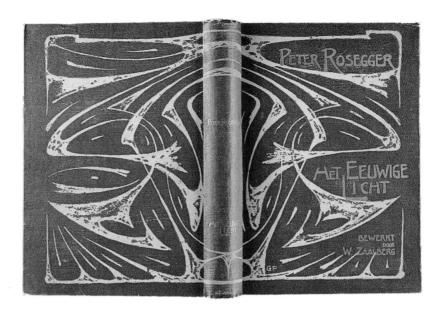

fig. 17
(right)
Gustaaf Frederik van de Wall Perné, book cover, designed 1902. From *Het eeuwige licht* (The Eternal Light) (Amsterdam: Van Holkema & Warendorf, third printing c. 1902).

fig. 18
(below)
Theodorus Johannes Josephus Neuhuys, book cover, designed 1901. From *Theorie en practyk van het Britsche vakvereenigingswezen* (Theory and Customs in the British Trade Union Practice) (Amsterdam: A. B. Soep, 1901).

exuberance. This is evidenced by his striking and lively 1902 binding for *Het eeuwige licht* (The Eternal Light) by Peter Rosegger (fig. 17). Sadly, Van de Wall Perné is by far one of the most underrated figures in Nieuwe Kunst book design, and most studies on this period either ignore him or treat him only as a footnote. To some extent, perhaps, this was because he entered the scene toward the end of the Nieuwe Kunst movement, but it was also because he could not be placed in a convenient category of book design history.

Combining interest in the East Indies and in geometry was T. J. J. Neuhuys, who worked in Amsterdam, The Hague, and East Aurora, New York. His 1901 design for *Theorie en practyk van het Britsche vakvereenig-*

ingswezen (Theory and Customs in the British Trade Union Practice) by Sidney and Beatrice Webb is typical of his bindings (fig. 18). It is characterized by delicate linear lacework extending from the spine, forming a frame for the letters. Though semigeometric, these patterns nonetheless suggest design motifs from the East Indies.

Having explored the stylistic variety of Nieuwe Kunst books, it is instructive to consider the process of their creation and the role of the publisher. Only rarely did one person design an entire book. Usually only the binding was commissioned, and the inner typography was left to the printer. Often the same binding designs were used for unrelated titles and had no relationship to the subject of the book. This was generally the case with Neuhuys's designs. On the other hand, distinct designs and color combinations were often used in different bindings for

fig. 19
Joris Johannes Christiaan
Lebeau, book cover,
designed 1900. From *De*
stille kracht **(The Hidden**
Force) (Amsterdam:
L. J. Veen, c. 1900).

the same title.[19] Some differences may be attributed to the availability of certain kinds or colors of paper. The designer did not always give precise instructions, but instead provided choices for the publisher. These were frequently ignored, and publishers often prevented designers from dealing directly with printers.[20]

When sales of a book increased unexpectedly, bindings were not selected for aesthetic reasons but instead for their availability, and if the original binding stock was depleted a replacement had to be found quickly.[21] To limit costs, publishers would resort to using existing binding stock that required only the insertion of a new title. Thus, a generic binding design that did not reflect the content could be easily used for various titles, and publishers would even resort to buying leftover bindings from competitors.[22]

The Amsterdam-based publisher Lambertus Jacobus Veen was a particularly important figure in the history of Dutch bookbinding, having commissioned works by several of the leading Nieuwe Kunst artists. Although Veen published a wide range of authors, he is best known for his titles by Louis Couperus (1863–1923), the prolific and immensely popular writer from The Hague, between 1892 and 1919. Couperus was first and foremost a novelist, but he also wrote short stories, travel journals, and a small amount of poetry. He was by far the greatest Dutch writer of the latter part of the nineteenth and beginning of the twentieth centuries. Couperus was very interested in the design of his bindings and often tried to play a role in the process. One of Veen's goals was to produce books of the highest quality in design, material, and execution. He was always fascinated by unorthodox techniques such as batik, and was the catalyst for the creation of one of the greatest Nieuwe Kunst bookbindings, *De stille kracht* (The Hidden Force).[23] This novel was based on a Dutch resident of Java's exploration of indigenous magical powers, and so batik was an apt choice (fig. 19).

Chris Lebeau, the designer of *De stille kracht,* was closely associated with the Arts and Crafts workshop at The Hague. In June 1900, he began

19. Van Vliet, *Versierde verhalen,* 75.
20. Ibid., 74.
21. Ibid.
22. Ibid.
23. Ibid., 207.

fig. 20
Jan Theodoor Toorop, book
cover, designed 1898.
From *Psyche* (Amsterdam:
L. J. Veen, c. 1898).

working at their Apeldoorn studio as a designer, and it was there that he produced his artwork for the novel. This was not his only version of *De stille kracht*, and one of his unused designs is in the collection of the Drents Museum in Assen. In October 1900, the definitive design was produced in batik and then stamped in gold before being made into the binding. In addition to the regular edition on cotton, a limited number of deluxe volumes of *De stille kracht* were printed on velvet. On the back, both the Amsterdam binder (Brandt) and the batik studio (Uiterwijk & Co. in Apeldoorn) are cited, an unusual gesture for this period that suggests their importance in the project. The vertical spine divides the symmetrical pattern on the front and the back. Although the design suggests flowers, it was actually made according to a mathematical system based on diamond shapes.[24] *De stille kracht* was printed in a large edition that reached thousands of readers, and as a result Lebeau and Veen further contributed to the popularity of batik in the Netherlands.

Veen was a personal friend of Jan Toorop and gave him many binding commissions. Toorop's style was well suited to the poetic, partially autobiographic, and symbolic tales of Couperus. In his bindings Toorop astutely implied the books' content through symbols.[25] His 1898 binding for *Psyche,* one of the many designs for Couperus, shows his adroitness in merging text with illustration, a device that Toorop continued to exploit to the fullest (fig. 20). *Psyche* is a symbolic, tragic, and erotic fairy tale

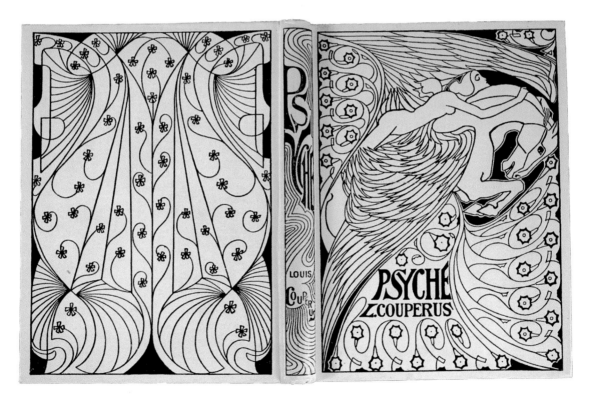

24. Ibid.
25. Ibid., 29.

fig. 21
(top)
Jan Theodoor Toorop,
book cover, designed
1903. From *God en goden*
(God and Gods)
(Amsterdam: L. J. Veen,
c. 1903).

fig. 22
(center)
Jan Theodoor Toorop, book
cover, designed 1899.
From *Egidius en de
vreemdeling* (Egidius and
the Stranger) (Haarlem:
De Erven F. Bohn, 1899).

fig. 23
(bottom)
Ludwig Willem Reijmert
Wenckebach, book cover,
designed 1895. From
Orchideeën (Orchids)
(Amsterdam: L. J. Veen,
second printing c. 1895).

about Princess Psyche, Prince Eros, and the winged stallion Chimera. While daydreaming on the ramparts of her father's palace, Psyche perceives in the shifting clouds the form of a knight on a winged steed. As depicted on the binding, Chimera eventually becomes real, and after Psyche's death carries her off through the wind and stars to the lands of her dreams.[26] The design, originally drawn in pencil and orange chalk, is filled with Toorop's "whiplash" lines, and the lettering, especially on the spine, blends in with the illustration. In contrast to the images on the front, the back is a symmetrical design suggesting a stringed instrument or peacock feathers. After reading the story, Toorop became very enthusiastic about the *Psyche* assignment and insisted upon seeing numerous proofs before approving the colors.[27] This created a constant struggle between him and the publisher, with the latter usually prevailing.

In general, the human figure has a small role in Nieuwe Kunst book design, and for this reason the bindings of Toorop are unusual.[28] In most of Toorop's bindings for Couperus, the figures are important but seem less apparent as they are integrated into the torrent of lines. In his 1903 design for *God en goden* (God and Gods)—two stories about gods titled "De zonen van de zon" (The Sons of the Sun) and "Jahve" (Jehovah)—a nude woman is draped in and framed by linear decorations; the lettering and illustration are in harmony (fig. 21). As evident in a letter to Veen, Couperus was very pleased with the design.[29] Toorop also designed bindings for other publishers. In 1899 he created for the Haarlem publisher De Erven F. Bohn the binding and illustrations for *Egidius en de vreemdeling* (Egidius and the Stranger) by W. G. van Nouhuys. Egidius, the heroine, is encased within the first letter of her name (fig. 22). The title, now so much a part of the surrounding decoration, is pushed almost to the point of illegibility, and the one illustrative element, the figure, has almost disappeared.[30]

L. W. R. Wenckebach also designed for Veen. His 1895 binding for the second edition of Couperus's *Orchideeën* (Orchids), a second compilation of his selected poems, is especially lyrical as the orchid motif extends over the back and front of the book (fig. 23). The design is constructed on a horizontal axis and divided on the spine by a vertical plant. There are examples with both green and gold lettering. Only on rare occasions did Wenckebach produce anything of a symbolic nature, such as his 1895 design for the cover of *Williswinde*, the third volume of poems by Couperus (fig. 24). In this illustration two lovers are depicted as entwined bushes or trees that support one another; should one die, the other is doomed as well.[31]

26. I. M. de Groot and M. Schapelhoumen, eds., *Rond 1900, Kunst op papier in Nederland Amster werk* (Amsterdam: Waanders Uitgevers, Rijksmuseum, 2000), 118.

27. Van Vliet, *Versierde verhalen*, 74.

28. Gans, *Nieuwe Kunst*, 59.

29. Braches, *Het boek als Nieuwe Kunst*, 178.

30. Gans, *Nieuwe Kunst*, 59.

31. Braches, *Het boek als Nieuwe Kunst*, 209.

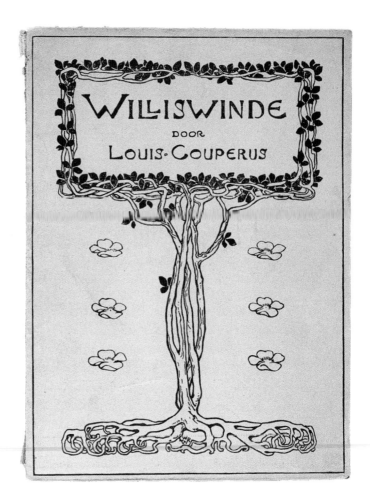

H. P. Berlage was one of the leading figures in the rebirth of Dutch architecture, but he also was active in the applied arts. *Hooge troeven* (High Trumps), designed in 1896, was the second Couperus binding Berlage made for Veen (fig. 25). Following *Majesteit* (Majesty) and *Wereldvrede* (World Peace), this is the third in a series of novels about royalty, all published in 1896. Each corner of the binding features one of the four suits associated with playing cards—a heart, club, spade, and diamond—picking up on the title of the book. The decoration of *Hooge troeven* is constructive, and the same design extends symmetrically to both the front and the back. One also sees in this binding a development toward geometrical abstraction.

By 1903, the glory and excitement of the experimental period of Nieuwe Kunst showed clear signs of having run its course as the movement assumed an established form. By 1910, Nieuwe Kunst had sadly digressed into mainly vapid commercial applications. In the end, the original discoveries were taken over by those who saw only the superficial aspects

fig. 25
Hendrik Petrus Berlage,
book cover, designed
1896. From *Hooge
troeven* (High Trumps)
(Amsterdam: L. J. Veen,
1896).

All illustrations from
The Mitchell Wolfson
Jr. Collection, The
Wolfsonian–Florida
International University,
Miami Beach, Florida.
All photographs
by Silvia Ros except
where noted.

of Nieuwe Kunst and they continued to exploit it as a fashionable decorative style, easy to manipulate and applicable to almost any end. However, Nieuwe Kunst book designs provided an aesthetic bridge between the nineteenth century and Modernism and served as a means to disseminate the style to a broad and diverse Dutch audience. Nieuwe Kunst's final and most significant impact was probably upon Art Deco design, its abstracted natural ornament having much in common with the decorative patterns of the later style. ✧

Acknowledgments
I would like to acknowledge the help of Francis X. Luca, Marianne Lamonaca, Joel Hoffman, Leslie Sternlieb, and Jacqueline Crucet of The Wolfsonian–Florida International University for their support of my research and the editorial assistance of Wilma Schuhmacher in Amsterdam.

RICHTER &

Thomas Row

Mobilizing the Nation: Italian Propaganda in the Great War

Thomas Row is resident assistant professor of history at the Johns Hopkins University Bologna Center in Italy. His most recent publication is a chapter on Italy during World War I in the *Oxford Short History of Italy* (2002). He was a Mitchell Wolfson Sr. Foundation Fellow at The Wolfsonian in 1997.

World War I marked a watershed in the modern development of propaganda. "Total war" required an unprecedented mobilization of national resources: material, moral, and psychological. As the conflict unfolded, each of the belligerent powers turned to the "arms of persuasion" to mold public opinion and uphold morale. As the costs of the war in blood and treasure mounted, the stakes of propaganda campaigns rose correspondingly. The result was an enormous increase in the output of propaganda, a transformation of its techniques, and the introduction of new kinds of "persuasive images." Beginning with the Great War, propaganda assumed an ever-increasing role in shaping mass opinion, a role that has had a lasting influence on the course of twentieth-century politics.[1]

The history of Italian propaganda in World War I is a relatively neglected subject.[2] Italy entered the war, initially against Austria-Hungary, in May 1915 and emerged victorious in November 1918. For Italy, the war was a crucial turning point: it produced the conditions that caused the collapse of Liberal parliamentary institutions and the rise of Fascism. Historians have, therefore, long recognized the importance of analyzing the transformation of state-society relations during the war. Propaganda is potentially an immensely revealing source for examining that relationship, for it is, in essence, a set of messages from the "state" to the "society." It is based upon and seeks to modify certain assumptions about popular behavior.

Detail of Mario Borgoni's *Prestito nazionale* (National Loan), postcard, 1918.

1. Maria Masau Dan and Donatella Porcedda, eds., *L'arma della persuasione. Parole ed immagini di propaganda nella grande guerra* (Gorizia: Provincia di Gorizia, 1991). Peter Paret, Beth Irwin Lewis, and Paul Paret, *Persuasive Images: Posters of War and Revolution from the Hoover Institution Archives* (Princeton, N.J.: Princeton University Press, 1992).

2. The seminal work is Nicola della Volpe, *Esercito e propaganda nella grande guerra (1915–1918)* (Rome: Stato Maggiore Esercito, Ufficio Storico, 1989).

DAPA 24

The broad aim of this article is to provide an introduction to the subject of Italian propaganda in World War I. In the first section, I will sketch out the historical context underlying wartime state-society relations. Next, some basic elements concerning the production and consumption of propaganda will be presented. These may serve as a basic model for analyzing propaganda messages. The final part of this article will be devoted to the empirical examination of selected propaganda images from The Wolfsonian–Florida International University and the Mitchell Wolfson Jr. Collection in Genoa, Italy. A unique strength of these collections is their capacity to support research in broad cultural and aesthetic contexts. One can, for example, study a subject across media, looking at posters, postcards, and calendars. By taking advantage of these rich resources, this essay seeks to provide a stimulating and impressionistic framework for viewing Italian propaganda during World War I, rather than a definitive history.

Italian State and Society in the Great War

When the Kingdom of Italy went to war in 1915, it had only been a unified nation-state for fifty-four years. Though slightly older than the German empire, Italy was considerably younger than the United States of America. The movement for national unification, the Risorgimento ("rebirth"), had been the work of only a minority of the people, and large segments of the population remained indifferent or hostile to the state. Vast regional differences separated not only the North from the South, but differences prevailed from province to province. Class and cultural divisions were strong as well. By 1915 a process of nationalization of the masses had only just begun in Liberal Italy.[3]

High politics were dominated by a restricted group of "insiders": King Victor Emmanuel III (1869–1947; ruled 1900–1946), army leaders, the prime minister, and the Liberal political class that ran local administration

---

3. For an overview of Italy's war, see Mario Isnenghi and Giorgio Rochat, *La grande guerra, 1914–1918* (Milan: La Nuova Italia, 2000).

and parliament. The concepts of nationhood, patriotism, monarchy, and "great power" status were for the most part important only to this elite. In the years before the war these values spread to parts of the urban middle classes, but remained alien to a great many Italians. The central political problem of prewar Italy lay in the fact that the minority of "insiders" had to govern the majority of often alienated and hostile "outsiders." These included Italy's Roman Catholics, who remained outside the political system because the rupture between the papacy and the Liberal state that was opened by national unification had not yet been healed. They also included the increasing number of industrial workers, organized by the trade unions and the Italian Socialist party. Another major group was the peasantry, a considerable force in a still-agrarian country. Thus the state-society problem was a crucial one.

Italy's decision to enter World War I brought this state-society tension to a head. A majority of Italians opposed intervention. But the variegated and highly mobilized minority of interventionists carried the day. These included the most militant nationalist segments of elite public opinion. King Victor Emmanuel III and Prime Minister Antonio Salandra (served 1914–1916) made the decision to enter the war without any significant prior consultation of parliament. Italy's war aims, as defined in the secret Treaty of London (April 1915), were narrowly diplomatic and dynastic: Italy was to go to war against Austria-Hungary in return for major territorial gains, including Trent and Trieste — the Austrian lands with significant Italian populations.

Thus millions of Italians found themselves engaged in a war they neither understood nor sought. They were pledged to make sacrifices for a king and a country toward which, in many cases, they felt no strong bonds. While one should not exaggerate the state-society division — after all, the Italians did, in fact, pull together in the war effort — it lay at the heart of the problem of mobilizing the nation for war. The Italian state had to convince or compel soldiers to fight and die; it had to convince or compel workers and farmers to produce. In a broad sense the state had two options: either it could rely on blind obedience, backed up by coercion; or it could seek consensus, backed up with persuasion. While these options were not mutually exclusive, the emphasis placed on one rather than the other proved crucial. Within this context, the role of propaganda came to be critical, as seen in a 1915 image showing Italy's initial war aims (fig. 1).

The first response of the Italian state and people was a cautious enthusiasm. The war was expected to be very short. Many volunteers imagined that they would soon find glory. The country was unprepared militarily and economically for war. In this situation, a large-scale propaganda effort was not a priority. Both the civil and military authorities intended to emphasize discipline and coercion. This was particularly true of the army, which,

fig. 2
Photographer unknown,
General Luigi Cadorna.
From *L'Italia e la sua
guerra* (Italy and Her War),
2d ed. (Milan: Studio
Editoriale Busetto, 1933).
The Mitchell Wolfson Jr.
Collection, The
Wolfsonian–Florida
International University,
Miami Beach, Florida.
Copy photograph
by Silvia Ros.

under the command of General Luigi Cadorna (1850–1928) (fig. 2) adopted a series of severe, repressive measures. Propaganda in the press, in satire, and in oratory emanated from the very active pro-intervention circles. Many of the individuals involved in these campaigns would figure in later, more organized, war propaganda.

The war did not resolve the tensions within Italian society; rather, it covered them up. As the conflict dragged on, Italy, like the other belligerent states, began to mobilize for total war (fig. 3). The large battlefront areas under military command were regimented, as was the rest of the country. The economy was rapidly reconfigured to support the war effort. Food, supplies, and currencies were controlled. Discipline was enforced in the booming war factories. The press was censored. Casualties began to mount.

It was in this context that Italy's wartime program of propaganda developed. It became necessary for the nation's leaders to enlist persuasion, in addition to discipline and coercion. Their efforts were conditioned by two strong general convictions. The first was that they had to win the war in order for the Liberal regime to survive. The second was that they could not fundamentally trust the masses, particularly the socialists, who had not been fully integrated within the Liberal system. Thus propaganda in Italy—as opposed to that in Britain, France, and Germany—developed rather slowly. It was not until 1917, when the ideological character of the war changed following the Italian army's defeat at Caporetto (enabling the Austrians to occupy much of the Veneto), that propaganda emerged as a major force. At Caporetto the Austrians and Germans broke through the Italian lines. The Italian position collapsed and the army retreated, only to regroup at the River Piave. The northeastern part of the country lay in enemy hands.

Propaganda can be many things, and there are numerous ways of understanding it.[4] On the one hand, propaganda can mean simply providing a certain kind of information. On the other hand, it can signify the manipulation of information to a specific end. Without entering into theoretical debate, propaganda will be considered here as the organized use of various media to attempt to shape mass psychology and, hence, behavior. From the above definition, four main questions emerge. First, what were the sources of propaganda? Second, what were the media of propaganda? Third, who were the targets of propaganda? And finally, the most difficult question, to what extent was the propaganda successful?

4. For a synthesis of theoretical perspectives, see Dan and Porcedda, *L'arma della persuasione.*
  A brilliant analysis using propaganda in a British case study is Nicoletta Gullace, "Sexual Violence and Family Honor: British Propaganda and International Law during the First World War," *American Historical Review* 102 (June 1997).

fig. 3
Raffaello Boschini,
La Pugna (The Battle).
From *L'Italia e la sua
guerra*. The Mitchell
Wolfson Jr. Collection,
The Wolfsonian–Florida
International University,
Miami Beach, Florida.
Photograph by Silvia Ros.

Looking ahead, we can see World War I as a first great step into the modern, industrial mass production of propaganda. The lessons learned would shape ensuing commercial advertising and political propaganda. Both would be perfected in the interwar years. Alas, the master of state propaganda would be none other than Benito Mussolini (1883–1945). In World War I, however, propaganda was in its nascent phase.

Sources

In analyzing propaganda it is of central importance to understand its sources.[5] Who was sending the messages? How was propaganda actually produced and disseminated? In the case of Italian propaganda during the Great War we can make a number of broad generalizations. The propaganda effort emanated from three focal points of the Liberal state. First, there was the government itself. Here prominent politicians issued statements, made speeches, and gave interviews. State agencies issued decrees, published manifestos, and funded private war-support groups. Government propaganda efforts tended to be traditional and limited in terms of media and message. Its overall effectiveness was questionable. The Liberal political class was not always inclined to address itself to the masses. Its members feared defeatism and subversion, and they hoped that discipline and coercion would keep the people on the home front in line.

The second center of propaganda was the army itself. Under Cadorna, the commander in chief, the distance between the leaders and the led was wide indeed. The army command felt little need to bolster troop morale. To a very large extent, it relied on iron discipline. Few efforts were initially made to provide relief centers for the soldiers. Food rations were abysmal. Given the historic rift between church and state in Liberal Italy, the army was slow to introduce chaplains and provide religious support. As the historian Giovanna Procacci has shown, Italian prisoners of war were deliberately denied aid (to discourage desertion by others).[6] This resulted in massive casualties. Instead, strict orders and coercion, including decimation, were the army's principal arms of persuasion. As with the politicians, the army leaders had an extreme fear of subversion. On the front, propaganda efforts initially were limited and traditional, including, for example, speeches by officers.

The third area of propaganda production was the amorphous world of civic society that was composed not only of groups of well-intentioned

5. della Volpe, *Esercito e propaganda;* and Gian Luigi Gatti, *Dopo Caporetto: Gli ufficiali P nella grande guerra: propaganda, assistenza, vigilanza* (Gorizia: Libreria Editrice Goriziana, 2000).

6. Giovanna Procacci, *Soldati e prigioneri nella grande guerra* (Turin: Bollati Boringhieri, 2000).

citizens, but of large economic interests as well. Throughout the country, and particularly in the main cities, organizations appeared in defense of the war effort. Bolstered later by the creation of regional industrial mobilization commissions, these came to form a network of support and propaganda (fig. 4). They were able to draw upon the intellectual resources of the interventionist elite. As the war developed, industrial and financial interests took on a primary role in supporting war propaganda. The arms maker Ansaldo, for example, heavily subsidized pro-war newspapers, including Mussolini's *Il Popolo d'Italia,* through advertising. Far and away the most important efforts concerned the war loan campaigns. In order to finance the war, Italy began to borrow money from its citizens by issuing a series of war bonds managed by the banks. The propaganda campaigns to encourage bond purchases were among the best and most sophisticated of the war (fig. 5).[7]

Thus the government, the army, and the Liberal civil and economic elite came together to form the nucleus around which propaganda production and distribution formed. The army, for example, had total control of press and propaganda efforts on the front. The government monopolized propaganda toward allied and neutral countries. Civil and economic propaganda appear to have worked in harmony with the state and army efforts. There was a degree of coordination among all three areas, although the specific arrangements, particularly the question of financing, remain obscure.

In sum, the sources of propaganda were the main bastions of the Liberal regime: the state, the army, the interventionist elite, and large economic interests. They had a common cause in promoting an aggressive war effort. They all had an uneasy relationship with the Italian masses, workers and peasants, socialists and Roman Catholics, men at the front and the people at home. As a general rule, they preferred discipline and coercion to persuasion. This tendency reflected the difficulties of state-society relations in Italy at the time.

The enormous Italian defeat at the battle of Caporetto in October 1917 brought about a revolution in Italian wartime propaganda. Until this catastrophe, Italian propaganda efforts had been limited in both quantity and quality. After Caporetto, a new activist prime minister,

---

7. Renato Breda, *Le cartoline dei prestiti di guerra 1915–1942* (Rome: Capo di Stato Maggiore, Ufficio Storico, 1992).

SOTTOSCRIVETE AL PRESTITO

Vittorio Emmanuele Orlando (served 1917–1919), came to power. Likewise, a new commander more sensitive to the morale of his men, Armando Diaz (1861–1928), replaced Cadorna. The country's citizens and industries mobilized in the face of enemy invasion. The Liberal regime realized that a major propaganda effort was now needed to bolster morale both on the home front and on the battlefield. In one of the few documented studies of a propaganda organization, the historian Gian Luigi Gatti has shown how a special division — Service P —was set up within the army to provide propaganda and to bolster the morale of troops, but also to keep them under surveillance.[8]

Media

A difficulty in propagandizing was that of selecting the correct medium for the correct target. The Liberal regime had various means at its disposal for disseminating propaganda, but in assessing them, we must keep in mind the character of early twentieth-century Italy. As noted, relations between the formal Italian state (the king, the army, the civil authorities) and the people were under stress and relatively weak. This meant that the gap between the producers of propaganda and the consumers was wide indeed, and very difficult to bridge. Modern means of mass communication — radio and television — were, of course, not yet available. In addition, the population was variegated, with differing degrees of education and literacy. Although great strides had been made, illiteracy remained high, particularly in the South and in the islands. Formal Italian remained a literary language, familiar in the towns and among the elite, but most Italians spoke a regional dialect. Propaganda therefore adapted traditional means of communication to new purposes. Some new technologies, however, such as the cinema, moved to the fore. Given this context the principal media of propaganda used images, the printed word, and the human voice. I have focused my research and analysis on propaganda images, believing they remain the most accessible.

fig. 5
Giovanni Capranesi, *Sottoscrivete al prestito!* (Subscribe to the War Loan!), postcard (from poster), 1918. From *La Pubblicità nei prestiti Italiani di guerra* (Advertising for Italian War Loans), vol. 1 (Milan: Risorgimento Grafico, 1918–1919). The Mitchell Wolfson Jr. Collection, The Wolfsonian–Florida International University, Miami Beach, Florida. Photograph by Silvia Ros.

8. Gatti, *Dopo Caporetto.*

fig. 6
(right)
Photographer unknown,
Arezzo street scene with
propaganda poster, 1917.
From *La Pubblicità nei
prestiti Italiani di guerra*,
vol. 1. The Mitchell
Wolfson Jr. Collection,
The Wolfsonian–Florida
International University,
Miami Beach, Florida.
Copy photograph by
Silvia Ros.

fig. 7
(far right)
Photographer unknown,
Monza street scene with
propaganda poster, 1917.
From *La Pubblicità nei
prestiti Italiani di guerra*,
vol. 1. The Mitchell
Wolfson Jr. Collection,
The Wolfsonian–Florida
International University,
Miami Beach, Florida.
Copy photograph by
Silvia Ros.

Posters. The poster was, and has until recently remained, one of the basic
media of communication in Italy. Large posters pasted on street corners
and buildings had been central to advertising, politics, and propaganda
for more than a century (figs. 6 and 7). Posters have the advantage of
communicating a basic message to a large number of people, unlike other
media, such as newspapers and books, that are aimed at the literate or
otherwise educated. Posters were a largely urban phenomenon, but one
that was highly effective in the dense array of cities and villages that
constitute Italy. Already by World War I, the poster had become a significant art form, providing many of the period's most compelling graphic
images. The commercial poster industry, its artists and printing plants,
soon turned to war propaganda. Poster designs were reused, adapted,
and transferred to other media, such as postcards. They form the corpus
of the most important graphic images of war propaganda.[9]

Postcards. It is difficult to underestimate the role of the humble postcard
in World War I. In the absence of widespread public telephone systems, the
postcard and the letter were the only significant means of communication
between the troops and their families and friends. The postcard, given its
economy and brevity, was essential. Many were not able to write letters at
all, let alone frequently, so the postcard was the vital communication link
binding Italians. Millions of postcards circulated during the war. As a tool
of propaganda, the postcard offered great possibilities, for the "picture"
side could be used to present persuasive images, including satiric political
cartoons. The enemy could be mocked, as in a caricature of the Emperor

9. Maurice Rickards, *Manifesti della prima guerra mondiale* (Milan: Alfieri and Lacroix, 1968);
   Mirtide Gavelli and Otello Sangiorgi, eds., "L'oro e il piombo: I prestiti nazionali in Italia nella
   grande guerra," *Bollettino del Museo del Risorgimento* 36 (Bologna: Comune di Bologna, 1991);
   Marzia Miele and Cesarina Vighy, eds., *Manifesti illustrati della grande guerra* (Rome: Fratelli
   Palombi editori, 1996); and Gessica Bone, Loretta Righetti, and Daniela Savoia, eds., *Immagini e
   documenti della grande guerra* (Cesena: Il Ponte Vecchio, 2000).

— Ecco una pillola che mi rimarrà indigesta!...

Franz Josef (fig. 8), who is presented with a bitter pill to swallow—an artillery shell. Often postcards celebrated particular military regiments. For the most part these were traditional images representing the soldiers or seals of these units; sometimes they were humorous. But as the war dragged on, a full array of images appeared. Given their number and circulation, postcards became, perhaps, the most popular and important propaganda medium.[10]

The Press. Italy's press played a distinct role in wartime propaganda. Italian newspapers were, for the most part, an elite affair, intended for educated urbanites. They also were firmly grounded in regional, economic, and political interests. With the outbreak of war, the military strictly controlled access to the front, and the government began to censor or repress those newspapers that opposed intervention. At the risk of over-generalizing, one can argue that the Italian press became a reflection of establishment propaganda for the war. Press propaganda served, above all, to hold the reading population together. Within the wartime press, one can trace the shifting stances and positions of the various factions and interests composing the Liberal regime. The press is less useful, however, in helping us understand the realities faced by the masses of Italians at war.[11]

Pamphlets. Fliers and pamphlets were a popular way of communicating with the people. Fliers, sometimes with graphic designs, were widely distributed for such purposes as issuing directives and promoting rallies. Pamphlets were aimed at those with basic literacy and could reach a population that might not have frequent access to newspapers. The contents of pamphlets varied widely, but their main goals were to explain to the people the meaning of the war, to inculcate hatred of the enemy, and to promise a better world ahead. The Roman Catholic catechism was adopted in one, for example, as the catechism of the nation.[12]

fig. 8
Aroldo Bonzagni, *Ecco una pillola che mi rimarrà indigesta!* (Here Is a Pill That Will Remain Undigested!), postcard, c. 1916. The Mitchell Wolfson Jr. Collection, The Wolfsonian–Florida International University, Miami Beach, Florida. Photograph by Silvia Ros.

10. Nicola della Volpe, *Cartoline militari* (Rome: Capo di Stato Maggiore: Ufficio Storico, 1994); and Luigi Amedeo de Biase, *Le cartoline delle brigate e dei reggimenti di fanteria nella guerra del 1915–1918* (Rome: Capo di Stato Maggiore, Ufficio Storico, 1994).

11. Mimmo Franzinelli, ed., *Giornali 1914–1918: La grande guerra* (Milan: Contemporanea, 1997); and Maurizio Pagliano, ed., *Le copertine della Domenica 1915–1918* (Milan: Rizzoli, 1975).

12. della Volpe, *Esercito e propaganda.*

Trench Newspapers. After Caporetto, and with the support of the special Service P, attempts were made to deliver propaganda directly to men at the front. Prior to this, officials had been wary that subversive tracts or expressions of soldier discontent would come to the fore. The solution was to launch the so-called trench newspapers, created by and for the fighting men, but still closely monitored by the authorities. *La Tradotta*, for example, was the paper of the Third Army. It was founded, in part, by an artist, Umberto Brunelleschi (1879–1949), and is a mixture of drawings, cartoons, verse, and jokes (some of them scatological). *La Tradotta*, like the other trench newspapers, gave voice to the hopes and fears of the soldiers while remaining within the limits imposed by those in command.[13]

Oratory and Cinema. In addition to printed images and texts, spoken words and moving images were important propaganda media. Oratory had a prominent role in Italian public life, where the piazza was central to all politics. With entry into the war, the interventionists had seized control of the piazza as a platform for war propaganda. Countless politicians, heroes, mutilated victims, civic leaders, and intellectuals delivered speeches during the war. Many of their remarks were later published in pamphlets and newspapers. On the front, officers and government officials also addressed soldiers. It is very difficult to assess the effectiveness of oratorical propaganda. Newspaper reports about them are not always reliable. A few accounts by soldiers are contradictory: sometimes an orator was considered effective; often the troops responded with cynicism.

The Italian film industry had already emerged on a world scale with director Giovanni Pastrone's *Cabiria* in 1914, an historic epic set in the third century B.C. Italy's entry into World War I quickly initiated a period of extraordinary growth for the film industry. Wartime films presented a whole gamut of patriotic themes, but did not represent a close-up view of the war. According to one critic, their distinctive feature was to create a sense of "distance and absence" from the conflict. State censors, who wished to see a sanitized version of the war, reinforced this tendency. Though immensely popular, Italian wartime films seldom attained the quality of the nation's prewar cinema. In fact, they tended to underscore the gap between the pro-war state and the rest of society.[14]

Taken together, these various media formed the arms of persuasion that were mobilized by the Liberal regime to shape opinion and mold public behavior during the war. Each medium was adapted and transformed for propagandistic purposes. Artists, journalists, writers, filmmakers, and printers all turned their talents to new purposes and targets.

13. See Mario Isnenghi, *Giornali di trincea, 1915–1918* (Turin: Einaudi, 1977); and *La Tradotta: Giornale della terza armata* (Milan: Mondadori, 1968).

14. Giovanni Nobili Vitelleschi, "The Representation of the Great War in Italian Cinema," in *The First World War and Popular Cinema*, ed. Michael Paris (New Brunswick, N.J.: Rutgers University Press, 2000).

Targets

A basic descriptive model of propaganda must, of course, take into account its targets. Whose opinion and behavior was to be shaped? Whose morale? In the case of wartime Italy, we can identify four target areas that were of particular concern to the Liberal state and its supporters. The first and most important was the battlefront. It included not only the soldiers in the frontline trenches and mountain outposts, but also those in the support trenches and supply lines in the rearguard. Moreover, much of northeast Italy was under military control as a war zone. Propaganda in this area was chiefly a military issue, and, as we have seen, the military preferred the stick to the carrot, at least until Caporetto.

The second major target was the home front, and this too was variegated and complex. Propaganda campaigns had to take into account class tensions, regional disparities, and differences between town and country. The war mobilization had clamped a lid on social conflicts, but these simmered beneath the surface. On the home front, the government, civic organizations, the press, and bankers and industrialists were most responsible for waging the propaganda war. One must also remember that the fence of censorship alternately separated and filtered the battlefront from the home front.

A third target of propaganda activity, the shaping of foreign public opinion, while a lesser priority, was nonetheless of great interest to the government. For the first few years of the war, the country tried to run a "parallel" war to that of the other allies. There was no unified command, and Italy did not declare war on Germany until 1916. But as the course of the conflict developed, and as Italy became ever more dependent on Britain and France for material and financial support, it became clear that Italy's war effort would rely on the help of its allies. Thus the government set up a propagandistic mission through the foreign office to sway foreign opinion in its favor, in particular to gather support for Italy's postwar territorial ambitions. When the United States entered the war in 1917, these efforts focused on securing the support of Italian Americans.[15]

Finally, Italy engaged in counter-propaganda against the enemy. At the front line this involved showering enemy troops with defeatist leaflets and folders. These sought, at best, to provoke desertions and, at least, discouragement. Some of this counter-propaganda was ingenious — enemy trench newspapers were, for example, recomposed with Allied messages. In the case of Austro-Hungarian troops, efforts were made to rally divisive nationalism within the ranks of this multinational empire. Other attempts at counter-propaganda were spectacular, such as the poet Gabriele D'Annunzio's (1863–1938) renowned air flight over Vienna to drop leaflets.

15. Luciano Tosi, *La propaganda italiana all'estero nella prima guerra mondiale. Rivendicazioni territoriali e politica delle nazionalitá* (Pordenone: Del Bianco editore, 1977).

fig. 9
A. Bertiglia, *Inutili*
***Offerte!* (Useless**
Offerings!), postcard,
1915. The Mitchell
Wolfson Jr. Collection,
The Wolfsonian–Florida
International University,
Miami Beach, Florida.
Photograph by Silvia Ros.

But what were the propagandists trying to say? Let us now turn to their messages.

Analyzing Messages

Analyzing historical propaganda messages presents a series of enormous methodological difficulties. Propaganda exists within a short and fleeting context. For the Italy of World War I (and particularly in the absence of modern opinion polls), it is practically impossible to determine with any precision either the intentions of the propagandists or the reactions of the recipients. While there are some clues about general morale (police reports documented political dissent, for example), there is little specific data with respect to overt propaganda. My analysis of propaganda centers on understanding and contextualizing materials, rather than on assessing their efficacy. For the most part I have studied images (posters, postcards, drawings) rather than messages conveyed in newspapers, pamphlets, or films. The emphasis has been on examining as many propaganda images as possible and identifying a representative sample. Based upon that sample, certain broad themes emerge, and these provide the organization for my analysis.

*1915 and 1918: **The Old and the New.*** Between the beginning of Italy's war in 1915 and the "victory" of 1918, the visual language of propaganda steadily evolved, reflecting the increasing stakes of the conflict. What began as a limited war for the conquest of Trent and Trieste ended as a clash of civilizations. G. Castiglioni's postcard *Trento e Trieste incoronano*

Strepitoso, inaspettato ed insuperabile
successo dei gas asfisianti di
marca italiana

fig. 10
S. Dattilo, *Fagioli Italiani*
(Italian Beans), postcard,
1915. The Mitchell
Wolfson Jr. Collection,
The Wolfsonian–Florida
International University,
Miami Beach, Florida.
Photograph by Silvia Ros.

l'esercito Italiano liberatore (Trent and Trieste Crown the Liberating Italian Army) well portrays the vision of the war and the country's war aims in 1915 (fig. 1). A valiant knight (a far cry from the reality of a muddy infantryman) smites the double-headed eagle symbolizing the Hapsburgs. In the background, gracious female figures draped in the colors of Trent and Trieste raise a laurel crown of victory over the warrior's head. This was the initial image of the war: a culminating battle of the Risorgimento against the traditional Austrian enemy to recover the *terre irredente* (unredeemed lands). By 1918 this vision of the conflict had been transformed. Total war demanded a broader and more powerful justification for the nation's sacrifice. Italy now was fighting not only for her survival but also for Western civilization against "barbarism." Giovanni Capranesi's 1918 postcard *Sottoscrivete al prestito!* (Subscribe to the War Loan!) shows in stark form the sharpness of this clash (fig. 5). Imploring citizens to lend financial support to the war effort, the postcard shows Italia herself, dressed in Roman armor, fending off the barbarian Teutonic invader (appearing in full Wagnerian glory) who dares to cross the Alps. Through the development of the images of propaganda we see the broadening of the war's aims and meanings.

A Short and Jolly War: Comic Images. At the outset, however, most Italians either expected or hoped for a short and jolly war. Vienna was to be captured in a matter of weeks. A. Bertiglia's postcard *Inutili Offerte!* (Useless Offerings!) dates to early 1915, the period of neutrality when the question of intervention was still hotly debated (fig. 9). It presents a comic view representative of early propaganda. Here, a young and flirtatious Italia (very different from that in fig. 5) is wooed by a series of suitors bearing gifts (Germany's Kaiser Wilhelm II, Austria-Hungary's Emperor Franz Josef, Britain's King George V, France's President Raymond Poincaré, Russia's Czar Nicholas II). On which side would the coquettish Italia intervene? The caption does not say; and war and intervention are on a par with a flirt. In a Dattilo postcard of 1915, *Fagioli Italiani* (Italian Beans), an Italian *bersagliere* (a member of the special regiment known for its ostrich-plumed helmets) blasts away the enemy in a humorous, scatological image (fig. 10). Italian beans will beat Austrian cannons: the soldier's fart knocks out the Emperor Franz Josef, whose flag bears the stain of the hangman. Unfortunately the realities of war, not least the horrors of gas warfare, would soon diminish the efficacy of comic images in propaganda. Stronger messages would be needed.

"Fate tutti il vostro dovere!"

LE SOTTOSCRIZIONI AL PRESTITO SI RICEVONO PRESSO IL

CREDITO ITALIANO

Everyone Do Your Duty. It was not until 1917 that Italian propaganda produced its most iconic image. This was Achille Luciano Mauzan's poster for the Credito Italiano bank's war loan campaign (fig. 11). The design had tremendous success both at home and abroad, and was reproduced in countless forms (figs. 6 and 7), including a giant version thirty meters square. What accounted for this success? Mauzan found a message and a way of representing it that transcended the troubled state-society relationship in Italy. In Britain, a comparably iconic image (by Alfred Leete) showed an authority figure (Lord Kitchener) pointing at the viewer with the caption, "Your Country Needs You." In the United States, James Montgomery Flagg likewise portrayed an authoritative Uncle Sam exclaiming, "I Want You for the U.S. Army." In Italy, where many mistrusted state authority, such appeals would have fallen flat. Mauzan's design shows us not a leader, but an ordinary infantryman, an "everyman." Against the background of battle and the silhouettes of his comrades the soldier points at the viewer (like Kitchener and Uncle Sam) and demands, "All of You Do Your Duty!" In Italy, representations of "everyman" held a broader appeal than those of authority figures.[16]

Success bred imitation, and the Banca Commerciale (the Credito Italiano's chief competitor) soon issued a war loan poster of its own (fig. 12). Like Mauzan's design, Anselmo Barchi's poster shows us an ordinary soldier pointing to the observer. "Help us win!" he exclaims. While the two images are similar, Banca Commerciale's was a propagandistic failure (as critics noted at the time). Barchi's soldier is disheveled, his collar undone; his look betrays more panic than resistance. In contrast to the approach adopted by Mauzan and Barchi is a rare poster in The Wolfsonian's collection (fig. 13).

16. This was true also in France, where Jules Abel Faivre's noted poster *On les aura!* (We Will Get Them!) adopts a similar iconography.

fig. 14
(right)
Mario Borgoni, *Prestito nazionale* (National Loan), postcard (from poster), 1918. From *La Pubblicità nei prestiti Italiani di guerra*, vol. 1. The Mitchell Wolfson Jr. Collection, The Wolfsonian–Florida International University, Miami Beach, Florida Photograph by Silvia Ros.

fig. 15
(opposite page)
Ugo Finozzi, *Cacciali via!* (Drive Them Out!), postcard (from poster), 1918. From *La Pubblicità nei prestiti Italiani di guerra*, vol. 1. The Mitchell Wolfson Jr. Collection, The Wolfsonian–Florida International University, Miami Beach, Florida. Photograph by Silvia Ros.

Here we do see an authority figure—Italian commander General Luigi Cadorna. The message reads: "Italy needs meat, grain, fats, and sugar. Eat very little of these foods because they must go to our people, and the troops of Italy." The explication of this poster depends upon its credit line, noted in small type at the bottom: United States Food Administration. In fact, this is a propaganda poster directed toward Italian Americans. Cadorna, a taciturn man and harsh disciplinarian, was not beloved in Italy. Nor could a people facing food scarcity be moved by an appeal to reduce consumption. Propaganda for Italians perforce differed from that for Italian Americans.

CACCIALI VIA!

SOTTOSCRIVETE AL PRESTITO

Caporetto and Resistance. After the defeat at Caporetto, the country was fighting for its survival, and the Italian propaganda machine shifted into high gear. Efforts were directed toward the soldiers, whose morale had to be restored, and to the home front. Italy's banks took the lead in general propaganda production as they sought to raise funds for the various war loan campaigns. Mario Borgoni's postcard design of 1918 (based on a poster) well demonstrates the message of post-Caporetto resistance (fig. 14). A soldier embraces the tricolor flag. The enemy is near: the corner of the flag is dragged out of the frame. We see only the soldier's eyes and the bridge of his nose over his arm as he reaches back to swing his sword. He clearly conveys the idea that the nation must be defended at all costs. Another 1918 image promoting war loans—and perhaps a more effective one in a country whose masses had not yet

been highly nationalized—is Ugo Finozzi's *Cacciali via!* (Drive Them Out!) (fig. 15). Instead of the national flag, we see the Italian family. A resolute soldier, dagger drawn, moves forward. Behind the soldier, touching his shoulder, is a female figure—not Italia, but a wife and mother, baby in hand. While *la Patria* (the nation) was often an abstract motivation for resistance, the family was something concrete to defend.

Fear and Loss. Two of the most powerful themes in propaganda are fear and loss. Fear—of the enemy, of the "other"—can motivate aggression. Anger over sacrifice and loss can be a potent instigation to revenge and resistance. Both feelings were frequent themes in Italian wartime propaganda. Two examples by the artist Aroldo Bonzagni (1887–1918) serve as illustration. One depicts a frightened woman carrying a child (fig. 16).

fig. 16
(right)
Aroldo Bonzagni, *Fratelli
salvatemi!* (Brothers
Save Me!), postcard,
c. 1918. The Mitchell
Wolfson Jr. Collection,
The Wolfsonian–Florida
International University,
Miami Beach, Florida.
Photograph by Silvia Ros.

fig. 17
(far right)
Aroldo Bonzagni, *...Ed ora
a voi, sottoscrivete!*
(...And Now, It's Up to
You — Subscribe!),
postcard (from poster),
c. 1918. From *La Pubblicità
nei prestiti Italiani di
guerra,* vol. 2. The
Mitchell Wolfson Jr.
Collection, The
Wolfsonian–Florida
International University,
Miami Beach, Florida.
Photograph by Silvia Ros.

fig. 18
(below)
Aroldo Bonzagni, book
cover, *Gli Unni...e gli Altri!*
(The Huns...and the
Others!) (Milan: Rava &
Co., c. 1916). The Mitchell
Wolfson Jr. Collection,
The Wolfsonian–Florida
International University,
Miami Beach, Florida.
Photograph by Silvia Ros.

Leering, beastly looking Austrian soldiers surround her. Gazing desperately
at the viewer she shouts, "Brothers Save Me!" The horrified viewer is left
to imagine the atrocity about to occur. In another, *...Ed ora a voi, Sottoscrivete!*
(...And Now, It's Up to You — Subscribe!) (fig. 17), we see a representation of loss. A young, decorated soldier (his dark complexion suggests
that he is a Southerner) raises a crutch with his right hand, while the left
crutch compensates for a missing leg. Like thousands of others, this soldier
had joined the ranks of the mutilated.

Aroldo Bonzagni was one of the most interesting fine artists of his generation, and the Wolfson collections in Miami Beach and Genoa provide a
representative sampling of his work as a whole. He was born in Cento
(Ferrara) and died during the Spanish influenza epidemic (which infamously
took more lives than the war itself). Before the war he was associated
with the Futurists, moving in the most avant-garde circles of his time.

Like many of his generation, he took
an active interest in the conflict and
became one of its most accomplished
propagandists. In addition to his
painting, Bonzagni was an accomplished
satirical draftsman, and it was this work
that led him into propaganda. In
1915, along with Marcello Dudovich,
Leonardo Dudreville, and others, he
published *Gli Unni...e gli Altri!*
(The Huns...and the Others!) (fig. 18) —
an anti-German satire that was followed

by his own, *I Comandamenti di Dio* (The Commandments of God).

Allies and Ideologies. Two events in 1917 further transformed the overall character of the war. The first of these was the Russian Revolution, which, after the Bolshevik victory, not only had strategic consequences — the withdrawal of Russia as a belligerent force — but ideological effects as well. Soviet Communism posed a challenge to the whole value system upon which the war had, until then, been fought. The prospect of revolution and peace, and of a new social and economic order, held a vast appeal for the war-weary masses. The second event was the entry of the United States into the conflict. Here, too, a new ideological system — that of Wilsonian liberalism — challenged preceding assumptions about the meaning of the war. Both the messages of Vladimir Lenin and of Woodrow Wilson resonated within Italy. The army high command developed an almost paranoid fear of "Red" subversion. Poor performance by the troops or insufficient support from the war industries was blamed on defeatism inspired by the political left. These fears, in fact, were ungrounded, yet the perceptions remained. Official attitudes toward Wilsonian liberalism were more favorable, even if they would ultimately contrast with the realpolitik war aims of the Italian state.

Propaganda images adapted to emphasize the changed ideological character of the war. They stressed its new, "positive" sense, the Wilsonian notion of a war that would make the world safe for democracy. At the same time, they came to counter war-weariness and defeatism by underlining the strength of a grand alliance. No longer was this just a national war, but a war of Allies. The American entry promised resources in men and weapons that would assure victory. In Armando Vassallo's 1918 poster *Libertas* (Liberty), the Statue of Liberty — a resonant image for the Italian nation that had experienced mass emigration — holds her torch high, against the rising sun of freedom (fig. 19). It pronounces that the Americans are

fig. 19
Armando Vassallo,
***Libertas,* poster, 46 x 34 cm,**
c. 1918. The Mitchell
Wolfson Jr. Collection,
The Wolfsonian–Florida
International University,
Miami Beach, Florida.
Photograph by Silvia Ros.

PER LA LIBERTÀ E LA CIVILTÀ
DEL MONDO
SOTTOSCRIVETE
AL PRESTITO
NAZIONALE
M. DUDOVICH
ATELIER
BUTTERI
TORINO

coming to bring victory and freedom. Above, the flags of the Allies (excluding Russia) form a secondary halo underscoring the message. A war loan poster by Marcello Dudovich, who was one of the country's masters in the graphic arts, also depicts a brilliant display of Allied strength and determination (fig. 20). An Italian *fante*, a French *poilu*, a British Tommy, and an American GI raise their rifles in defiance against the (unseen) forces of barbarism. As the inscription notes, theirs is a crusade "For the Freedom and Civilization of the World."

The Home Front. Throughout the war there was a sharp distinction between the battlefront and the home front. Italy's military campaigns were for the most part in the far northeast of the country, far away, say, from the world of a southern Italian farmer. The battlefront came under the strict jurisdiction of the military command. Given the nature of trench warfare, it was a terrible and unique environment, a special universe, separated from the "normal" world. In the course of the war the home front changed too, as mobilization for total war altered traditional social relations. The connections between the home front and the battlefront were important, as problems of morale emanating from one of these, it was widely feared, would have an impact on the other.

One of the most popular propaganda campaigns directly addressed ties between the warring nation's dual fronts. It consists of two designs by Aldo Mazza for the Credito Italiano bank's war loan campaign. In the first, a young *alpino* sits writing a letter to his parents (fig. 21). The *alpini* are a special branch of the Italian army. As their name implies they are mountain troops, locally recruited for warfare in the Alps. Their distinctive badge is the peaked cap, notable for its feather. Here, the viewer sees

fig. 23
Giovanni Greppi, *A me resistere, A tutti sottoscrivere!* (It's Up to Me to Resist, It's Up to Everybody to Subscribe!), poster, 100 x 70 cm, 1917. The Mitchell Wolfson Jr. Collection—Fondazione Regionale Cristoforo Colombo, Genoa, Italy.

another everyman, a son, shivering on the mountain battlefield while writing a letter to his parents on the home front. The message: "Invest your savings in the national war loan. Do this for your own interest, for me, and for the country." The order of priority is revealing. Family self-interest comes first, the son second, and the country third. This is a shrewd assessment of family mentalities in a still-traditional society. Mazza portrays the other side of the story in what may be considered a companion piece (fig. 22). Here, in the warmth of their home, the father and mother examine with satisfaction the war bond they have purchased with their savings. A portrait of their son, the *alpino,* rests on the desktop. Again the message is repeated: "For our interest, for him, and for the country."

The Home Front: Work. One of the touchiest social issues that arose during the war centered on the industrial working classes. Labor relations had never been easy in Italy, but the economic mobilization necessary for total war introduced new elements. First, there was the spectacular growth of war industries and the consequent demand for labor. Second, the state began to play a more active role in managing the economy and in mediating labor disputes. Fear of defeatism by the socialists (who had adopted the policy of "neither adherence nor sabotage" when Italy entered the war in 1915) was widespread in government circles. Fear of revolution increased after the Russian example in 1917. At the same time, there was a considerable amount of friction between the fighting men and the workingmen,

fig. 24
Giovanni Greppi, *Prestito
per la vittoria, Operai
sottoscrivete* (Loan
for Victory, Workers
Subscribe), poster,
66 x 94 cm, 1917.
The Mitchell Wolfson Jr.
Collection, The
Wolfsonian–Florida
International University,
Miami Beach, Florida.
Photograph by Silvia Ros.

the latter being accused of dodging the war. Perhaps because of this touchy issue, scenes of industrial life are extremely rare in Italian war propaganda.

The Wolfsonian collections contained the two most important propaganda images that dealt with the problem of soldier-worker relations. Both are war loan campaign posters commissioned by the Lombardy Industrial Mobilization Committee and designed by the artist Giovanni Greppi (1884–1960), whose non-propaganda work also is represented in the collections. In one we see a heroically posed soldier addressing a crowd of workers; around him are numerous war widows shrouded in black (fig. 23). His message is clear: "It's my task to resist the enemy. Everyone should subscribe to the war loan." The soldier and the widows (those who bear the direct costs of the war) are in the forefront. Working-men (often suspected of defeatism) dominate the background—while a superb depiction of factories rises behind them. The rather heavy-handed implication is that the workers' material support for the war should let them "off the hook" from the accusation of draft dodging or of having an "easy" war.

Greppi's other image is a much subtler treatment of the same theme (fig. 24). In this design, the sharp contrast between the fighting man and the workingman is removed. Here the soldier does not strike a heroic pose with arched back, but rather is "at ease"; his contrast with the amiable workers is downplayed. Yet with his left hand the soldier points toward a billboard bearing the persuasive headline "Loan for Victory." The message emphasizes solidarity between labor and the military. Both are contributing to the war effort, albeit in different ways. Greppi's prewar etching of the industrial factories at Pozzuoli near Naples shows a clear link between his general artistic work and his propaganda designs

fig. 25
(above)
Giovanni Greppi, *Factories at Pozzuoli,* etching, 58 x 46 cm, c. 1900–1910. The Mitchell Wolfson Jr. Collection, The Wolfsonian–Florida International University, Miami Beach, Florida.

fig. 26
(below, right)
Umberto Brunelleschi, *Tram Conductor,* postcard, 1918. The Mitchell Wolfson Jr. Collection, The Wolfsonian–Florida International University, Miami Beach, Florida. Photograph by Silvia Ros.

fig. 27
(far right)
Umberto Brunelleschi, *Barber,* postcard, 1918. The Mitchell Wolfson Jr. Collection, The Wolfsonian–Florida International University, Miami Beach, Florida. Photograph by Silvia Ros.

(fig. 25). His vivid portrayals of smokestacks appear in all three images.

The War and Gender: Women. It is clear that the war altered traditional gender roles. On the home front women took on ever more responsibility in the absence of young men. They entered the work force in increasing numbers, often assuming traditionally male jobs. The female tram conductor became a familiar trope. On the battlefront, soldiers lived in a universe of men, where patterns of male bonding were essential for military cohesion. Longings for and anxiety about women were thus a great preoccupation for the average soldier. The artist Umberto Brunelleschi created a fascinating series of postcards depicting women at work in men's jobs. These were directed toward men at the battlefront, and all portray attractive women, chaste precursors of the pin-ups of World War II. I believe the general purpose of these images was to assuage men who were fearful that women were taking their place in society while they were away. The attractive women in Brunelleschi's postcards appear to be "playing" at their jobs. His depiction of a "lady" tram conductor serves two purposes: first she is a "fashion model" image (pin-up), a morale booster for the troops; second, she doesn't really suggest a threat—her tram and her pose have a fairy-tale quality (fig. 26).

fig. 28
Artist unknown, *Pro patria*, postcard, c. 1917. The Mitchell Wolfson Jr. Collection, The Wolfsonian–Florida International University, Miami Beach, Florida. Photograph by Silvia Ros.

A more complicated image from the same series is Brunelleschi's depiction of a female barber (fig. 27). This design openly refers to what might be considered castration anxiety—and does nothing to minimize the threat. The female barber is sharpening her razor on a phallically stretched strop as she looks at herself in the mirror. Her threatening manner is reminiscent of depictions of the Old Testament heroine Judith, who saved her people by beheading Holofernes. Reflected in the background we see an alarmed and lathered male customer in the chair. Perhaps he is a draft dodger. It is hard to say, for in this image we are presented once again with the difficulties of interpreting propaganda imagery and its reception.

The War and Gender: Men. The question of the war's impact on male gender roles also is complicated, and firm conclusions are hard to draw from propaganda representations. Far and away the most common images were those of men as soldiers, usually assuming heroic poses. Each army, regiment, and division developed a series of postcards that celebrated or commemorated the unit. As the war dragged on, however, what might be identified as a sub-genre of male propaganda images emerged. These were depictions of sacrifice, of the fallen. For example, one postcard shows a nude youth standing within a classical tomb structure (fig. 28). He upholds the lintel bearing the inscription "Pro patria." Behind him are a pagan sacrificial altar and a stylized crown of thorns. Youth, sacrifice, *patria*—these are the themes that would become central to the later sacralization of the Great War and would strongly influence the design of its resulting memorials.

Artists and the War. In the course of the war, many of Italy's artists joined the effort, largely as soldiers—such as the Futurist painter Umberto Boccioni (1882–1916)—but also as propagandists. As a whole, we know little about the artists who produced propaganda images, although research at The Wolfsonian provides some clues. While many artists remain unknown, most were professional illustrators who shifted their work from creating peacetime posters and illustrations for the press to wartime propaganda. A number, including Aroldo Bonzagni, Umberto Brunelleschi, and Giovanni Greppi were "fine artists" who also produced propaganda. Their propaganda work has been little noticed in analyses of their output as a whole.[17]

17. Enzo Cassoni, *Il cartellonismo e l'illustrazione in Italia dal 1875 al 1950* (Rome: Nuova Editrice Spada, 1984); and *Catalogo Bolaffi del manifesto italiano. Dizionario degli illustratori* (Turin: Giulio Bolaffi editore, 1995).

fig. 29
(above)
Giulio Aristide Sartorio,
La Battaglia del Fratta
(The Battle of Fratta),
offset lithograph,
54 x 76 cm, post-1915.
The Mitchell Wolfson Jr.
Collection, The
Wolfsonian–Florida
International University,
Miami Beach, Florida.

fig. 30
(above, far right)
Giulio Aristide Sartorio,
Trieste Miramare, Pumo
e mar Timavo, **offset**
lithograph, 54 x 76 cm,
post-1915. The Mitchell
Wolfson Jr. Collection,
The Wolfsonian–Florida
International University,
Miami Beach, Florida.

Some artists more subtly imbued their work with persuasive messages. Giulio Aristide Sartorio (1860–1932), for example, combined a deeply personal, painterly approach to the war with the needs of propaganda. Sartorio was one of the country's most prominent artists of the older generation. In 1915, at the age of fifty-five, he volunteered for active service at the front. There he began to execute a series of paintings that were widely reproduced in prints and postcards. Sartorio's depiction of war focused on nature and the sublime. One lithograph depicts a long line of soldiers hauling a cannon up a steep slope — but they are dwarfed by the stupendous mountain range in the background that is equally the subject of this work (fig. 29). In another lithograph, Sartorio represents a romantic landscape, with a white castle and the sea in the background (fig. 30). Only the informed viewer would know that we are looking out from a trench toward Trieste, a territorial objective never reached during Italy's participation in the war.

Final Considerations

This cursory and selective view of some of the mechanisms, themes, and images of wartime propaganda can yield some general conclusions. In the course of World War I, Italy had its first experience with modern propaganda. Motivated by wartime leadership, propaganda organizations used the means at their disposal to mobilize targeted populations for war. Italy's experience of war took place within the context of a strained and fragile state-society relationship. Wartime propaganda responded to and reflected this. Propaganda, whatever its form, was a complex web of messages sent, on a broad level, from the authorities to the people, and on a micro level, among individuals and within social groups. The images we have examined provide insight into the "ideal world" that the wartime establishment hoped to project to the nation. They reflect, in some measure, the hopes, fears, and anxieties of the leaders and the led. It was not, however, until after the war that the full legacy of Italy's propaganda experience became apparent.

On 4 November 1918 Italy signed an armistice with Austria-Hungary; the war was over, and the Italian nation was victorious. Despite the strains of conducting total war, despite the great defeat at Caporetto, the Italian state had held firm. Italy was not to collapse into revolution like Russia, nor was it to disintegrate, as did Austria-Hungary and the Ottoman Empire. But what had the country "won"? Italy had entered the war without a national consensus on its aims; it ended the war with no unified notion of victory, as its territorial aims were only partially realized. The costs in men and material were tremendous. The war unleashed fierce social forces for change. The Liberal regime sought to maintain its hegemony in the face of challenges by a mobilized workers' movement, a new mass Catholic Party, and militant nationalism. For four years the country was convulsed by the economic, social, and political problems of re-establishing a stable order. In the end, the Liberals failed; in 1922 they yielded to the "man of providence"—Benito Mussolini.

Fascism itself was a product of the Great War. Much of its strength as a "political religion" lay in its ability to draw upon and mobilize the symbols and myths of war.[18] At the heart of the matter was the nation, for which so much had been sacrificed. Italy was a country fragmented by regionalism, class, differing degrees of economic development, and varying historical experiences. The unified national state had only been created half a

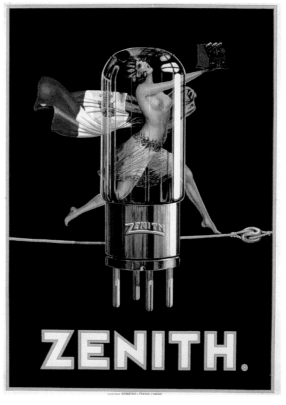

18. Emilio Gentile, *The Sacralization of Politics in Fascist Italy* (Cambridge, Mass.: Harvard University Press, 1996).

BRUNELLESCHI
L'ART ITALIEN
XIXE
XXE
SIECLES
15 MAI-JUIN-JUILLET
JEU DE PAUME-TUILERIES

fig. 33
Umberto Brunelleschi,
L'Art Italien XIX–XX siècles
(Italian Art of the
Nineteenth and Twentieth
Centuries), poster,
156 x 118 cm, 1935.
The Mitchell Wolfson Jr.
Collection, The
Wolfsonian–Florida
International University,
Miami Beach, Florida.

century before the Great War. "Making Italians" or the "nationalization of the masses" were processes that were far from complete. In this light, the experience of the Great War was the first moment in which the entire nation had been drawn into a common, albeit tragic, struggle.

The figure of Italia, like Marianne for France, was a key representation of the nation *(la Patria)* before, during, and after the war. A war loan poster of 1918 (fig. 31) shows a classic Italia as a goddess of victory pointing the soldiers on to combat. She is wrapped in the tricolor flag, which forms her wings, while she literally holds Nike (victory) in her hands. The symbolic power of Italia continued after the war, but in some cases the images employed were less than reverential. Thus, in a Zenith advertisement poster of the 1920s (fig. 32), we see a bare-breasted flapper illuminated by a Zenith radio tube. Consumer goods, modernity, and desire had replaced the sacrifice and hardship of the war years.

Fascism restored order.[19] Wartime artist Umberto Brunelleschi's great triumphal design of 1935 portrays an Athena-Italia (fig. 33), once more bearing Nike, but this time with the fasces in the background. Propaganda was of central importance to the Fascist dictatorship, and Fascist propaganda drew upon and grew from the Italian propaganda experience of World War I. Fascism inherited the legacy of the Great War and transformed it for its own totalitarian purposes. ✧

Acknowledgments

For their advice and assistance with this article, the author would like to thank David Ellwood, Robert Evans, and Patrick McCarthy, in Bologna; Marilyn Young in New York; Gianni Franzone and Matteo Fochessati, in Genoa; and Cathy Leff, Joel Hoffman, and Bill Kearns, in Miami Beach.

19. Dennis Doordan, "Political Things: Design in Fascist Italy," in *Designing Modernity: The Arts of Reform and Persuasion, 1885–1945,* ed. Wendy Kaplan (New York: Thames and Hudson, 1995), 225–255.

OF

TRIPOLI

Brian L. McLaren

The Tripoli Trade Fair and the Representation of Italy's African Colonies

Brian L. McLaren is an assistant professor in the Department of Architecture at the University of Washington. He holds a Ph.D. from the Massachusetts Institute of Technology, where he wrote his doctoral dissertation on the architecture and culture of Italian colonialism in North Africa. McLaren conducted research for this essay as a Wolfsonian Fellow in 1997.

The most significant exhibition to be organized in the Italian colonies was the Tripoli Trade Fair—an annual display of metropolitan and colonial goods held between 1927 and 1939. This series of exhibitions closely paralleled the representation of Italy's colonies at similar events held in Italy and elsewhere in Europe during the same period. Indeed, all of these exhibitions were intended to communicate the value of Italy's colonial possessions to a wider audience, while also establishing stronger economic and commercial ties between Italy and North Africa. However, the Tripoli Trade Fair also was a crucial medium through which an image of Italian society was disseminated to the indigenous populations of North Africa. There was, thus, a relationship between the Tripoli Trade Fair and its potential audiences that was more complex than that at fairs in the metropole. It not only represented Italian industry and culture in the colonial context, it was also the mechanism for a complex process of exchange between Italian and North African culture. Using a wide range of material—from postcards, posters, and publicity photographs to pamphlets and catalogues—this essay examines the Tripoli Trade Fair as a constantly evolving hybrid of metropolitan and colonial identities. In this discussion, the designations "metropolitan" and "colonial" can be understood as both descriptive terms and analytical categories—typically used by cultural critics and historians—that identify a basic dichotomy between the culture of the colonizer and that of the colonized.[1]

The Tripoli Trade Fair and other contemporary colonial exhibitions should, first of all, be viewed against the backdrop of the larger Italian colonial project. Although a latecomer to the so-called scramble for Africa that

1. The use of the terms "metropolitan" and "colonial" to describe the relationship between colonizer and colonized is most common in discussions of the French in Africa—the first term coming from the French "metropole," meaning "home country." See Gwendolyn Wright, "Introduction," in *The Politics of Design in French Colonial Urbanism* (Chicago: University of Chicago Press, 1991), 1–13.

Detail of Tripoli Trade Fair poster, 1930.

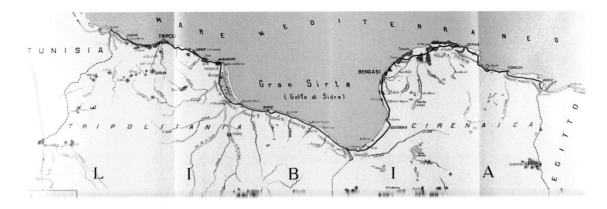

fig. 1
Foldout map of the north coast of Africa. From *La strada litoranea della libia* (The Libyan Coastal Road) (Verona: A. Mondadori, c. 1936). The Mitchell Wolfson Jr. Collection, The Wolfsonian–Florida International University, Miami Beach, Florida. Photograph by Silvia Ros.

began in the 1880s, Italy consolidated its long-standing interest in Africa by founding the East African colonies of Eritrea in 1890 and Somalia in 1905.[2] Italian politicians argued that these colonies would represent an affirmation of the country's status among the great powers of Europe and provide a solution to its problem of mass emigration. Italy's invasion of the Libyan colonies of Tripolitania and Cyrenaica in 1911 was, likewise, supported by these assertions as well as the popular belief that conquest of this region was part of Italy's destiny, due to its much earlier Roman occupation (fig. 1). Behind this imperialist rhetoric the Italians also had a strategic aim in colonizing North Africa. With the British foothold in Egypt and the French protectorate in Tunisia, the Libyan colonies would provide Italy with a beachhead that could solidify the nation's economic stake in the Mediterranean region. The Italian presence in Tripolitania and Cyrenaica in the 1920s reflects this combination of economic and political demands. Following a ten-year period in which the Italian authorities attempted to govern by collaboration with the Libyans—a period characterized by guerrilla warfare and civil unrest—they pursued a more authoritarian direction. Largely based on the earlier efforts of General Hubert Lyautey in the French colony of Morocco (served 1912–1925), Governor Giuseppe Volpi in Tripolitania (served 1921–1925) combined firm military and political control with an aggressive program of economic development. The "rebirth" of Tripolitania under Volpi—which supported local industries while also creating stronger connections to Italy— established an economic and political climate in which metropolitan and colonial interests could freely interact. The relative success of Volpi's program in Tripolitania was the impetus for Benito Mussolini's (1883–1945) visit to this region in April 1926 and the subsequent organization of the first Tripoli Trade Fair in February 1927.[3]

2. J. M. Roberts, *Europe 1880–1945* (New York: Longman, 1989), 105–118; and Martin Clark, *Italy 1871–1982* (New York: Longman, 1984), 99–101.

3. Angelo Piccioli, ed., *La rinascità della Tripolitania. Memorie e studi sui quattro anni di governo del Conte Giuseppe Volpi di Misurata* (Milan: Casa editrice A. Mondadori, 1926).

The potential of the Tripoli Trade Fair as a vehicle of economic and cultural exchange between Italy and North Africa was recognized from its inception. Conceived as a presentation of Italian goods similar to the various trade fairs throughout Italy, the Tripoli fair was intended to "promote commerce and trade between the Colony and the Mother country."[4] The exhibition of Italian products at the Tripoli Trade Fair also was widely viewed as an act of patriotism—a concept linked to its function as an instrument of colonial propaganda. According to the governor of Tripolitania at the time, Emilio De Bono (served 1926–1928), the exhibition was intended to foster a colonial consciousness in Italy by "cultivating the understanding, the sentiment and the colonial passion in a people who... still do not have it, or... do not have enough of it."[5] This propagandistic dimension of the Tripoli fair was understood as relating to both metropolitan and colonial audiences. The fair was conceived as a demonstration to Italians and foreigners of Italy's promise as a colonizing nation that would encourage the continuing development of this region. The Tripoli Trade Fair also was expected to convince the Libyans of Fascist Italy's technical advancement and political strength, thereby justifying the nation's colonial politics. The Italian government expressed a deep and abiding concern for the response of local populations to the exhibition. According to De Bono, the Libyans were more than grateful recipients of Italy's benign leadership; they were "pervaded by the spirit of Fascism"—their relationship to the Italian authorities being one of incorporation, rather than mere association.[6]

The hybrid quality of the Tripoli Trade Fair was closely tied to the politics of Italian colonialism in North Africa. The "indigenous politics" were initially developed under the guidance of Governor Volpi. The first component of these government policies was a program to modernize the colony's public infrastructure and improve its economy.[7] As part of this program, the Italian government made a considerable effort to create a viable system of roads and public institutions that would serve both military and domestic needs. The improvement of Tripolitania's economy was linked primarily to agriculture. To facilitate this initiative, the Volpi government enacted laws to allow private companies to claim uncultivated land and provided incentives for them to develop agricultural estates.[8] The second component of Volpi's indigenous politics called for the preservation of the Roman and Muslim historical patrimony of Tripolitania—a policy that was largely aimed at appeasing the local populations. This program initially involved the creation of a commission to study buildings and objects of

4. Emilio De Bono, "La prima Fiera Campionaria di Tripoli sarà una grande affermazione coloniale (Nostra intervista con il generale De Bono)," *La Tribuna*, 19 September 1926, 2.

5. Ibid.

6. "L'inaugurazione della Fiera," *L'Italia Coloniale* 4 (March 1928): 44.

7. Sergio Romano, *Giuseppe Volpi. Industria e finanza tra Giolitti e Mussolini* (Milan: Bompiani, 1979), 102–112.

8. Claudio Segrè, *Fourth Shore. The Italian Colonization of Libya* (Chicago: The University of Chicago Press, 1974), 47–56.

historic, artistic, and archeological interest and to develop strategies for their eventual restoration. One specific initiative that resulted from this preservation policy was the creation of the Ufficio Governativo delle Arte Applicate Indigene (Government Office of Indigenous Applied Arts) to enhance Tripolitania's indigenous artisanal industries, including jewelry making, metalworking, and carpet weaving.[9]

Inaugurated by the Italian government on 15 February 1927, the first Tripoli Trade Fair conveyed an optimistic image of the economic and political possibilities of Italy's North African colonies. According to the official program, the exhibition was intended to have a "strictly national character"—featuring the products of Italian and colonial industries— with the intention of increasing trade between Tripolitania and Italy.[10] This national representation also was aimed at educating the local population as potential consumers—"to introduce [Italian] products to the natives"—and at indoctrinating them as colonial subjects—"to give [them] ... a broad and concrete understanding of the power and greatness of Italy."[11] The metropolitan status of the first Tripoli Trade Fair is reflected in both its location and its organization. The exhibition was housed in a series of temporary buildings in a park-like setting along the Lungomare Conte Volpi, a seafront boulevard that connected the most significant public buildings and tourist facilities constructed by the Italians in the mid-1920s.[12] The displays of Italian products were organized by industry and also by geography. The more prevalent industry-based displays were housed largely in neutral frameworks that gave this segment of the exhibition the appearance of a marketplace—a quality that is shown in an aerial view of the first Tripoli Trade Fair (fig. 2). The collective displays that presented materials by geographical origin included submissions by the chambers of commerce of individual provinces and cities in Italy such as Calabria, Genoa, and Rome. These displays of local products were housed in pavilions that conveyed the identity of their city or region.

The method of organization of the first Tripoli Trade Fair was based largely on metropolitan precedents. The annual exhibition in Milan, for example, was ordered by individual industries—including those presenting chemistry, electricity, art and applied arts, and agriculture.[13]

9. Renato Bartoccini, "Gli edifici di interesse storico, artistico ed archeologico di Tripoli e dintorni," in *La rinascità della Tripolitania*, ed. Piccioli, 350–352; and Francesco Rossi, "Le Piccole industrie indigene," in *La rinascità della Tripolitania*, ed. Piccioli, 513–519.

10. *Prima Esposizione Fiera Campionaria di Tripoli. Programma* (Spoleto: Arti grafiche Panetto & Petrelli, 1927), 6.

11. Letter from Il Presidente del Comitato Esecutivo, Prima Esposizione Fiera Campionaria di Tripoli, Tripoli, June 1926. Central State Archive, Rome. PCM 1927-14.1.316. Sottofascicolo 1. Decreto di autorizzazione della Fiera Campionaria.

12. Marida Talamona, "Città europea e città araba in Tripolitania," in *Architettura italiana d'oltremare, 1870–1940*, eds. Giuliano Gresleri, Pier Giorgio Massaretti, and Stefano Zagnoni (Venice: Marsilio editori, 1993), 256–277.

13. *Ente Autonomo Fiera di Milano. VII Fiera di Milano. 12–27 aprile 1927* (Milan: Arti grafiche Pizzi e Pizio, 1927), 5–6.

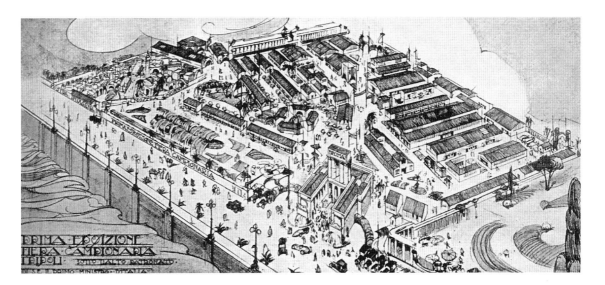

fig. 2
Aerial view, Tripoli Trade
Fair, 1927. From *L'Italia*
Coloniale, **February 1927.**

This organization was given form through a series of large permanent pavilions that were dedicated to these industries, providing the site a refined urban character. In Tripoli, the general exhibits were influenced by the modest size of the fair—only one-eighth that of the Milan event—and by the impermanence and anonymity of its structures. The Italian fairs also provided a precedent for regional representation at the first Tripoli Trade Fair. At the Milan fairs, the predominant structure of large pavilions was overlaid by a series of modest buildings that presented the products of individual Italian provinces, thereby giving these displays a regional identity. In Tripoli, this secondary structure of regional pavilions was the sole architectural counterpoint to an otherwise undistinguished fabric of decorated industrial sheds. By presenting Italy's different regions in pavilions that expressed their distinctive architectural traditions, the Tripoli Trade Fair was not merely copying the precedent of Italian fairs. Given the task of representing Italy in the colonies, it was instead responding to what one contemporary commentator referred to as "the multiform attitude of Italy, a nation of many peoples."[14]

The Governorate of Rome, the most important metropolitan contributor to the first Tripoli Trade Fair, was represented in the exhibition's most prominent pavilion, designed by the architect Felice Nori. The Roman Pavilion was the ceremonial entrance to the fair and a symbolic representation of the municipal activities of Rome. Two rectangular wings of display space flanked a sequence of courtyards that carried visitors into the exhibition grounds—the center marked by a monumental architectural fragment that referred to antique sources (fig. 3). Located along the previously mentioned Lungomare Conte Volpi, this pavilion was described as a "solemn affirmation of the return of Italian possessions to Rome."[15]

14. Angelo Piccioli, "La Fiera di Tripoli," *Gli Annali dell'Africa Italiana* 1 (August 1938): 503–505.

15. N. Ciampi, "Roma alla prima Fiera coloniale. Tripoli–febbraio–marzo 1927," *Capitolium* 10 (January 1927): 569–578.

fig. 3
Felice Nori, Pavilion of
Rome, Tripoli Trade Fair,
1927. From *Capitolium,*
January 1927.

The Roman Pavilion thus exemplified *romanità* — a term used by artists and critics during the Fascist period (1922–1943) to refer to the use of classicism as a political statement. The reference to classical Rome is consistent with contemporary architectural discourse in the Libyan colonies — a discourse that was dominated by the architect Armando Brasini. The reclining figures that adorned the Roman Pavilion's façade were based on the first-century A.D. statues of the Nile and the Tiber that flank the staircase of the Palazzo Senatorio on the Campidoglio (Capitoline Hill) in Rome. This historical representation was reinforced by displays within the pavilion, consisting of information on contemporary Roman activities — including public works projects, archeological research, and artisanal industries. This project can, therefore, be understood as a gesture of aesthetic and cultural colonization. It was a reification of Fascist colonial politics, which viewed the present activities of Italy in North Africa as a continuation of ancient practices.

The first Tripoli Trade Fair also included a substantial presentation of colonial goods. The colony of Tripolitania was represented by the so-called Colonial Village — a form of display that had appeared much earlier in Italian exhibitions. In the Turin International Exhibition of 1911, the Italian colony of Eritrea was represented by a Coptic Church and a series of six round *tukul* huts — a vernacular dwelling with mud walls and a conical roof of bound reeds. This Eritrean village was located just outside the neoclassically inspired Colonial Pavilion along the banks of the Po River — creating a setting in which the characteristic craft production of this colonial possession could be demonstrated in a seemingly authentic

environment.[16] Similarly, the Colonial Village at the first Tripoli Trade Fair was an eclectic collection of pavilions presenting products of the various regions of Tripolitania. Located on the far eastern end of the exhibition site, this walled precinct was intended to "offer a summarizing but extremely faithful vision of the Tripolitanian landscape" through a collection of buildings that included display spaces, artisanal workshops, an Arab house, and a *suq*—a vaulted market space traditionally found in North African cities.[17] One example of the formal presentation of Tripolitania at this event was the Pavilion of Zliten, dedicated to the city east of Tripoli, which exhibited the products of local craftsmen in a contextual setting, reflecting the influence of displays in the Colonial Museum in Rome (established 1923) (fig. 4).[18] While the Colonial Village offered an experience of the native culture that was consistent with those of previous exhibitions in Italy, there was a very important difference. This indigenous village was located within the very context that it purported to represent. The Colonial Village at the first Tripoli Trade Fair was a heterotopic enclave of authentic native culture, screening out all aspects that were contradictory to the colonial order, such as the religious practices of the local populations.

The first Tripoli Trade Fair was thus a combination of a metropolitan representation for a colonial audience and a colonial representation for a metropolitan one. The hybridization of these identities was communicated

16. Ministero delle Colonie, *Le Mostre coloniali all'Esposizione internazionale di Torino del 1911. Relazione generale* (Rome: Tipografia nazionale di G. Bertero e Compagnia, 1913), 46–47.

17. M. M. "L'Esposizione di Tripoli," *L'Italia Coloniale* 3 (December 1926): 232.

18. F. M. Rossi, "La Fiera e le piccole industrie tripolitane," *L'Italia Coloniale* 4 (April 1927): 67–70.

fig. 5
(right)
Tripoli Trade Fair, postcard,
1927. The Mitchell
Wolfson Jr. Collection,
The Wolfsonian–Florida
International University,
Miami Beach, Florida.
Photograph by Silvia Ros.

fig. 6
(opposite page)
R. Franzi (e) Authonomous
*Organization of the
Sample Fair of Tripoli,*
poster, 100 x 70 cm,
Tripoli Trade Fair, 1930.
The Mitchell Wolfson Jr.
Collection, The
Wolfsonian–Florida
International University,
Miami Beach, Florida.
Photograph by Silvia Ros.

in the various promotional efforts associated with this exhibition. Press reports in periodicals, newspapers, and other publications ranged from straight news stories and political commentary to romantic travelogues that combined patriotic assertions of Italian colonization with a fascination for the exotic qualities of indigenous culture.[19] This composite image of the first Tripoli Trade Fair was also conveyed in the various posters, catalogues, postcards, and postage stamps issued to commemorate the event. A particularly compelling example of this fusion of identities is the image used on the catalogue, poster, and postcard developed for the 1927 fair (fig. 5). This vividly colored illustration depicts a monumentalized woman in Roman costume saluting with her right hand while leaning on a fasces — the symbol of Fascist Italy — with her left. In the distance, one side of the image contains fragments of Roman antiquity while the other reveals the palm trees of an oasis landscape. The tension between *romanità* and local culture is perfectly expressed in the framing of the scene with an Islamic horseshoe arch.

The interaction between metropolitan and the colonial identities within the Tripoli Trade Fair underwent a substantial transformation over the course of its thirteen-year history. What had begun in 1927 as a relatively modest exhibition of largely regional significance opened in 1930 under the designation "First Inter-African Exhibit." The new format involved the participation of African free states, colonies, protectorates, and mandates, such as Algeria, the Belgian Congo, Morocco, and South Africa, desiring to present their products to an international audience. Several European nations interested in trade with these African states also participated, resulting in the construction of pavilions for Belgium and France.[20] The organizing committee of the Tripoli Trade Fair unquestionably made its

19. See Angelo Piccioli, "Dopo la Fiera di Tripoli: La Nuova Italia d'Oltremare," *Rassegna Italiana* 19 (June 1927): 609–612; Enrico Niccoli, "Le Materia prime alla Fiera Campionaria di Tripoli," *Rivista delle Colonie Italiane* 1 (November 1927): 25–52; Filippo Tajani, "Alla vigilia della solennità di Tripoli per l'inaugurazione della Fiera-Esposizione," *Corriere della Sera,* 15 February 1927, 6; and Roberto Cantalupo and Filippo Tajani, "L'affermazione dell'Italia coloniale a Tripoli. Il Duca delle Puglie inaugura la Fiera campionaria," *Corriere della Sera,* 16 February 1927, 1.

20. Ente Autonomo Fiera Campionaria di Tripoli. IV. *Manifestazione. Prima rassegna internazionale in Africa. XX febbraio – XX aprile MCMXXX–VII.* Catalogo (Rome: Arti grafiche Fratelli Palombi, 1930), 125–150.

exhibition international in scope to compete with the larger European colonial exhibitions such as those in Marseilles (1922), Lausanne (1925), Antwerp (1930), and Paris (1931). This competitiveness was particularly evident during the International Colonial Exhibition in Paris of 1931, when the group responsible for the Tripoli Trade Fair organized the first International Exhibition of Colonial Art, which opened in Rome in October of the same year.[21] In its new configuration, the Tripoli Trade Fair projected contemporary fascist colonial politics, which were increasingly oriented around international ambitions. These aspirations were given visual form in the poster of the fourth Tripoli Trade Fair of 1930, depicting a continuous stream of international flags spiraling outward from an Italian flag marked with the fasces (fig. 6). The fact that this poster and other promotional materials were printed in English, French, German, and Italian further underscores the international dimension.[22]

The character of this "internationalism" was defined by a number of significant modifications to the Tripoli Trade Fair. One of the most important changes was its relocation in 1929 along the Corso Sicilia, a thoroughfare in a newly established residential and commercial quarter to the west of the old city. The site became the permanent home of the event — marking a conceptual shift in the status of this exhibition and its relationship to the city of Tripoli.[23] This choice reflects a new stage in the planning of the city, which was no longer solely defined by its seafront façade. According to contemporary initiatives issued by the municipality, Tripoli was to be a combination of metropolitan urbanity and the environmental qualities of the indigenous landscape. The plan of the Tripoli Trade Fair was a microcosm for this larger urban development in its combination of a regularized grid system and unstructured open spaces. A second factor in defining the new character of the event was the initiation of a program for constructing permanent pavilions. This policy resulted in a decisive change in the design of pavilions, moving away from the scenographic and toward a more serious consideration of formal and material issues — allowing these buildings to engage more directly with contemporary architectural discourse.

The architect Alessandro Limongelli, who succeeded Armando Brasini as the main architect for the municipality of Tripoli in 1929, exemplified this new approach to the design of pavilions at the Tripoli Trade Fair.[24] His Roman Pavilion of 1929 both represented Italy's capital city and acted as the entrance to the exhibition site (fig. 7). The exterior consisted of a monumental mass, designed to suggest a triumphal arch, flanked by

21. "La I Mostra d'Arte Coloniale inaugurata dal Duce," *L'Oltremare* 5 (October 1931): 400.

22. Letter from Ente Autonomo Fiera Campionaria di Tripoli dated 28 October 1929. Archivio Centrale dello Stato-Segreteria Particolare del Duce, Seria Alfanumerica. B. 5, f. 155.1.

23. Piccioli, "La Fiera di Tripoli," 510.

24. Gian Paolo Consoli, "The Protagonists," *Rassegna* 51 (September 1992): 56–57.

fig. 7
Alessandro Limongelli,
Pavilion of Rome, Tripoli
Trade Fair, 1929. From
Architettura e Arti
***Decorative*, July 1929.**

two low horizontal blocks, each articulated with an abstract pattern of pilasters and niches. The formal references for this project are to classical Rome, including Amleto Cataldi's central bronze statue of Dea Roma — a deified personification of Rome as a female warrior. This was flanked by sculptures on the pair of freestanding pilasters, representing the Roman symbols of the eagle, the fasces, and the Capitoline wolf. The central vaulted space had a marble fountain and served as the ceremonial entrance, while the two side galleries contained material documenting the activities of the municipality of Rome.[25] Limongelli's Roman Pavilion was the product of an evolving discourse on the nature of modern colonial architecture, which in this case was linked to Roman sources. However, the architect's use of classical references contrasted strongly with the theatrical staging of antique influences in the first Roman Pavilion of 1927. Limongelli's *romanità* offered a classicism viewed through the lens of a modern aesthetic sensibility. In the simplicity of its exterior volume and its use of local materials, this project was a tentative first step toward harmonizing with the colonial environment. This approach to colonial architecture — one that called for a more careful consideration of the North African context — would become more pronounced in Limongelli's later works, eventually emerging as the dominant paradigm in the new architecture of this colony by the 1930s.[26]

25. Virgilio Testa, "Il Padiglione di Roma alla Fiera di Tripoli," *Capitolium* 5 (March 1929): 225–228.
26. Consoli, "The Progatonists," 57.

fig. 8
View of one of two main streets, Tripoli Trade Fair, 1939. Photographic archive of Azione Coloniale. The Mitchell Wolfson Jr. Collection–Fondazione Regionale Cristoforo Colombo, Genoa, Italy.

Limongelli's Roman Pavilion also contributed to the creation of a specifically urban image for this exhibition. The project established a formal face to the city of Tripoli through its frontage along Corso Sicilia. This façade, with its carefully articulated surface and urban scale, acted as the formal transition from the city into the streets and open spaces of the exhibition. The urban spaces of the Tripoli Trade Fair also related to contemporary concepts of colonial urbanism in the city of Tripoli. The exhibition was organized around two parallel streets linking the large open spaces at opposite ends of the site (fig. 8). The first of these open spaces was an irregular zone near the main entrance along Corso Sicilia that accommodated the triangular shape of the site; the second was a piazza, formed by the surrounding buildings, which marked the far end of the site. A series of secondary open spaces was overlaid on this general pattern, introducing some visual and spatial relief. One such space was the Lake and Boat Exhibition, where a large reflecting pool suggested an oasis environment (fig. 9). The Tripoli Trade Fair had thus become a hybrid urban space — combining the regularity of a metropolitan street and the variability of the Tripolitanian landscape. This quality was enhanced by the lack of systematic separation between metropolitan and colonial pavilions. Such heterogeneity is consistent with urban design strategies in the regulatory plan of Tripoli by Alpago-Novello, Cabiati, and Ferrazza of 1933, where no absolute separation was maintained between Italian and indigenous populations.[27] This approach to urban design has a visual corollary in

27. Maurizio De Rege, "Il nuovo piano regolatore di Tripoli," Urbanistica 3 (May–June 1934): 121–128.

**fig. 9
(above)
Lake and Boat Exhibition,
Tripoli Trade Fair, 1939.
Photographic archive of
Azione Coloniale. The
Mitchell Wolfson Jr.
Collection–Fondazione
Regionale Cristoforo
Colombo, Genoa, Italy.**

**fig. 10
(above, far right)
Alessandro Limongelli,
proposal for restructuring
of Piazza Italia, 1931.
From *Rassegna
di Architettura*,
September 1933.**

Alessandro Limongelli's 1931 proposal for the restructuring of Piazza Italia in Tripoli (fig. 10). Working with the existing walls of the old city of Tripoli and the scale and materials of its open spaces, Limongelli's project exemplified a condition of hybridity where the urban image of the Italian state met the historic architecture and characteristic landscape of the colonial context.

The interaction of metropolitan and colonial identities in the architecture of the newly international Tripoli Trade Fair was subject to its own internal transformations. The first stage in this development culminated in the mid-1930s with the fusion of modern and indigenous forms into a unified expression. This resulted in the kind of hybridity that, according to architectural historian Patricia Morton, the French assiduously avoided in the architecture of the 1931 Paris International Colonial Exhibition. Citing cultural theoretician Homi Bhabha's 1985 essay "Signs Taken for Wonders," Morton states: "The final consequences of hybridization are the erasure and blurring of the boundaries between races and the dissolution of the codes of difference established by colonialism."[28] She, in turn, connects the French authorities' desire for separation of metropolitan and colonial in this exhibition to the fear of mixing race imbedded in the French colonial policy of association, which maintained the strictest separation between the European and indigenous populations. Hybridity within the French pavilions of the Paris exhibition was, according to Morton, a threat to the hierarchies of separation between "the native" and "the civilized"— one that "had to be contained, neutralized, or at least countered by a distracting reference back to the purely (cleanly) divided colonial world."[29] In the Tripoli Trade Fair, hybridity was used as a tactical gesture consistent with the colonial order. In the Libyan colonies, Italian authorities embraced the cultural traditions of the local populations while, at the same time, redefining them according to the standards of modern Italian society.

28. Patricia Morton, "The Civilizing Mission of Architecture: The 1931 International Colonial Exposition in Paris" (Ph.D. diss., Princeton University, 1994), 12–13, 96.

29. Ibid., 88.

fig. 11
(above)
**Florestano di Fausto,
Pavilion of Collective
Exhibits, Tripoli
Trade Fair, 1935.
Photographic archive
of Azione Coloniale.
The Mitchell Wolfson Jr.
Collection–Fondazione
Regionale Cristoforo
Colombo, Genoa, Italy.**

fig. 12
(above, far right)
**Exhibition of Provincial
Council of Milan, Tripoli
Trade Fair, 1935.
Photographic archive of
Azione Coloniale. The
Mitchell Wolfson Jr.
Collection–Fondazione
Regionale Cristoforo
Colombo, Genoa, Italy.**

The hybrid was, in this case, not an undermining of Italian authority, but rather the reification of its politics of incorporation of the native into the modern.

Hybridity was not limited to the Roman Pavilion or the plan of the Tripoli Trade Fair, but was similarly infused into the architecture and exhibitions of other pavilions in this period. The presentation of products from Italy's various regions was organized, by 1936, under the banner of the Consigli Provinciali dell'Economia Corporative (Provincial Councils of the Corporative Economy). This organization, part of the economic system instituted by the Fascist government, was a union of industry, labor, and the state that allowed for "the complete organic and totalitarian regulation of production."[30] The exhibits of these provincial councils were organized by region and contained a combination of consumer goods and industrial products. In 1935 architect Florestano di Fausto designed a pavilion for these collective exhibitions (fig. 11). It was composed of a simple undecorated wall, suggesting the modest exteriors of indigenous rural constructions. Superimposed over this continuous wall were two large glazed elements with the appearance of a metropolitan storefront. The pavilion's lofty and austere interior was defined through its structural frame and limited use of walls. The display within this space by the Provincial Council of Milan was stark, appearing more like a museum of technology than a bustling marketplace (fig. 12). This presentation of Milanese industrial products thus acted as a seemingly objective affirmation of the cultural advancement of the metropole.

The representation of Italy's colonies at the Tripoli Trade Fair began with pavilions dedicated to individual colonial authorities. The earliest permanent building of this type was the Pavilion of Tripolitania, which was constructed for the third fair in 1929. This building was joined in 1932 by the pavilion for the eastern Libyan colony of Cyrenaica.

30. Benito Mussolini, "Discorso per lo stato corporativo," 14 November 1933, in *Opera Omnia di Benito Mussolini*, eds. Edoardo and Dulio Susmel (Florence: La Fenice, 1958), 16: 85–96.

fig. 13
Pavilion of Tripolitania,
Tripoli Trade Fair, 1929.
Photographic archive of
Azione Coloniale. The
Mitchell Wolfson Jr.
Collection–Fondazione
Regionale Cristoforo
Colombo, Genoa, Italy.

These two governments—eventually united as the colony of Libya in 1935—were represented throughout the duration of the fair. During the initial period, the governments of Tripolitania and Cyrenaica presented information on Italy's activities in these territories—including agricultural colonization, public works projects, educational programs, and indigenous craft production—assuming the form typical of contemporary colonial exhibitions in Italy.[31] These displays combined the supposedly objective practices of such exhibitions with the proclivity for excess found in the colonial marketplace. The exterior of the Tripolitanian Pavilion was carefully conceived in relation to this composite approach to exhibiting material, in that it was an abstract representation of the region's architecture (fig. 13). Its vernacular references included the simple cubic massing and unadorned exterior volumes, the use of traditional door and window treatments, and allusions to battered-wall construction.

Also organized by Italian colonial authorities was the 1936 Pavilion of Libyan Artisanry, designed by the architect Pietro Lombardi. This pavilion contained exhibits related to the colony's indigenous artisanal production— a production that had undergone considerable restructuring under the Fascist authorities. Artisanal industries were incorporated into the corporative structure of the Libyan economy during aviator Italo Balbo's (1896–1940) term as governor of the Libyan colonies (served 1934–1940). The new status of these industries was formalized with the creation of the Istituto Fascista degli Artigiani della Libia (Fascist Institute of Libyan Artisans)

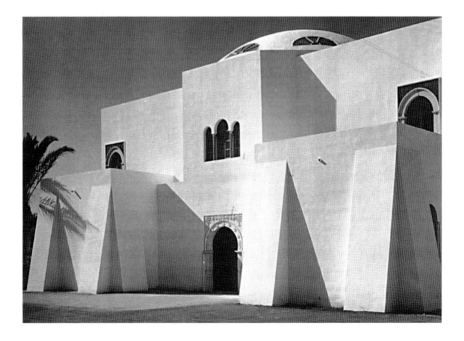

31. Ente Autonomo Fiera Campionaria di Tripoli, *VI. Manifestazione. Terza rassegna internazionale in Africa. 8 marzo – 8 maggio. MCMXXXII–X. Catalogo* (Rome: Arti grafiche Fratelli Palombi, 1932), 259–276.

fig. 14
Pietro Lombardi, interior of the Pavilion of Libyan Artisanry, 1936. Photographic archive of Azione Coloniale. The Mitchell Wolfson Jr. Collection–Fondazione Regionale Cristoforo Colombo, Genoa, Italy.

in March 1936—an organization that provided both artistic and technical assistance.[32] The exhibition of native crafts at the Tripoli Trade Fair showcased developments of this industry. Displays included drawings and photographs of artisanal works as well as the best products from all regions of Libya, such as furnishings, jewelry, metalwork, ceramics, and carpets. The most important exhibit was the display of the Campionati di Mestiere (Champions of the Trades), the winners of a competition in twelve different categories of artisanal products.[33] In the interior displays, the distinctive arts of each region were represented in the manner of an ethnographic museum exhibit, with a combination of wall units and freestanding cabinets again creating a seemingly objective and distanced representation (fig. 14). This approach is not surprising, as these artisanal traditions had themselves been constructed through scholarly research and education initiatives undertaken by the Italian authorities. Beginning with the governorship of Volpi, the Italians had studied Libyan craft production to restore what they deemed to be more authentic practices and to modernize sales and distribution.[34] Both these artisanal products and their means of representation were as modern as the radios and scooters presented by the Provincial Council of Milan. The presentation of the indigenous culture of Libya in the Tripoli Trade Fair was inextricably connected with metropolitan society. In the same way that the Italian presence was given the benign appearance of a vernacular construction in the pavilion of Tripolitania, the colony's indigenous culture was being "modernized" to incorporate it into the political and economic structures of Italian society.

Italy's East African colonies also were represented at the Tripoli Trade Fair. The appearance of Eritrea in this exhibition began as early as 1928, with the involvement of the Governorate, its Public Works Office, and several public and private companies seeking to establish trade with Tripolitania and Italy. Although the presence of Eritrea and Somalia at this event was solidified with the realization of a permanent pavilion in 1931, it was not until the construction of a second building in 1934 that these colonies gained prominence within the exhibition. This latter building was designed by the architects Sebastiano Larco and Carlo Enrico Rava.

32. Guglielmo Quadrotta, "Sviluppo e realizzazioni dell'artigianato in Libia," *Rassegna Economica dell'Africa Italiana* 25 (July 1937): 956–957.

33. Ente Autonomo Fiera Campionaria di Tripoli, *XI Manifestazione internazionale intercoloniale. Prima mostra coloniale dell'Impero fascista* (Rome: Arti grafiche Fratelli Palombi, 1937), 210.

34. Quadrotta, "Sviluppo e realizzazioni," 960–961.

Like their earlier project for the Colonial Pavilion at the Milan Fair of
1928, this project was closely tied to theoretical discourses within
contemporary Italian architecture. Indeed, the Pavilion of Eritrea and
Somalia confirmed Rava's theorization of a more "independent" direction
for Italian Rationalism in the colonies, where modern, North African, and
Roman references could be fused into a single expression. The trajectory
of these views was mapped out in the publication *Nove anni di architettura
vissuta,* an anthology of essays on contemporary architecture written by
Rava from 1926 to 1935.[35] The collage that adorns the cover of this book
gives visual expression to Rava's writings, as it carefully combines his firm's
metropolitan and colonial projects into a unified composition (fig. 15).

Larco and Rava's pavilion for Eritrea and Somalia was clearly situated within
contemporary discourse on the use of indigenous references in the creation
of a modern colonial architecture (fig. 16). It was a simple two-story block
with a central open courtyard. The architects responded to site conditions
by locating the building's formal entrance along the main avenue and
creating a covered verandah on the second floor facing a small open space.

35. Carlo Enrico Rava, *Nove anni di architettura vissuta, 1926 IV– 1935 XIII* (Rome: Cremonese
editore, 1935).

fig. 16
(opposite page)
Sebastiano Larco and
Carlo Enrico Rava,
Pavilion of Eritrea and
Somalia, Tripoli Trade
Fair, 1934. From *Nove anni
di architettura vissuta,
1926 IV–1935 XIII*.
The Mitchell Wolfson Jr.
Collection, The
Wolfsonian–Florida
International University,
Miami Beach, Florida.
Copy photograph by
Silvia Ros.

fig. 17
(above, right)
Sebastiano Larco and
Carlo Enrico Rava,
courtyard of the Pavilion
of Eritrea and Somalia.
From *Architettura*,
August 1934.

fig. 18
(above, far right)
Sebastiano Larco and
Carlo Enrico Rava,
entrance view of the
Pavilion of Eritrea and
Somalia. From *Nove anni
di architettura vissuta,
1926 IV–1935 XIII*.
The Mitchell Wolfson Jr.
Collection, The
Wolfsonian–Florida
International University,
Miami Beach, Florida.
Copy photograph by
Silvia Ros.

This verandah acted as both a filter through which the courtyard opened to this adjacent space and a means of exterior connection between the two levels of gallery spaces—the latter achieved through a large open staircase (fig. 17). An article in *Domus* magazine alluded to the relationship between this project and the indigenous architecture of Africa, noting that the entrance portal was of Somalian derivation, and the *masharabbia* (wooden screens) and tile-floor pattern of the patio of Eritrean inspiration. The author argued that the arcaded courtyard space was a point of connection between the building's vernacular references and Roman sources, which he referred to as "the classic scheme, both Latin and African, of the houses of the south."[36] This project also was seen to relate to the Libyan context through what was referred to as its "Mediterranean intonation"—in both general appearance and specific elements. For Rava, the environmental dimension of the Libyan vernacular—including the covered verandah and courtyard—was a fundamental constant to which all Mediterranean architecture should respond, connecting indigenous constructions, ancient precedents, and modern rational architecture.[37] This *mediterranietà* of the Pavilion of Eritrea and Somalia is particularly well expressed in the photographs taken after its construction, photographs that primarily depict the ambiance of the building's exterior spaces (fig. 18).

The Pavilion of Eritrea and Somalia also represented an important development in the organization and presentation of indigenous culture. The Somalian exhibition contained displays of both natural and agricultural products, including cotton, bananas, and salt, and manufactured and

---

36. "Per la moderna architettura coloniale italiana," *Domus* 7 (June 1934): 11–13.
    Masharabbia are the wooden screening devices found in Islamic domestic architecture.

37. Carlo Enrico Rava, "Di un'architettura coloniale moderna, parte prima," *Domus* 4 (May 1931): 39–43, 89; and "Di un'architettura coloniale moderna, parte seconda." *Domus* 4 (June 1931): 32–36.

fig. 19
Cover of *Tripoli,* tourist
brochure, 1935.
The Mitchell Wolfson Jr.
Collection, The
Wolfsonian–Florida
International University,
Miami Beach, Florida.
Photograph by Silvia Ros.

handmade items, such as incense and leather goods. A similar range of
material was collected for the Eritrean exhibition, including coffee,
canned meat, flax seed, and artisanal products, such as wood carvings and
silverware. A second and equally important aspect of the Eritrean and
Somalian exhibits was a presentation of colonial fauna and a collection of
ethnographic objects. The exhibition catalogue to the eighth Tripoli
Trade Fair in 1934 states that the ethnographic material "represents that
form of art through which the natives express their inventive capacity and
which gives the sensation of the progress achieved in the mentality of this
population during the Italian occupation."[38] As a "permanent pavilion and
ethnographic museum," this project purported to present material in
accordance with the most rigorous scientific practices. The same can be
said of the building's architecture, which demonstrated the vernacular
influences and characteristic building materials of these colonies. However, if the Pavilion of Eritrea and Somalia can itself be regarded as an
ethnographic object, not unlike those that it displayed, what culture was
it intended to represent? This project combined the vernacular influences
of Italy's East African colonies with a general Mediterranean character
derived from its North African context. It addressed the issue of the Italian
representation of Eritrea and Somalia in Libya by creating a hybrid of all

38. Ente Autonomo Fiera Campionaria di Tripoli, *VIII. Manifestazione. Quarta rassegna
    internazionale intercoloniale in Africa. 11 marzo–11 maggio. MCMXXXIV–XII. Catalogo*
    (Rome: Arti grafiche Fratelli Palombi, 1934), 255–257.

fig. 20
Interior pages from
Tripoli, tourist brochure,
1935. The Mitchell
Wolfson Jr. Collection,
The Wolfsonian–Florida
International University,
Miami Beach, Florida.
Photograph by Silvia Ros.

of these references, articulated through a contemporary metropolitan language. It was a cultural expression of the complex exchange of metropolitan and colonial identities found in the politics of Italian colonization — an architecture where the modern and the indigenous coincided perfectly.

The synthesis of identities in the Tripoli Trade Fair is particularly evident in publicity from the period. One such example is a tourist brochure from the fair of 1935 (fig. 19). The cover of this publication, entitled *Tripoli*, depicts indigenous Libyan culture — a merchant in traditional dress, with artisanal wares placed around and draped over his camel. The opening pages of this publication introduce the native culture in a romanticized narrative accompanied by images documenting the *suqs* of the old city and their artisans.[39] The Tripoli Trade Fair was subsequently shown as a form of metropolitan commerce that was carefully integrated with the colonial landscape. The accompanying text is prosaic, emphasizing the role of this event in "attracting people and products from every part of the world interested in trade with Africa."[40] Images of the fair depict the presentation of Italian industrial goods side by side with vignettes of native culture (fig. 20). These promotional materials reflect the perception that there was no contradiction between modern Western society and the local culture of Libya within Italian colonial politics.

In the late 1930s the representation of the metropolitan and the colonial at the Tripoli Trade Fair underwent a decisive shift — largely the product of changes in the Fascist authorities' approach to colonial politics. The Italian Fascist government called for the invasion of Ethiopia in October 1935 in an effort to gain a trophy of overseas expansion and to erase Italy's stunning defeat by the army of the Abyssinian Emperor Menelik at Adowa in 1896. The conquest of the Ethiopians was quickly followed by

39. Ente Autonomo Fiera di Tripoli, *Tripoli. IX. Manifestazione. VI. Rassegna coloniale internazionale in Africa*, text by Temi Agostini (Milan: S. A. Arti grafiche Bertarelli, 1934), 1–6.

40. Ibid., 25.

XIᴬ FIERA DI
TRIPOLI
PRIMA MOSTRA COLONIALE DELL'IMPERO
1937-XV-E.F.

Mussolini's declaration of an Italian empire in Africa in May 1936—an event that dramatically changed the relationship between Italy and other European nations. In part due to the sanctions imposed by the League of Nations in Geneva, the foreign presence at the Tripoli Trade Fair decreased considerably; Luxembourg and Belgium were the only official participants in 1936.[41] In reaction to international disapproval, this exhibition was widely viewed by Italian commentators as a vehicle through which the Fascist government could affirm Italy's new imperial status. This affirmation was clearly manifested in the eleventh Tripoli Trade Fair in 1937, called the "First Colonial Exhibition of the Fascist Empire." This imperial dimension of the Tripoli fair was greatly reinforced by Mussolini's voyage to Libya in March of that year—a well-publicized visit that, notably, included his appearance at the inauguration of this exhibition. Mussolini's lengthy and politically significant public statement to his "Comrades of Tripoli" was a carefully measured affirmation of empire, aimed at stirring Italian nationalism while extinguishing what was described as "the continual neurotic alarmism" of other European powers. In seeking to dismiss the fears of other nations, he stated:

> We arm ourselves on the sea, in the sky and on the ground, because this is our irresistible duty in the face of the armament of others, but the Italian people demand to be left alone, because they are intent on a long and difficult labor.[42]

The itinerary of Mussolini's visit to the Tripoli Trade Fair was as polemical as his speech, including carefully choreographed stops at the pavilions of Germany, France, and Italy's colonial possessions in North and East Africa.

The Tripoli Trade Fair had evolved from a national exhibition affirming the politics of colonial expansion into an imperial forum espousing the politics of war. These "politics" were given graphic expression on the cover of the catalogue to the 1937 fair, which shows the winged Roman goddess of victory cautiously offering an olive branch in an outstretched hand while brandishing a sword in the other (fig. 21). The initial section of this catalogue makes explicit the connection between the Tripoli fair and Fascist colonial politics by including images of Mussolini's first visit to Tripolitania in 1926. The text underscores this connection by noting: "every year the Tripoli Trade Fair, faithful to the trust given by Mussolini, has progressively improved, to become a political and economic instrument always more valid and appropriate to the dynamic rhythm of Italian life."[43] The transformation of this exhibition over the course of its ten-year span was thus seen to coincide with the politics of Mussolini in this region.

41. Ente Autonomo Fiera Campionaria di Tripoli, *XI Manifestazione internazionale intercoloniale*, 54.

42. Benito Mussolini, "Ai camerati di Tripoli" (17 March 1937), in *Opera Omnia di Benito Mussolini*, eds. Edoardo and Dulio Susmel (Florence: La Fenice, 1959), 28: 143–145.

43. Ente Autonomo Fiera Campionaria di Tripoli, *XI Manifestazione internazionale intercoloniale*, 29.

The connection between the Tripoli Trade Fair and the politics of empire are clearly demonstrated in a particularly compelling two-page spread from this catalogue. While the text describes the organization and content of the first imperial edition of this exhibition, images depict both the labor and military strength of Italian colonization efforts (fig. 22). This visual presentation is accompanied by a quotation from Mussolini: "The Italian people created the Empire with their blood. They will develop it with their work and defend it against anyone with their weapons."[44]

The architectural manifestation of this display of imperial rhetoric was the Tripoli Trade Fair's third and final permanent pavilion constructed to represent Italy's East African colonies. Designed by the architect Pietro Lombardi, the Pavilion of Italian East Africa was completed for the eleventh fair in 1937, an exhibition that was enthusiastically described by Alessandro Melchiori, president of the organizing committee, as "an integral part of the work of empowering our Empire."[45] Indeed, this pavilion was an important means of asserting the politics of Mussolini's newly founded colonial empire in Africa. In so doing, its first task was to validate Italy's claims in East Africa by documenting what one scholar of colonialism described as the "laborious and glorious historical process through which Italy conquered its 'place in the sun' in Africa."[46] This pavilion also had a clear economic mission that was tied to the role of the Tripoli fair as a vehicle for facilitating trade between Western nations and the Italian colonies. It was intended to "present to the Italian and foreign visitor a complete picture of what the territories of the Empire could offer to the Mediterranean markets." However, these declarations should be regarded as largely

44. Ibid., 46–47.
45. Alessandro Melchiori, "Premessa," *XI Manifestazione internazionale intercoloniale*, 25.
46. Piccioli, "La Fiera di Tripoli," 558.

fig. 23
(right)
Pietro Lombardi, Pavilion
of Italian East Africa,
Tripoli Trade Fair, 1937.
Photographic archive of
Azione Coloniale. The
Mitchell Wolfson Jr.
Collection–Fondazione
Regionale Cristoforo
Colombo, Genoa, Italy.

fig. 24
(below)
Pietro Lombardi, entrance
view of the Pavilion of
Italian East Africa.
Photographic archive of
Azione Coloniale. The
Mitchell Wolfson Jr.
Collection–Fondazione
Regionale Cristoforo
Colombo, Genoa, Italy.

rhetorical, because Italy sought self-sufficiency in trade and economic matters in reaction to the sanctions by the League of Nations after the invasion of Ethiopia.[47]

Lombardi reacted to this political context by creating his pavilion for Italy's East African colonies as a sober volume, articulated only with alternating bands of rough and smooth marble and a continuous strip window at the height of the ceiling (fig. 23). The entrance was marked by two large monoliths commemorating Mussolini's founding of the Italian empire in 1936. Avoiding any synthesis of the indigenous architecture of the East African colonies, this project suggested an archaic religious monument. It also strongly conveyed the military dimension of the Italian empire in East Africa through the prominent positioning of weapons framing the entrance (fig. 24). The exhibits within this pavilion provided depth to this

vision of empire by presenting both the Italian victory in Ethiopia and contemporary colonization efforts throughout the East African territories. In so doing, the image of conquest was fused with that of economic and public life. This intersection of war and secular society was invoked in the catalogue of the twelfth Tripoli Trade Fair in 1938, which asserted that "the evocation of the glorious military conquest is perfectly harmonized with that, no less glorious and always heroic, of the civil conquest."[48]

47. Ente Autonomo Fiera Campionaria di Tripoli, *XI Manifestazione internazionale intercoloniale*, 53.

48. Ente Autonomo Fiera Campionaria di Tripoli, "La 2ª Mostra dell'Impero," *XII Manifestazione Internazionale-Intercoloniale. 20 febbraio–5 aprile 1938–XVI. Seconda Mostra dell'Impero* (Rome: Società anonima tipografica Luzzatti, 1938), 139.

fig. 25
Pietro Lombardi,
general interior view
of the Pavilion of
Italian East Africa.
Photographic archive of
Azione Coloniale. The
Mitchell Wolfson Jr.
Collection–Fondazione
Regionale Cristoforo
Colombo, Genoa, Italy.

Within the Pavilion of Italian East Africa, the Italian conquest of Ethiopia was documented in maps, technical drawings, and photographs. Italian accomplishments in East Africa were evidenced in an equally "objective" manner, through the display of products intended for export to Italy and the presentation of colonization efforts, such as public works projects and agricultural development. This exhibition space was subdivided into separate geographically defined areas, with materials presented by their place of origin. A continuous shelf on the perimeter wall—containing pottery, busts, and agricultural products—visually unified these areas (fig. 25). Above this shelf, the upper portion of the room was dedicated primarily to a series of large murals that thematically portrayed each of the East African colonies, combining the colonial landscape with images of military power. According to the exhibition catalogue, the artifacts and images were displayed "in an organized and convincing form with the evidence and immediacy of facts, without any artifice or rhetorical pandering."[49] This approach to the material was based on the most exacting contemporary practices of institutions like the Colonial Museum in Rome. However, the seeming objectivity of these institutions had already been completely compromised by the same imperial politics that this exhibition purported to represent—the Colonial Museum itself having mounted an exhibition related to Italian military activities in Ethiopia in 1935.[50]

The Pavilion of Italian East Africa at the Tripoli Trade Fair signaled a decisive shift in the representation of indigenous culture of the Italian colonies and, as a consequence, in the politics of colonialism. Instead of

49. Ibid., 139.

50. The new home of the Colonial Museum opened on 21 October 1935, less than three weeks after Italy's invasion of Ethiopia. Both in its organization and in its content, this imperial museum placed great emphasis on the military dimension of the Italian colonial enterprise — an emphasis that coincided with the contemporary activities of the Italian military in Ethiopia.

conveying these cultures through a synthesis of their vernacular traditions, as had been done with Larco and Rava's 1934 Pavilion of Eritrea and Somalia, this project offered monumental proof of the Italian empire's political force. The representation of indigenous culture had been completely permeated with images of conquest, and the modernity of the hybrid had been replaced by a more singular aesthetic of war and subjugation. Indeed, what had begun in 1928 as an exhibition of metropolitan and colonial goods set in North Africa—one whose role as an instrument of colonial propaganda was fully integrated with its potential for encouraging economic and cultural exchange—by 1937 had become a more powerful, albeit limited, expression of a Fascist politics of empire. Despite the success of the Tripoli Trade Fair in stimulating the economic development of this region over the course of its thirteen-year history, the legacy of this event in the North African context was determined, at least in part, by the Fascist leadership's politics of war. This connection is perhaps most ironically conveyed in the story of this exhibition's eventual demise. The fourteenth Tripoli Trade Fair, planned for March and April of 1940, was suspended shortly after Germany's invasion of Poland in September 1939. Had it occurred, this event would have ended shortly before the start of conflict between the British and Italians in North Africa, during which Governor Italo Balbo was shot down by his own forces over the skies of Tobruk in eastern Libya. ✧

Acknowledgments
The research for this essay was conducted at The Wolfsonian library in Miami Beach in February of 1997 and the Mitchell Wolfson Jr. Collection in Genoa, Italy, in May 1997. I would like to thank the following people at The Wolfsonian for their assistance: in Miami Beach—Cathy Leff, Joel Hoffman, Pedro Figueredo, and Neil Harvey; and in Genoa—Gianni Franzone, Silvia Barisione, Matteo Fochessati, and Susanna Cappai. This specific topic is part of my recently completed Ph.D. dissertation, entitled "Mediterraneità and Modernità: Architecture and Culture during the Period of Italian Colonization of North Africa" (Massachusetts Institute of Technology, February 2001).

James Wechsler

From World War I to the Popular Front: The Art and Activism of Hugo Gellert

James Wechsler was assistant curator for works on paper at The Wolfsonian–Florida International University. He is a specialist in American leftist art of the 1920s and 1930s. Wechsler is currently finishing his doctoral dissertation, "Embracing the Specter of Communism: The Art and Activism of Hugo Gellert," at the Graduate Center of the City University of New York. Wechsler conducted research for this essay as a Wolfsonian Fellow in 1998.

During the 1930s, Hugo Gellert (1892–1985) was a well-known figure in American art. Today he is recognized primarily by specialists of the period between the two world wars. Gellert is perhaps more famous for his passionate, unwavering commitment to the American Communist Party (CPUSA) than for his important artistic contribution. Yet Gellert strongly disavowed any distinction between his politics and his art. He declared, "Being a Communist and being an artist are the two cheeks of the same face and, as for me, I fail to see how I could be either one without also being the other."[1] Gellert and his views on the political role of art became influential in America during the 1930s, when artists, impelled by economic crisis and the subsequent threat of world fascism, assumed a less-isolated place in society. Not only did Gellert produce a vital, socially engaged body of work, he also occupied a crucial position in the important artists' organizations that proliferated during the Great Depression. In order to better understand Gellert's evolution to a position of leadership during the 1930s, when artists found a strong, collective voice that often blurred the boundaries between art and activism, one must also examine his development during the 1910s and 1920s.

Gellert was born Hugo Grünbaum on 3 May 1892 to a Jewish family in Budapest, Hungary. In 1905 his father, a tailor, brought the family to the United States. He changed their name to Gellert, and they settled in New York City. From 1909 through 1914, Hugo Gellert received a traditional art education at the conservative National Academy of Design. Gellert enrolled in numerous life drawing classes and studied composition,

Detail of Hugo Gellert's
Self-Portrait, c. 1923.

1. Hugo Gellert, unpublished draft of speech probably for an Artists for Victory function in the early 1940s. Hugo Gellert Papers, Archives of American Art, Smithsonian Institution, Washington, D.C. (hereafter AAA).

painting, and etching. Though he was suspended once for not submitting his final examination drawings, by the time he finished the program Gellert had won a noteworthy total of nine awards, four of which included cash prizes.[2] According to the artist, his social conscience developed when he visited relatives in Budapest after the outbreak of World War I.[3] There he witnessed the effects of war on the home front as families received word of casualties and deaths. When Gellert returned to New York he became involved with socialism through his younger brother Ernest and the Hungarian-American workers' movement. He contributed drawings to the weekly supplement of the movement's Hungarian-language newspapers *Elöre* (Forward) and *Uj Elöre* (New Forward) and participated in related cultural events, outings, and picnics. In the winter of 1915, Gellert moved to Greenwich Village, where he supported himself as a poster designer for a commercial lithography company. When Gellert refused to accept a pay cut after the busy season ended, he was fired. Finding himself unemployed, the young socialist artist soon became involved with the radical journal *The Masses*. In Gellert's own words:

> I picked up two of my black and white drawings, and I took them down to *The Masses*, because they were against the war, as I was. When the next issue appeared, it had my drawings and I became a regular contributor.[4]

Gellert worked in an Art Nouveau style that proved to be very popular. His drawings soon began to appear on the covers of *The Masses*. Gellert's early work may seem incongruous with the very political, very confrontational art for which he later became known. As Dorothy Day (1897–1980), leftist journalist and founder of *The Catholic Worker* noted, "When he wasn't drawing pictures of marching workers in overalls grasping their tools like weapons, he was making lovely pictures of goats and frolicking kids."[5] While Day's implication that Gellert's idyllic scenes are concurrent with his communist-themed signature style is inaccurate, others shared the point she made regarding the disparity between these different aspects of his work. Gellert's friend, the writer Mike Gold (1893–1967), remarked:

> His drawings seemed out of another world. They were serene country idylls from some lost and forgotten golden age: beautiful little white goats with their kids resting gracefully under the trees; or lovely young girls in Greek robes who danced by a river to the piping of dark young shepherds while the sky shed happiness on all the world.[6]

2. National Academy of Design School of Fine Arts Records, Archives, National Academy of Design, New York.

3. Hugo Gellert, "Europe Summer of 1914," in *This Noble Flame: An Anthology of a Hungarian Newspaper in America 1902–1982*, ed. Zoltan Deak (New York: Heritage Press, 1982), 72–74.

4. Hugo Gellert, interview by Jeff Kisseloff, c. 1985, in Jeff Kisseloff, *You Must Remember This: An Oral History of Manhattan from the 1890s to World War II* (San Diego, New York, London: Harcourt Brace Jovanovich, 1989), 438.

5. Dorothy Day, *The Long Loneliness: The Autobiography of Dorothy Day* (New York: Harper, 1952), 71.

fig. 1
Hugo Gellert, *Fantasie*.
From *The Masses*, August
1917. Courtesy of
Reference Center for
Marxist Studies, New York.

Later in life, Gellert also disparaged his early, less-political works. Referring
to *Fantasie*, a work appearing in the August 1917 issue of *The Masses*
(fig. 1), he stated in a 1984 interview:

> As far as *The Masses* was concerned I made some allegorical drawings
> against the war. For instance, I had a man with an arrow and an animal
> he was aiming at. Someone came between him and the animal to protect
> it. That was my decorative way of expressing anti-war political cartoons.[7]

For Gold and Gellert, who made these remarks long after the beginning of
their adherence to communist dogma, "decorative" was synonymous with
politically noncommittal. It was something to be avoided. Yet Gellert's
early style is quite radical. It is a form of modernism rare in the history of
American art.

Unlike other early American modernists—who broke from tradition by
working in Paris and Berlin, by attending the 1913 Armory show, or by
frequenting Alfred Stieglitz's gallery, 291, or informal gatherings at the
apartment of collectors Louise and Walter Arensberg—Gellert consciously
drew his modernist style from Hungarian art. In the 1890s Hungarian
modernism grew from the Viennese Secession—the Austrian version of
Art Nouveau—which challenged the dominant, academic style. By the
turn of the century, modernists insinuated motifs derived from Hungarian

6. Michael Gold, "Salute to Hugo Gellert," *Masses and Mainstream* 8 (January 1955): 27.

7. Hugo Gellert, interview by Paul Buhle, 4 April 1984, transcript, oral history project, AAA.

fig. 2
(right)
Béla Lajta, detail of
doorway at School and
Students' Hostel
(formerly Institute for
the Blind), Budapest,
Hungary, 1908.
Photograph by the author.

fig. 3
(far right)
Hugo Gellert, cover of
Pearson's magazine,
August 1922. Courtesy
of Mary Ryan Gallery,
New York.

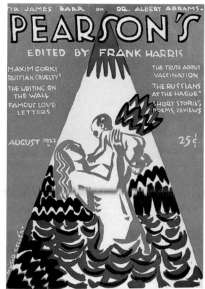

folk art into Secessionist-inspired designs. When Gellert visited Hungary in the summer of 1914, the revival of vernacular forms by avant-garde artists was at its peak. Geometric folk designs were incorporated into many of prewar Budapest's newest architectural projects—including schools, hospitals, gravestones, churches, and synagogues (fig. 2). The naïve, brightly colored geometric flowers, birds, prancing stags, and abstract zigzag border designs in Gellert's decorative work of the 1910s and early 1920s are derived directly from traditional Hungarian peasant arts and crafts, or through familiarity with the avant-garde (fig. 3). Gellert's early work is not at odds with his later, overtly political work. The use of indigenous forms in prewar Hungarian art had political connotations. At that time Hungary was part of the Austro-Hungarian Empire. Use of the vernacular was a rejection of official Austrian culture. It was an anti-imperialist statement. The subject matter may not be revolutionary, but the subtext is.

More explicit leftist political statements generated by the Hungarian avant-garde group known as Aktivisták (the Activists) also affected Gellert's production. Formed during the war by the poet Lajos Kassák (1887–1967), the Activists included other artists of Gellert's generation such as Mihály Bíró (1886–1948), Sándor Bortnyik (1893–1976), Gyula Derkovits (1894–1934), János Tábor (1890–1956), and Béla Uitz (1887–1972), who all supported the short-lived Hungarian Communist revolution of 1919 led by Béla Kun (1886–1937). Because the Activists wanted to communicate to a broad audience—including the working class as well as intellectuals—they used posters to depict scenes of leftist agitation. Gellert was aware of the Activists through the radical Hungarian-American

fig. 4
(below)
Mihály Bíró, *A háború borzalmai ellen...* (Against the Horrors of War...), poster, 126 x 95 cm, 1912. Collection of the Magyar Nemzeti Múzeum Legújabb Kori Föosztálya, Budapest, Hungary.

fig. 5
(below, center)
Hugo Gellert, untitled lithograph, 58 x 39 cm, 1933. From *Karl Marx Capital in Pictures*, edition 133. The Mitchell Wolfson Jr. Collection, The Wolfsonian–Florida International University, Miami Beach, Florida. Photograph by Silvia Ros.

fig. 6
(below, far right)
Mihály Bíró, cover of *The Masses*, July 1916. Courtesy of Reference Center for Marxist Studies, New York.

community and *Uj Elöre,* which published Kassák's writings.[8] Bíró's posters are the source for a number of Gellert's works. In 1912 Bíró created an antiwar poster depicting the image of a uniformed skeleton shoveling tiny people into the back of a cannon (fig. 4); Gellert appropriated this image for his 1933 portfolio *Karl Marx Capital in Pictures* (fig. 5). Other American radicals also knew Bíró's work. His image of a red, sledgehammer-wielding, hulking figure was used for a cover of *The Masses* in July 1916 (fig. 6).

America's entry into the war in late 1917 altered the political climate in the United States, further polarizing the left from the American mainstream. A number of artists and writers involved with *The Masses* were tried for propagating sedition and treason because of their published works. Though these individuals were acquitted, *The Masses* was suppressed under the 1917 Espionage Act, which empowered the postmaster general to prevent the mailing of subversive material. In the wake of *The Masses's* demise, Gellert became more active in the radical press. He immediately joined *The Liberator* magazine as a contributing editor—his drawing of a Russian peasant sowing red seeds appeared on the cover of the inaugural issue. The artists and writers of *The Liberator* were virtually the same as those of *The Masses,* but the editorial staff strove to protect their new journal from the fate of its predecessor. Indeed, the cartoonist Art Young (1866–1943), who was associated with both publications, remarked, "Looking over a bound volume of *The Liberator* for 1918, it is easy to discern that the soft pedal was being used, in contrast to the outspokenness of *The Masses.*"[9] Almost no direct attacks on America's involvement in the war were included in *The Liberator.* Events in Russia took center stage.

8. In the early 1920s, *Uj Elöre* published numerous poems by Kassák as well as his essay "Aktivista művészet és forradolom" (Activist Art and Revolution), *Uj Elöre,* 2 June 1922, 6.

9. Art Young, ed. John Nicholas Beffel, *Art Young: His Life and Times* (New York: Sheridan House, 1939), 330.

FOUR HOURS IN THE SNOW—ERNEST GELLERT BEFORE HIS SUICIDE.

fig. 7
Maurice Becker, *Four Hours in the Snow— Ernest Gellert Before His Suicide,* lithograph. From *The Workers Monthly,* June 1925. Courtesy of Reference Center for Marxist Studies, New York.

In fact, the journal was hastily formed two months after *The Masses* folded in order to publish John Reed's (1887–1920) reports of the Russian Revolution.[10] The editors shifted the tone of their magazine away from discord and pessimism toward a unified, optimistic vision of revolutionary Russia. They even featured works by Vladimir Lenin (1870–1924); the Soviet Commissar of Enlightenment, A.V. Lunacharsky (1875–1933); author Maksim Gor'ky (1868–1936); and other Russian literati.

During this transitional period, Gellert's brother Ernest was drafted into the American armed forces. A conscientious objector, he was confined to military prison for insubordination. Ernest Gellert described his objections to the war in socialist terms:

> They requested me to state my views… I replied that I considered the present war the logical result of the mad ambitions for commercial and territorial expansion on the part of the ruling classes of the European nations involved—that wars are only made possible through the control of the political machineries, and all channels for forming public opinion, by those unscrupulous minorities…[11]

On 8 April 1918 Ernest died at Fort Hancock in New Jersey. The Gellert family was informed that he committed suicide. According to the official account, he had acquired a rifle. Using a stick to pull the trigger, he shot himself through the chest. As Dorothy Day described:

> The report was that he had taken his own life, but we could not believe it. He was a happy youth, friendly with the guards who smuggled his violin to him so that he could play to them. Hugo insisted he had been murdered.[12]

This traumatic event confirmed Gellert's belief that where capitalism dominated, freedom and human rights were mere illusions that vanished when the system was threatened. For Gellert, Ernest's incarceration and death stood in direct contrast to contemporary events in Russia. After all, the revolution was driven by Russian soldiers who, like Ernest, refused to obey orders to fight for the government. Gellert's unwavering, lifelong defense of Soviet Russia did have ideological roots, but on a psychological

10. Rebecca Zurier, *Art for The Masses: A Radical Journal and Its Graphics* (Philadelphia: Temple University Press, 1988), 25, 27.

11. Ernest Gellert, draft of six-page typed statement, Gellert Papers, AAA.

12. Day, *Long Loneliness,* 71–72.

level Gellert's zealousness also can be seen as an attempt to address his loss. The artist Maurice Becker (1889–1975) portrayed Ernest's plight in a lithograph from a series on Americans who refused to obey military authority. In *Four Hours in the Snow—Ernest Gellert Before His Suicide,* a gaunt, underdressed boy shivers as a large uniformed soldier with a rifle guards him (fig. 7). Although Hugo Gellert never depicted the incident in his own art, he dedicated *Karl Marx Capital in Pictures*

> To the memory of my very dear brother Ernest, brave and faithful soldier of the proletarian cause, born at Budapest on January 12, 1896, died in military confinement at Fort Hancock, N.J., on March 8, 1918.[13]

Gellert did not join the American Communist Party until 1934; however, he considered himself a communist from 1919 when "the most advanced members of the Socialist Party formed the Communist Party."[14] He and other like-minded artists and writers paid close attention to the revolutionary experiment in Russia, attempting to discover a model on which to base their work. They found this model in Soviet Proletkult, a program conceptualized by members of the Bolshevik party in mid-1917 to encourage the working class to create new forms of culture suitable for the communist state. A government subsidy was provided under Proletkult's auspices for theater workshops, art studios, literary circles, and adult education. But the post-revolutionary civil-war period proved too unstable to maintain such an experiment. In 1921 Proletkult lost its state support.

Soon, similar ideas about engineering a working-class culture entered the American discourse. Early in 1921 Mike Gold announced:

> The art ideals of the Capitalist world isolated each artist as in a solitary cell, there to brood and suffer and silently go mad…. Proletcult [*sic*] is Russia's organized attempt to remove the economic barriers and social degradation that repressed that proletarian instinct during the centuries.[15]

Gellert championed this "proletarian instinct" in his lyrical drawing *Proletarian Poet,* which, through its title, suggests the role of industrial workers as producers of art (fig. 8). However, in Proletkult terms, Gellert's style of facile draftsmanship was derived from modernist, intellectual—and therefore bourgeois—traditions. Thus, it was not entirely successful as

Proletarian Poet

13. Hugo Gellert, *Karl Marx Capital in Pictures* (White Plains, N.Y.: Privately printed, 1933), dedication. Although Gellert wrote here that Ernest died on 8 March 1918, Ernest's grave bears the death date 8 April 1918.

14. Gellert, unpublished draft of speech, Gellert Papers, AAA.

15. Irwin Granich [Mike Gold], "Towards Proletarian Art," *The Liberator* (February 1921): 20–24.

The Angel of the Lords

The Knight of the Round Belly

**fig. 9
(right)
Hugo Gellert, *The Angel of the Lords,* crayon.
From *The Liberator,*
August 1922. Courtesy of Mary Ryan Gallery, New York.**

**fig. 10
(far right)
Robert Minor, *The Knight of the Round Belly,*
crayon. From *The Liberator,* July 1922.
Courtesy of Mary Ryan Gallery, New York.**

an expression of the revolutionary class. Turning to *Masses/Liberator* cartoonist Robert Minor (1884–1952) for inspiration, Gellert began to close the gap between style and political theory in his art. He wrote:

> Armed with a jumbo-sized black marking crayon, Bob [Minor] would grunt and groan as he put all his might into a drawing. When he finished the work he looked like a gladiator emerging from combat. His drawing, reduced to the barest essentials, verily flashed its message.[16]

Gellert continued to work in the colorful, eye-catching, modernist style to produce magazine covers, but in his political cartoons he adopted Minor's physical, unrefined method. Compare, for example, Gellert's *The Angel of the Lords* to Minor's *The Knight of the Round Belly,* both published in *The Liberator* in 1922 (figs. 9 and 10).

Gellert's style developed further with his introduction to the Russian avant-garde in the mid-1920s. Gellert's friend and *Liberator* colleague, the Russian-American painter and graphic artist Louis Lozowick (1892–1972), spent the early 1920s in Europe and knew many of the Russian Constructivists. Upon his return to New York in 1923, Lozowick became the leading authority on the Russian avant-garde, writing and lecturing on the subject of modern art. His precisionist, machine-age style, which incorporated principles of Constructivist-inspired abstraction and urban realism, had a strong effect on Gellert. Although Lozowick also was a communist sympathizer, Gellert's work was generally more explicitly political. Lozowick's cityscapes, factoryscapes, and mechanical abstractions implied his leftist orientation (fig. 11). Gellert, however, incorporated ideological elements of communist agit prop. In *The Noon Hour,* for instance, he positions workers in the foreground, concentrating on the human element of labor and class struggle (fig. 12).

In the summer of 1925, Gellert met the Soviet poet Vladimir Mayakovsky (1893–1930) in New York, after the latter's brief stay in Mexico with the muralist Diego Rivera (1886–1957).[17] Cofounder of the avant-garde Russian Futurist movement, Mayakovsky developed a radical modernist

16. Hugo Gellert, "The Poor Man's Art Gallery," *American Dialog* (Spring 1967): 17.

17. Wiktor Woroszyiski, *The Life of Mayakovsky* (New York: Orion Press, 1970), 364–368.

The Noon Hour

poetry that glorified technology, revolution, and the new Soviet society.[18]
With his booming voice, shaved head, "broad shoulders, thin torso, and
long legs of a Dempsey,"[19] Mayakovsky made a commanding impression
on the circle of radicals who welcomed him. The poet was struck by the
degree to which New York was industrially advanced, but he criticized
the metropolis as unorganized, maintaining, "intellectually, New Yorkers
are still provincials. Their minds have not accepted the full implications
of the industrial age."[20] Gellert and Mayakovsky spent time together in
August 1925, discussing this subject. Gellert drew a portrait of Mayakovsky
for Gold's *New York Sunday World* interview (fig. 13), and Mayakovsky,
in turn, even drew one of Gellert.[21] In Gellert's drawing, an abstracted
industrial vignette rises behind the poet's head.[22] At the center of this
vignette, a rushing figure becomes a cog in a greater machine, symbolically
illustrating Mayakovsky's communist ideal of "real industrial civilization"
in which the populace works in tandem with technology.

Soviet cultural figures of Mayakovsky's stature rarely visited New York
during the 1920s. However, conceptual and formal innovations such
as those associated with Proletkult and Constructivism, emerging in
post-revolutionary Russia, filtered into New York through Americans
who spent time in Russia. Early in 1925, Mike Gold went to Europe.
While in London he met Huntly Carter, who had just written the first
English book on modern Soviet drama, *The New Theatre and Cinema of
Soviet Russia* (1924). Gold recalled, "He gave me a copy, and to my own
amazement, some latent passion for theatre cropped out in me... and I
took a freight boat to Leningrad."[23] Gold then returned to America and

18. Disillusioned with political, social, and cultural developments in Soviet Russia under Stalin,
    Mayakovsky committed suicide in 1930.

19. Joseph Freeman, *An American Testament: A Narrative of Rebels and Romantics*
    (New York: Farrar and Rinehart, 1936), 367.

20. Vladimir Mayakovsky, interview by Mike Gold, c. August 1925, "Russia's Dynamic Poet Finds
    New York Tame: We're Old-Fashioned, Unorganized, to Mayakovsky," *New York Sunday World,*
    9 August 1925, 3E.

21. See Hugo Gellert, "Drawing Mayakovsky," in *Noble Flame,* ed. Deak, 73–74.

22. Upon publication, the drawing was cropped to include only Mayakovsky's head.

New PLAYWRIGHTS Theatre
presents
the third production of the season
at the
52nd STREET THEATRE
"FIESTA"
A comedy of the Mexican Revolution
by MICHAEL GOLD

Staged by
ROBERT MILTON

Settings designed by
CLEON THROCKMORTON

Original costumes procured in Mexico by Mordecai Gorelik
Additional costumes by Evelyn Clifton

fig. 14
Hugo Gellert, detail of program for the New Playwrights Theatre production of Michael Gold's *Fiesta*, 1929. Courtesy of Billy Rose Theatre Collection, New York Public Library for the Performing Arts, Astor, Lenox, and Tilden Foundations.

shared his admiration for Vsevolod Meyerhold's Constructivist theater, which featured revolutionary subjects and innovative set designs of abstract, geometric forms with moving platforms. Along with the artists and writers Paul Peters, Arturo Giovannitti, William Gropper (1897–1977), Louis Lozowick, Florence Rau, and Bertram Wolfe, Gellert became involved with the Workers' Drama League, the theater group Gold organized in 1925.[24]

This was not Gellert's first contact with the performing arts. He had done illustrations in promotional materials for productions at the Penderton and Schubert theaters. During the late 1910s and early 1920s, he designed and painted scenery for performances at the Elöre Culture Club and illustrated *Szinházi Ujság* (Hungarian Theatrical Journal). By the early 1920s, Gellert was known for "his posters, his magazine covers, his stage designs."[25] Furthermore, through his association with *The Masses* and bohemian Greenwich Village, Gellert had been involved with the Provincetown Players, the experimental theater company. He made sketches of George Cram Cook (1873–1924), Eugene O'Neill (1888–1953), Paul Robeson (1898–1976), and Mike Gold for Provincetown Players productions, and designed a poster for the 1924 production of O'Neill's *All God's Chillun Got Wings*. But, in the Workers' Drama League, Gellert found a company whose political and creative desires were directly modeled after those of post-revolutionary Russia.

The Workers' Drama League was to be a new American theater that used modernist techniques to deliver politically revolutionary messages. It staged a number of productions in 1925, including a mass pageant, *The Paris Commune,* and Gold's own play *Money.*[26] By all accounts, the Workers' Drama League fell far short of creating a revolution in American theater. It did succeed, however, in capturing the attention of millionaire Wall Street financier and philanthropist Otto Kahn (1867–1934). In the fall of 1926, playwrights Em Jo Basshe, John Dos Passos (1896–1970),

23. Michael Gold, "My Life," c. 1928, manuscript, Gold Clippings File, Billy Rose Theatre Collection, The New York Public Library for the Performing Arts, Astor, Lenox, and Tilden Foundations.

24. See Freeman, *American Testament*, 372.

25. Egmont Erens, foreword to checklist for Gellert's exhibition at Kervorkian Galleries, 40 West Fifty-seventh Street, New York, 1–31 May 1923, Gellert Papers, Mary Ryan Gallery, New York.

26. See Virginia Hagelstein Marquardt, "Centre Stage: Radical Theatre in America, 1925–1934," *RACAR Revue d'art canadienne* 19 (1992): 112–122.

Francis Faragoh, John Howard Lawson, and Mike Gold received backing from Kahn to reorganize the Workers' Drama League into a non-profit corporation, the New Playwrights Theatre. The name made direct reference to the Provincetown Players' original Playwrights Theatre that was located in a MacDougal Street brownstone in Greenwich Village. Kahn was known as an art collector and generous patron to theater companies and musicians in the 1920s. According to Gold, Kahn had "the strangest, most inexplicable instinct for all that [was] new, experimental and revolutionary," and had "little respect for the bourgeois art authorities, but a youthful and warm and unforced sympathy for the young fledgling self-doubting art worker."[27] Kahn gave the New Playwrights Theatre more than fifty thousand dollars over a two-year period. He also lent Gellert money to purchase property in Westchester, New York.[28]

Reaction to the New Playwrights Theatre proved disappointing. As Dos Passos later recalled:

> One attempt to buck the tide and put on plays dealing with industrial life around us in a novel experimental manner, the new Playwrights Theatre, found no support in the kind of interest and enthusiasm that kept the Provincetown Players going in the early days, and failed after two seasons. Still, I think it may eventually be remembered as a crude forerunner of a new type of theatre.[29]

Reviews of New Playwrights Theatre productions in the mainstream press were unkind. However, they did describe an attempt to emulate Soviet avant-garde productions. *New York Times* critic J. Brooks Atkinson quipped that Paul Sifton's *The Belt* was "more racket than drama," while his review of John Howard Lawson's *The Loud Speaker* noted that the stage design was "constructivist to the last daub of red paint."[30] The extent of Gellert's involvement in New Playwrights Theatre Constructivist stage design is yet unknown. He did contribute his skills as a graphic artist, producing designs for programs and letterhead. His 1929 program for Mike Gold's *Fiesta*, subtitled "a comedy of the Mexican Revolution," shows a male figure with a sledgehammer, fully integrated with the mechanical environment around him (fig. 14). In late 1928, along with a group of other artists and designers, Gellert organized the EN-PI-TI Shops out of the West Fourteenth Street theater.[31] A phoneticization of "NPT," for New Playwrights Theatre, the EN-PI-TI Shops was a "design and

27. Michael Gold, "My Life."

28. Otto Kahn Papers, Princeton University; and Gellert Papers, AAA. Copies of receipts from Kahn indicate Gellert made a number of interest payments to Kahn from February through April 1929.

29. John Dos Passos, "The American Theatre: 1930–31," *New Republic*, 1 April 1931, 171, in Malcolm Goldstein, *The Political Stage: American Drama and Theater of the Great Depression* (New York: Oxford University Press, 1974), 11.

30. J. Brooks Atkinson, *New York Times*, 20 October 1927, 33; and 3 March 1927, 27.

31. The others were Louis Lozowick, George Granich, Yosel Cutler, Remo Bufano, William Gropper, Morris Pass, Arthur Segal, Henry Glintemkamp, and Art Young.

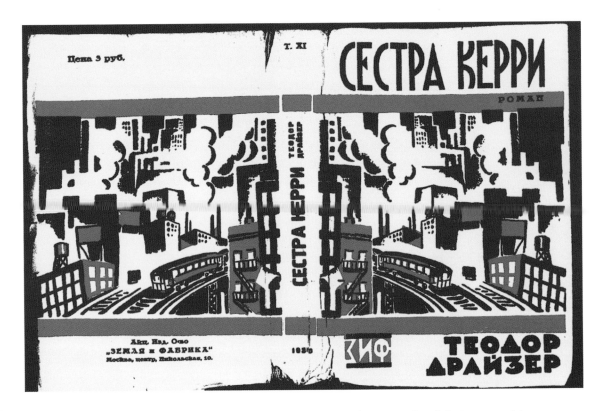

fig. 15
Hugo Gellert, book
jacket for the Russian
publication of Theodore
Dreiser's *Sister Carrie*
(Moscow: State
Publishing House, 1930).
Courtesy of Annenberg
Rare Book and
Manuscript Library,
University of
Pennsylvania,
Philadelphia.

construct" business, advertising "skyscraper bookshelves, machine-age furniture, bookends, bookplates, modernist window displays, signs, posters, screens, and letterheads… in any material from your own or our own designs."[32] Despite the fact that it existed within capitalist society, the EN-PI-TI Shops was a self-conscious emulation of Soviet productivist ideas that artists should design functional products suitable for the new, post-revolutionary society.

Gellert had the opportunity to participate directly in a Soviet productivist project the previous year when, in the fall of 1927, he made his first trip to Russia to attend the Tenth Anniversary Celebration of the October Revolution. Many other foreigners were in Moscow at this time, including Gellert's comrades Robert Wolf and William Gropper, the American novelist Theodore Dreiser (1871–1945), and the Mexican muralist Diego Rivera. Gellert met a number of important exiled Hungarian communist cultural and political figures, such as the former Activist artist Béla Uitz, the critic Alfred Kemény (1895–1945), the art historian János Mácza (1893–1974), and even the revolutionary leader Béla Kun himself. Uitz had recently become a professor at the Soviet VKhUTEIN (High

32. *Theatre 1929: A Magazine Published by the New Playwrights Theatre* (January 1929): 2, New Playwrights Theatre Clippings File, Billy Rose Theatre Collection, The New York Public Library for the Performing Arts, Astor, Lenox, and Tilden Foundations.

33. From 1930–1935, Uitz was secretary of the International Bureau of Revolutionary Artists (IBRA), which established contact with communist artist groups outside the Soviet Union. Gellert returned to the USSR at the end of 1932, and it is likely that Uitz and IBRA were involved with Gellert's commission to paint an eight-square-meter mural in Moscow in honor of the fifteenth anniversary of the revolution (whereabouts unknown). Russian contract, Gellert Papers, AAA.

State Art-Technical Institute) and was well connected with many of the state agencies and artist organizations that comprised the Moscow art world.[33] It may have been through Uitz that Gellert received a commission from the State Publishing House to design book jackets for Russian translations of Dreiser's novels and stories.[34] Gellert's illustration for *Sister Carrie* (fig. 15), Dreiser's novel about a working girl's struggles and eventual rise to success on the New York stage, depicts different strata of the American urban landscape. In the foreground are an elevated train, factories, and tenements with drying laundry. In the background, visible through the cloud-like smoke, are the skyscrapers of the well-to-do.

During the late 1920s, Gellert's ideas on the function of art and the political obligation of artists coalesced around the Communist Party. In 1926 he became one of the founding editors of the journal *New Masses*, contributing to the revival of the *Masses/Liberator* tradition. However, where *The Masses* and *The Liberator* were not specifically communist journals, Gellert helped point *New Masses* toward the Communist Party line. After Gellert and Mike Gold emerged as the dominant forces behind the publication in 1928, *New Masses* became the cultural voice of the CPUSA. In *New Masses* Gellert not only found a forum for his political drawings, but he also published criticism articulating his support of communism.

He began in January 1927 with a scathing attack on Constantin Brancusi (1876–1957), condemning the Romanian sculptor for remaining "vague and noncommittal" during the world war, striving for an expression that was "pure [and] above the battle":

> What is it that Brancusi worked on in 1916 during the war in Paris? What had he to say? He cut a huge phallus into marble that is what he had to say! Men are slaughtered, men are crazed…the artist, the divine, toys with the phallus.[35]

In a letter to *New Masses* defending Brancusi, the poet Ezra Pound protested "why the HELL should Brancusi, a Roumanian [*sic*] peasant by birth, take sides in a war between [the] German Empire and two capitalist arms firms?"[36] Gellert replied by declaring, "I did take it for granted that Roumanian [*sic*] peasants were humans and that it would disturb them to have other humans murdered."[37] This epitomized the

---

34. The Russian publication of Dreiser's *Sister Carrie*, for which Gellert designed the jacket, is dated 1930. It is unclear if Gellert made this drawing while in Moscow in 1927 or at a later date. David Shapiro wrote that, during Gellert's 1927 trip, he "created a series of book jackets for numerous translations of Dreiser's work." See David Shapiro, "Hugo Gellert: Political Activist, Political Artist," in *Hugo Gellert, 1892–1985: People's Artist*, eds. Zoltan Deak, James Gellert, Susan Joseph, Charles Keller (New York: Hugo Gellert Memorial Committee, 1986), 10. However, Ruth Apperson Kennel, Dreiser's personal secretary during the writer's visits to Russia, only specifically mentioned that in 1927 Gellert designed the jacket for *Chains*, Dreiser's volume of short stories. See Ruth Apperson Kennel, *Theodore Dreiser and the Soviet Union 1927–1945: A First Hand Chronicle* (New York: International Publishers, 1969), 20.

35. Hugo Gellert, "A Literary Debate with Ezra Pound," in *Noble Flame*, ed. Deak, 87.

36. Ibid.

212

fig. 16
Hugo Gellert
Self-Portrait, **oil and**
graphite on board,
59 x 40 cm, c. 1923.
The Mitchell Wolfson Jr.
Collection, The
Wolfsonian–Florida
International University,
Miami Beach, Florida.

communist position that those not directly involved with the social struggle automatically aligned themselves with the status quo. Tina Modotti (1896–1942), the communist, expatriate American photographer in Mexico, sided with Gellert. Modotti commented in a letter to the photographer Edward Weston that in the March 1927 *New Masses* there was "an interesting controversy between Ezra Pound and Hugo Gellert — I daresay the latter got the better of it."[38]

Through his exchange with Pound, Gellert threw down the gauntlet against modernist formalism, which seemed to have no clear social message. Later that year, en route to Moscow, Gellert sent a brief dispatch to *New Masses* from Paris advancing his position. In it he contradicted the notion that artistic freedom was guaranteed in capitalist societies. Gellert wrote that while he and an unnamed "individualist" artist sat in a Montparnasse café, discussing issues of artistic freedom in Russia, the "individualist" suddenly ran out into the street. When the artist returned, he explained to Gellert that an art dealer had passed. "And you," Gellert replied, "the individualist, ran after him. If a fat art patron would show you the color of a thousand-franc note you would drop on your knees." Gellert noted that he then asked, "If someone offered you a large sum of money would you refuse to paint the kind of picture he would demand of you?" The "individualist" replied that he would "probably give him the picture he wanted."[39] The points Gellert made in these 1927 anecdotes would become central to the platform of the Artists' Union in the 1930s. As painter Stuart Davis (1892–1964) pronounced:

> The artist of the immediate past was an individualist, progressive or reactionary, in his painting theory, working within the framework of middle class culture and marketing his product through channels set up by the middle class. His economic condition in general was poor and he was exploited by art dealer and patron alike.[40]

37. Ibid., 88

38. Tina Modotti, letter to Edward Weston, 22 March 1927, in "The Letters of Tina Modotti to Edward Weston," *The Archive* (Center for Creative Photography, University of Arizona) 22 (January 1986): 49–50. I thank Lic. Antonio Saborit of the Instituto Nacional de Arte y Historia, Mexico City for bringing this letter to my attention.

39. Hugo Gellert, "I Meet an Individualist," *New Masses* (September 1927): 25.

40. Stuart Davis, "The Artist Today: The Standpoint of The Artists' Union," *The American Magazine of Art* (August 1935). In *Social Realism: Art as a Weapon*, ed. David Shapiro (New York: Frederick Ungar Publishing Co., 1973), 112.

fig. 17
(below)
Hugo Gellert, *The
Communist Party Leads
Us,* poster, 97 x 64 cm,
c. 1932. The Mitchell
Wolfson Jr. Collection,
The Wolfsonian–Florida
International University,
Miami Beach, Florida.
Photograph by Silvia Ros.

fig. 18
(below, far right)
Hugo Gellert, *Vote
Communist,* poster,
75 x 34 cm, 1928.
The Wolfsonian–Florida
International University,
Miami Beach, Florida.

Supporting his written position as an artist of the communist cause, Gellert renounced his own earlier history as an "individualist." Through the mid-1920s Gellert had been a modernist painter as well as a graphic artist. He exhibited paintings and drawings in commercial venues such as the Kervorkian Galleries in 1923, and the New Art Circle in 1925 and 1927. His *Self-Portrait* (fig. 16) from the early 1920s reveals ambivalence between abstraction and figuration. In it he is literally situated between the two approaches. To one side is an abstract, rainbow-like wave pattern, to the other a rural landscape, an airplane, and, directly above his head, a nude woman. A flat, Cubist-like, transparent rectangle emanates from the middle of his forehead. By 1928 Gellert abandoned easel painting as an elitist form and concentrated entirely on media that were accessible to a wide audience, with the specific purpose of leftist agitation. He took his art to the street, designing posters promoting the Communist Party (fig. 17), its leaders — including Communist presidential candidate William Z. Foster (1881–1961) (fig. 18), and its newspaper, the *Daily Worker* (fig. 19).

While posters enabled Gellert to communicate the Party's official stance, events in Europe led him to take more direct political action. In 1927, under the military dictatorship of Admiral Miklos Horthy (1868–1957), Hungary signed a friendship treaty with Mussolini's Fascist Italy.

DailyWorker

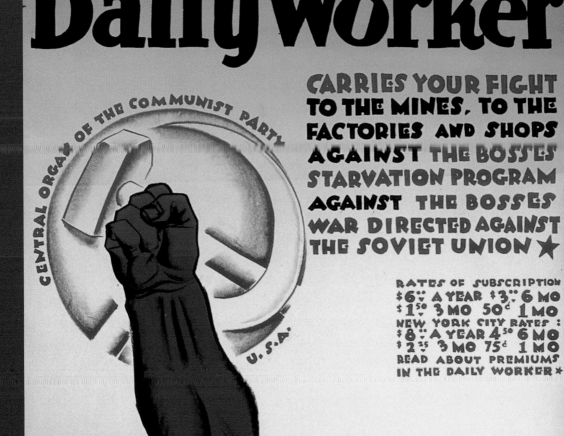

CARRIES YOUR FIGHT TO THE MINES, TO THE FACTORIES AND SHOPS AGAINST THE BOSSES STARVATION PROGRAM AGAINST THE BOSSES WAR DIRECTED AGAINST THE SOVIET UNION ★

CENTRAL ORGAN OF THE COMMUNIST PARTY U.S.A.

RATES OF SUBSCRIPTION
$6⁰⁰ A YEAR $3⁰⁰ 6 MO
$1⁵⁰ 3 MO 50ᶜ 1 MO
NEW YORK CITY RATES:
$8⁰⁰ A YEAR 4⁵⁰ 6 MO
$2²⁵ 3 MO 75ᶜ 1 MO
READ ABOUT PREMIUMS
IN THE DAILY WORKER ✶

HELP TO GET SUBSCRIPTIONS **ORGANIZE** NEIGHBORHOOD SQUADS TO SOLICIT SUBS ∿ **BUILD** GROUPS OF FRIENDS OF THE DAILY WORKER AROUND EVERY LARGE FACTORY, MINE AND FARMING DISTRICT!

HUGO GELLERT

5000 YEARLY SUBSCRIPTIONS WILL PUT THE DAILY WORKER ON A SOUND FINANCIAL BASIS

As *New Masses* reported:

> When Premier Count Stephan Bethlen de Bethlen [*sic*] of Hungary returned from two weeks visiting Signor Mussolini at Rome he said "my government will undertake in the immediate future a thorough study of the fascist system, especially its social aspects…we shall adopt those fascist reforms which have been tested and found practicable."[41]

Subsequently, with a number of other Hungarian immigrants, including the artist Wanda Gág (1893–1946), Gellert organized the Anti-Horthy League to oppose the Hungarian admiral's regime. In March 1928, when a group of Hungarian delegates arrived in New York to dedicate a monument to Louis Kossuth (1802–1894), leader of the 1848–1849 Hungarian revolution, the Anti-Horthy League was prepared. Labeling Horthy "Hungary's Bloody Mary," the League was enraged by the dictator's "reign of terror," which "managed to kill off, or imprison, or exile, or shut up, intimidate and castrate, every decent contemporary exponent of the arts and sciences."[42] They regarded the Horthy regime's gift of the Kossuth monument as nothing less than "pimping":

> The gesture is calculated to produce two results: one is that the poor Hungarian workingmen of this country, blinded by the glorious name, will fork up the shekels; the other, that the American bankers will so much more readily cock their eyes in the direction of Hungary.[43]

The Anti-Horthy League also took action. According to the *New York Times:*

> Warned by the demonstrations alleged to have been staged by the Anti-Horthy League, the Hatvany Defense Committee and their sympathizers on Tuesday night, the city sent forth such an army of its blue clad soldiers of peace that any possibly contemplated disturbance developed no further than the silent circulation of Anti-Horthy handbills.[44]

But, the following day at the dedication ceremony, an elaborate disturbance did develop. Gellert and writer Charles Yale Harrison (1898–1954) "made arrangements with an ace pilot of the war to fly [them] over the unveiling ceremony" so they could disperse the anti-Horthy handbills.[45] Gellert recalled of the preparation:

> We arrived in New Jersey with a bundle of leaflets to meet the pilot. A few of the leaflets had nothing but "Greetings to the Mayor" printed on them. We showed one of them to the pilot.[46]

41. "In Hungary," *New Masses* (June 1927): 21.
42. "Hungary's Bloody Mary," *New Masses* (February 1927): 25.
43. Ibid.
44. "Hundreds of Police Guard Hungarians," *New York Times*, 15 March 1928, 12.
45. Hugo Gellert, "The Anti-Horthy League," *Noble Flame,* ed. Deak, 84.
46. Ibid.

What they didn't reveal to the pilot was that the greater proportion of leaflets were printed with Gellert's drawing "showing how Horthy had transformed the gallows into a statue of Kossuth" (fig. 20).[47] From the air Gellert and Harrison showered the monument's formal unveiling ceremony with the artist's anti-fascist propaganda. The *New York Times* described the incident as a minor disturbance:

> The only trace of discord at the unveiling ceremonies was the hum of an airplane circling above the Hudson River to scatter anti-Horthy leaflets. Most of these floated on the breeze to some other section of the city. A few, however, fell into the crowd and found their way to the speaker's stand, just north of the monument. They were copies of the same leaflet distributed at the City Hall exercises on Wednesday when the more than 500 "Kossuth Pilgrims" were welcomed by Mayor Walker.[48]

This event fueled Gellert's search for a new, diverse audience outside the traditional dealer/patron/collector system, leading him to explore other forms of public art. In the late 1920s and early 1930s, Gellert followed in the tradition of the Mexican muralists, using this medium as a political vehicle. As an editor of *New Masses* he championed the Mexican mural movement, regularly featuring the works of Diego Rivera, José Clemente Orozco (1883–1949), Rufino Tamayo (1899–1991), and Xavier Guerrero (1896–1974). Emulating these artists, Gellert painted a monumental mural for the cooperative cafeteria of the Workers (Communist) Party on New York City's Union Square East in 1928 (fig. 21). Eight feet high, Gellert's mural covered one eighty-foot-long wall, and a facing wall with roughly thirty feet of usable space. The long wall included a frieze of heavily mus-cled, idealized laborers carrying placards. One of them echoed the communist slogan "WORKERS OF THE WORLD UNITE!" Another warned, "DON'T SCAB!" The central panel of the mural was devoted to steel workers and coal miners. While Orozco's 1930 mural for the New School for Social Research, and Rivera's notorious 1933 fresco, *Man at the Crossroads,* for Rocke-feller Center are well known for

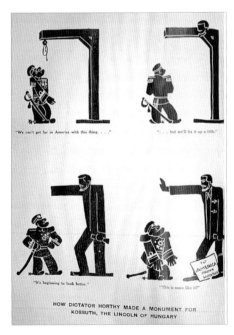

HOW DICTATOR HORTHY MADE A MONUMENT FOR
KOSSUTH, THE LINCOLN OF HUNGARY

47. Ibid.

48. "Two Nations Unveil Statue of Kossuth," *New York Times,* 16 March 1928, 3.

fig. 21
(above)
Hugo Gellert, detail
from mural for Workers
(Communist) Party
Cafeteria, New York, 1928
(destroyed). Courtesy
of Mary Ryan Gallery,
New York.

fig. 22
(below, far right)
Hugo Gellert, detail from
mural depicting Lenin
for Workers (Communist)
Party Cafeteria, New York,
1928 (destroyed). From
New Masses, January
1929. Courtesy of
Reference Center for
Marxist Studies, New York.

their depictions of Lenin, Gellert's cafeteria portrait preceded these works and was the first mural representation of the Bolshevik leader in New York. Opposite the central panel was a life-size depiction of Lenin, demonstratively muscular through his three-piece suit (fig. 22). Lenin was joined by portraits of other prominent radicals, including the journalist John Reed; the first general secretary of the Communist Party, Charles Ruthenburg (1882–1927); and the recently electrocuted anarchists Nicola Sacco (1891–1927) and Bartolomeo Vanzetti (1888–1927). As one would expect, *New Masses* hailed the mural as "probably the finest example of modern art in America."[49] However, even the mainstream press praised Gellert's work. A review in the *New Yorker* raved that

> the Gellert murals are the only ones on this continent except those of Rivera in Mexico City that are really contemporary. We have been shameful in our failure to use artists in our buildings, and the Proletcos [*sic*] cafeteria may start something… The labor party is fortunate in having a spokesman as articulate as this artist.[50]

The *New Yorker* clearly meant this comparison as praise; however, press coverage of the Mexican influence on American artists was by no means uniformly laudatory. In 1930, when Rivera arrived in San Francisco to paint a mural for the stairwell of the Pacific Stock Exchange Social Club, the *San Francisco Chronicle* printed an illustration epitomizing what many feared would result if the foreign communist artist were allowed to realize the project. The *Chronicle's* illustration — captioned

49. *New Masses* (January 1929): 4.

50. *New Yorker* (10 November 1928): 105. The *New Yorker's* critic's use of the term "Proletcos" suggests that this cafeteria was also was known by that name, which emulates the anagram titles of Soviet organizations.

fig. 23
(right)
Diego Rivera, *Wall Street Banquet,* fresco, 1926. Court of the Fiestas, Secretaría de Educación Pública, Mexico City. Courtesy of El Instituto Nacional de Bellas Artes y Literatura.

fig. 24
(opposite page)
Hugo Gellert, *Us Fellas Gotta Stick Together (Last Defenses of Capitalism),* chalk on celotex and plaster, 217 x 125 cm, 1932. The Mitchell Wolfson Jr. Collection, The Wolfsonian–Florida International University, Miami Beach, Florida. Top row depicts, from left to right, President Herbert Hoover, J. P. Morgan, John D. Rockefeller Sr., Henry Ford, and Al Capone; at bottom right, Tom Mooney.

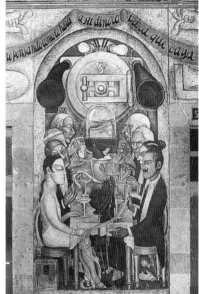

"Will Art be Touched in Pink?" — showed a photograph of the stock exchange stairwell, doctored to include a superimposed image of Rivera's 1926 fresco *Wall Street Banquet*, as if this were the image destined for the space. One of the most notorious of Rivera's works, *Wall Street Banquet* (fig. 23) featured caricatures of the famous American capitalists John D. Rockefeller Sr. (1839–1937), J. P. Morgan (1837–1913), and Henry Ford (1863–1947).[51] The accompanying article observed:

> And so the controversy rages! The artistic world as well as the leading financiers of San Francisco, are all waiting with great interest — and some with a bit of apprehension — to see what Rivera will produce when a Communist is called upon to decorate the walls of a temple of capitalism.[52]

When Rivera's mural was completed these fears were allayed. It contained no disrespectful portraits of prominent capitalists. As a result, the Communist Party was outraged. The following year, when Rivera was given a one-man retrospective at the Museum of Modern Art in New York, *New Masses* denounced him as a counter-revolutionary for "accepting commissions from the wealthy bourgeoisie he once so savagely caricatured."[53] Gellert joined in the attacks. He deemed it disgraceful that Rivera, who professed to be an artist for the working class, included no references in his San Francisco mural to Tom Mooney (1892–1942) and Warren Billings (1893–1972) — two anarchists who were arrested in that city for bombing a 1916 parade advocating United States intervention in World War I. To Gellert, an artist of Rivera's stature became complicit in the "Mooney-Billings frame-up" by not declaring its injustice.[54]

When Gellert was invited to participate in the Museum of Modern Art's May 1932 exhibition of *Murals by American Painters and Photographers,* he engaged the very same issues he faulted Rivera for ignoring. Moreover, he

51. From 1923 to 1928, Rivera decorated the walls on three levels of the Ministry of Education with scenes from the Mexican Revolution and scenes depicting his current sociopolitical concerns. Located on the third floor in the colonnaded Court of the Fiestas, *Wall Street Banquet* appears with a series of other images depicting the overindulgence of capitalists. These panels were contrasted with images of poverty and communist revolution.

52. *San Francisco Chronicle,* 25 September 1930.

53. Robert Evans [Joseph Freeman], "Painting and Politics, The Case of Diego Rivera," *New Masses* (February 1932): 25.

54. See Raquel Tibol, *Diego Rivera, Arte y Política* (Mexico City: Editorial Grijalbo, S.A., 1979), 436. I thank Lic. Raquel Tibol for bringing this to my attention.

fig. 25
(right)
William Gropper,
The Writing on the Wall,
1932 (lost). From *New
Masses*, June 1932.
Courtesy of Reference
Center for Marxist
Studies, New York, with
permission of the Estate
of William Gropper.

fig. 26
(far right)
Ben Shahn, *The Passion
of Sacco and Vanzetti*,
tempera on canvas,
215 x 122 cm, 1931–1932.
Collection of the Whitney
Museum of American Art,
New York, © Estate of
Ben Shahn/Licensed
by VAGA, New York.

fig. 27
(opposite page)
Hugo Gellert, *Us Fellas
Gotta Stick Together
(Last Defenses of
Capitalism)*, first
submission, chalk on
celotex and plaster,
126 x 216 cm, 1932.
The Mitchell Wolfson Jr.
Collection, The
Wolfsonian–Florida
International University,
Miami Beach, Florida.
Shown, from left to right,
President Herbert Hoover,
J. P. Morgan, John D.
Rockefeller Sr., Henry
Ford, and Al Capone.

used the opportunity to address anti-communist accusations that Russian artists did not have the creative freedom of their counterparts in the United States. To prove his point that there existed in America boundaries that artists could not transgress, Gellert submitted a work deliberately designed to offend some of the most powerful men in the country. His piece, *Us Fellas Gotta Stick Together (Last Defenses of Capitalism)*, generated controversy when it was rejected from the exhibition because of the insulting depictions of John D. Rockefeller Sr., J. P. Morgan, Henry Ford, and President Herbert Hoover (1874–1964) guarding bags of money (fig. 24). Also rejected were William Gropper's *The Writing on the Wall* (fig. 25) and Ben Shahn's (1898–1969) well-known *Passion of Sacco and Vanzetti* (fig. 26). Gellert's portable mural linked the most powerful figures of industry and government to the gangster Al Capone (1899–1947), who stands by their side. Beneath the capitalist/politician/criminal alliance, a Wild West lawman, soldiers, and uniformed police throw tear gas while standing over and guarding the jailed Tom Mooney. Its implications were clear: corrupt money bought the power to suppress dissent.

This version of Gellert's mural study was actually a reworking of his first submission, which depicted only the Hoover, Morgan, Rockefeller, Ford, and Capone figures (fig. 27). The original was rejected outright, ostensibly because the horizontal format did not conform to the rules of the exhibition specifying that each entry had to be seven feet high by four feet wide. Immediately after the first version was rejected, a museum representative contacted Gellert and suggested that he change not only the format, but also the subject matter. By willfully disregarding this suggestion and

reworking the same theme into a different format, Gellert deliberately set out to make the kind of trouble that the communists accused Rivera of avoiding. Gellert's mural study depicting capitalists with the spoils of their corrupt and exploitative system is a virtual quotation of Rivera's *Wall Street Banquet*. Helen Appleton Read, critic for the *Brooklyn Daily Eagle,* noticed the similarity:

> Rivera's and Orozco's invectives against capitalism painted on the walls of the Secretariat and the High School in Mexico City in which Morgan, Ford, and Rockefeller appear as symbols of the system, were probably regarded as artistic precedent for the unreasonable inclusions [55]

But the relationship to Rivera went deeper. In fact, the entire concept of the Museum of Modern Art's *Murals by American Painters and Photographers* exhibition developed directly from another scandal centered on the Mexican artist. *Murals by American Painters and Photographers* opened in May 1932. It was the inaugural exhibition at the museum's first home on West Fifty-third Street, following Rivera's enormously successful retrospective at the former space. During Rivera's exhibition, rumors began to circulate throughout the New York art world that he, along with the Spanish painter José Maria Sert (1876–1945), and the British painter Frank Brangwyn (1867–1956), had been commissioned to create murals in the newly completed Rockefeller Center complex. *Art Digest* reported:

> The rumor that the murals for Radio City, the Rockefeller project in the heart of New York, were to be commissioned to Rivera, Sert and other foreign artists has stirred [up] a tempest. Advocates of the "American Movement" broke into print with bitter attacks of alleged discrimination... others argued for an open competition.[56]

Gellert was by no means a supporter of the "American Movement," but he did advocate open competition. His June 1932 article in *New Masses* explained:

> Rockefeller Center with its huge wall spaces loomed big as a mural decoration possibility for many an artist. They awaited the completion of the buildings with impatient expectancy. Then came the news: these walls had been assigned without any competition... The architects of Rockefeller Center issued a statement denying that the contracts were assigned. Upon the heels of this upheaval, the Museum of Modern Art, of which Mrs. John D. Rockefeller Jr. is treasurer, invited artists to participate in an exhibition of mural decorations.[57]

55. Helen Appleton Read, "Mural Projects Shown at Modern Museum Fail to Reveal Potential Talent," *Brooklyn Daily Eagle,* 8 May 1932, Museum of Modern Art Archives, New York.

56. "The Mural Tempest," *Art Digest,* 15 February 1932.

57. Hugo Gellert, "We Capture the Walls," *New Masses* (June 1932): 29, in *Social Realism: Art as a Weapon,* ed. Shapiro, 39–41.

Indeed, the exhibition did seem to materialize as an afterthought to redress negative publicity. It allowed artists only six weeks to prepare their entries. The critic Henry McBride remarked in the *New York Sun* that the "wall painting experiment seems to have found artists unprepared."[58] In this context, the offensive nature of works by Gellert, Gropper, and Shahn can be seen as returning the slap in the face, which Rockefeller Center/Museum of Modern Art officials dealt to these less-established artists. There is evidence that this slap was felt keenly by the museum's administration. A. Conger Goodyear, president of the board of trustees, threatened to resign if these mural studies were included in the show. A few days before the exhibition was scheduled to open, the museum's board met in Goodyear's absence. They decided to include the offending paintings rather than face a scandal in the press, prompting the museum's director, Alfred Barr, to send Goodyear a telegram on 28 April, explaining:

> We have had ten days of hell over these pictures… the decision of [Samuel] Lewinson, [Stephen] Clark, and Nelson [Rockefeller] was made after the most careful consideration and after Mrs. Rock [Abby Aldrich Rockefeller]… agreed to leave them in… I implore you not to make a hasty decision but to talk with Mrs. Rock as well as Clark and Lewinson. Please keep this telegram confidential.[59]

Goodyear, no doubt, did keep the telegram confidential, but the day before the exhibition opened the story leaked to the press. On 2 May a headline in the *New York World* announced: "Insurgent Art Stirs Up Storm Among Society; Murals for Modern Museum Rejected as Offensive, Then Accepted, Linked Hoover to Al Capone." The article reported:

> The advisory committee of the museum, headed by Nelson Rockefeller, son of Mr. and Mrs. John D. Rockefeller Jr., took the part of the three artists whose work was at the center of the storm, while the majority of the more venerable trustees opposed hanging the murals.[60]

Abby Aldrich Rockefeller (1874–1948) was "understood to have maintained an attitude of neutrality." Gellert and Gropper both were quoted confirming "the existence of a controversy about their work":

> The tide was finally turned in their favor, they said, by a revolt among other artists invited to contribute murals. Soon after receiving the notices of rejection, they said, they told the others of their fate, and eight or ten declared that they also would withdraw, if the murals by Gellert, Gropper and a third by Shahn, dealing with the Sacco-Vanzetti case, were not hung.[61]

58. Henry McBride, *New York Sun*, 7 May 1932.

59. Alfred Barr, telegram to A. Conger Goodyear, 28 April 1932, Museum of Modern Art Archives, New York.

60. "Insurgent Art Stirs up Storm Among Society," *New York World Telegram*, 2 May 1932.

61. Ibid.

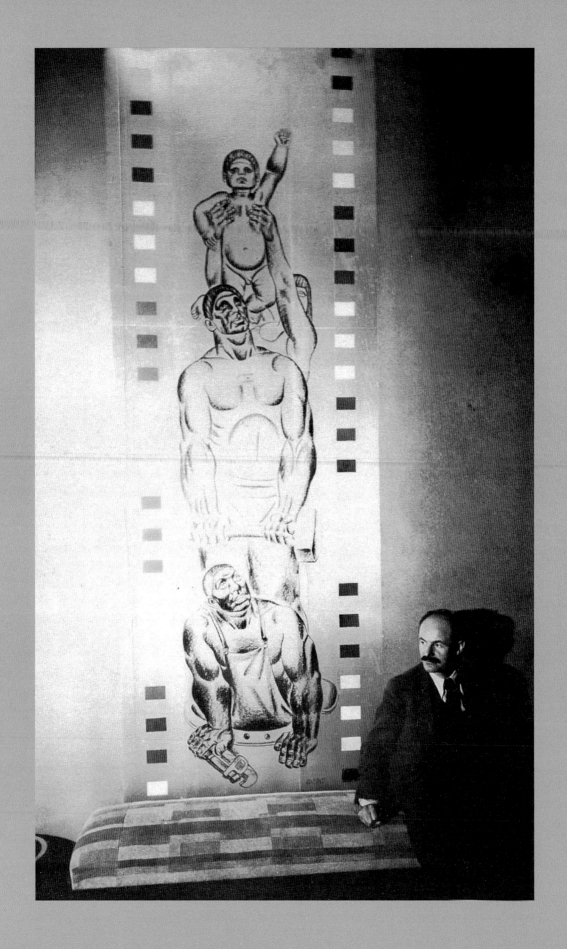

The "disagreeable" works by Gellert, Gropper, and Shahn were included in the exhibition; however, they were not photographed for the catalogue. In a decade known for politically based artistic groups, this incident set a precedent for American artists organizing against censorship. In addition, because Nelson (1908–1979) and Abby Aldrich Rockefeller did not actively oppose the inclusion of such militantly communist artworks in the museum that they sponsored, the incident demonstrated that the Rockefellers would tolerate, and even support, works of art that made damaging statements about capitalism, a system the Rockefeller family epitomized. Rivera certainly would have known about this controversy, if not from accounts in the press then from Ben Shahn, whose Sacco-Vanzetti paintings Rivera championed, and who was one of Rivera's assistants on his *Man at the Crossroads* fresco for Rockefeller Center. The fact that the Rockefeller family sided with Gellert, Gropper, and Shahn must have had some bearing on Rivera's decision to include the Lenin portrait in *Man at the Crossroads.*

The *Murals by American Painters and Photographers* exhibition was understood to be a forum for raising the profile of American muralists. One would assume that through the offensive nature of Gellert's submission, and through the scandal it caused, he would have essentially disqualified himself as a competitor for mural commissions. As Helen Appleton Read observed: "It suffices to say that the panels sent in by Gellert, Shahn… and Gropper had no place in an exhibition purporting to discover material with which to 'enrich the walls of modern buildings.'"[62]

Not everyone agreed. Shortly after the 1932 exhibition closed, Eugene Schoen (1880–1957), an interior designer hired by the Rockefeller Center Corporation, contacted Gellert. Schoen informed the artist that Wallace Harrison (1895–1981), one of the Center's architects, had been impressed by Gellert's Union Square cafeteria mural and wanted him to paint a mural for the Center Theater, a cinema within the Rockefeller Center complex. The choice seems surprising in light of the events at the Museum of Modern Art, and nobody was more astonished by it than Gellert himself. However, because of his cafeteria mural, Gellert was still recognized as a leading modern muralist at the time, despite the controversy.[63] Furthermore, Schoen's original concept for the Center Theater project involved portraits of leading movie stars. Gellert was well known for the modernist, graphic portraits he drew for the *New Yorker*, the *Daily World*, *Pearson's,* and other journals of the day. The movie star concept was eventually abandoned. Instead, Gellert used the motif of a filmstrip, complete with sprocketed edges that emerged from the floor, went across the ceiling,

62. Read, "Mural Projects."

63. According to the *New York Times*, Gellert had "an important mural commission, already executed, to speak for him. The walls of the Workers' Cafeteria in Union Square were decorated some four years ago with designs in Gellert's simple, dynamic style." See "Mural Projects on View at Decora Gallery," *New York Times*, 13 March 1932, 4.

fig. 29
Hugo Gellert, *Workers of All Lands Unite!,* **litho-graph, 58 x 39 cm, 1933. Frontispiece from** *Karl Marx Capital in Pictures,* **edition 133. The Mitchell Wolfson Jr. Collection, The Wolfsonian–Florida International University, Miami Beach, Florida. Photograph by Silvia Ros.**

and down the opposite wall (fig. 28). Developing the theme "man the builder," Gellert depicted laborers with building tools on the two side walls. On the ceiling, he recalled, "there was a moon, which looked like a silver dollar. To the moon was tied a man, his hands tied behind him with ticker tape." Another man reached for one of the large red stars that dominated the background. Because of the hidden subversive message, cultural critic Lewis Mumford compared Gellert's mural to "the Aztec idols the Indian workman used to hide under the altars of the Christian churches in Mexico."[64] Unlike Rivera's *Man at the Crossroads* mural, Gellert's less-prominent work survived for a number of years before it was destroyed in the late 1940s, when the Center Theater was torn down. By the time Rivera's Rockefeller Center mural was threatened with destruction in 1934, Gellert had acquired a certain expertise in exploiting controversial situations. Despite the fact that a few months earlier he had joined in the denunciations of Rivera, Gellert now led the protests against "Rockefeller vandalism," speaking out through the Artists' Committee of Action, the organization he co-founded, in part, to protest the destruction.

64. Gellert's description of the Center Theater mural from Hugo Gellert, interview by Sofia Sequenzia, 1981, audiotape, Gellert Papers, AAA. For Mumford, see Robert Wojtowicz, ed., *Sidewalk Critic: Lewis Mumford's Writings on New York* (New York: Princeton Architectural Press, 1998), 92.

fig. 30
(right)
Hugo Gellert, untitled
lithograph, 58 x 39 cm,
1933. From *Karl Marx
Capital in Pictures,*
edition 133. The Mitchell
Wolfson Jr. Collection,
The Wolfsonian–Florida
International University,
Miami Beach, Florida.
Photograph by Silvia Ros.

fig. 31
(center, right)
Hugo Gellert, untitled
lithograph, 58 x 39 cm,
1933. From *Karl Marx
Capital in Pictures,*
edition 133. The Mitchell
Wolfson Jr. Collection,
The Wolfsonian–Florida
International University,
Miami Beach, Florida.
Photograph by Silvia Ros.

fig. 32
(below, right)
Hugo Gellert, untitled
lithograph, 58 x 39 cm,
1933. From *Karl Marx
Capital in Pictures,*
edition 133. The Mitchell
Wolfson Jr. Collection,
The Wolfsonian–Florida
International University,
Miami Beach, Florida.
Photograph by Silvia Ros.

Also in the early 1930s, Gellert turned to printmaking, exploring themes consistent with his murals. On a technical level, his graphic style lent itself to lithography. On a theoretical level, Gellert's prime concern was to make communist dogma accessible. Printmaking was an important means to realize these ends. Where illustrations in magazines and posters displayed in the streets are ephemeral, and murals can only be experienced *in situ,* editioned prints, through their numbers and archival qualities, are ubiquitous and indelible. They can be easily disseminated, exhibited simultaneously in multiple locations, and preserved in libraries and museums. Prints allowed Gellert to create a portable, organized, permanent record of many of the images he explored in other media. For the frontispiece of the 1933 portfolio *Karl Marx Capital in Pictures,* for example, Gellert reworked *Us Fellas Gotta Stick Together* to create *Workers of All Lands Unite!* (fig. 29). Though Hoover and Capone no longer appear, and another figure was added to the lower register, the image still makes the point that America does not adhere to the ideals of democracy. Capitalism ensured that the rich would remain in control, and for this system to thrive it needed to suppress threatening forces.

Through the portfolio format, Gellert was able to work with text in series. Individually, each print makes a direct statement. As a group, the prints can be read in relation to the text and to each other. In *Capital,* Gellert first presents conditions under capitalism. Henry Ford can lock out his workers should they demand more pay or fewer work hours. But if the labor force organizes through a strong union, they can eventually achieve the ultimate goal, control of the means of production (figs. 30–32). This positive message in a publication that did not pander to the needs of an unsympathetic patron set the tone for Gellert's art-related activism later in the decade.

Art in America underwent an intense transformation during the 1930s. A relatively small movement toward the left by politically radical artists in the 1920s prevailed as a unifying factor among artists when the Popular Front Against Fascism was announced at the Seventh Congress of the Communist International in August 1935. Through this political and cultural initiative — intended to amass support under the growing Nazi threat — the Communist Party began to court relations with the liberals, intellectuals, and socialists it had once denounced. Because Gellert's development as a young artist during the 1910s and 1920s coincided with the development of the Communist Party in America, he became a seminal figure in many of the significant events that characterized American art during the turbulent 1930s. Gellert was a founding member of the John Reed Club, the communist group that strove "to give [the revolutionary workers' movement] in the arts and letters greater scope and force, to bring it closer to the daily struggle of the workers."[65] He was a fundamental co-organizer of The Artists' Committee of Action and The Artists' Union. These two pivotal institutions united artists around interrelated problems of private patronage and censorship, greatly contributing to the instigation of the federally funded Works Progress Administration (WPA) art programs. He served on the editorial committee of *Art Front*, the Artists' Union's official publication. Gellert helped arrange the American Artists' Congress of 1936, at which he presented the paper "Fascism, War, and the Artist", he spoke at the second Congress in 1937 as well. That same year Gellert became involved with the Artists' Coordination Committee for the National Exhibition of Contemporary American Art at the 1939 New York World's Fair. Not only did he paint a mural for the fair (now lost), but he also oversaw the formation of a labor union to protect the rights of muralists and their assistants.[66]

Hugo Gellert contributed to the diversity of American art during the early twentieth century. His interpretation of modernism was informed by the Hungarian idiom, American leftist cartoons, and by Soviet art, all channeled through communist ideology. For Gellert, communism offered a program for the betterment of mankind, and the function of art was to serve the communist cause. Gellert distrusted the American government because of the circumstances surrounding the loss of his brother, the influence of big business on public policy, the ill treatment of minorities, and the persecution of leftists. This distrust allowed him to dismiss as hostile propaganda all negative reports about the Soviet Union. Though the Nazi-Soviet Non-Aggression Pact in 1939 ended the Popular Front,

65. "Draft Manifesto of the John Reed Club," *New Masses* (June 1932): 14, in *Social Realism: Art as a Weapon*, ed. Shapiro, 42–46.

66. That labor union was Local 829, Mural Artists Guild of the United Scenic Artists, AFL-CIO. Gellert, interview by Sequenzia, Gellert Papers, AAA.

Gellert remained passionate and unswerving in his commitment to the Communist Party until his death in 1985. He adamantly defended communism as the only system that could offer justice for the repressed classes. In his art and in his life Gellert continued to work toward that goal, despite the hardships of the more conservative eras. As he frankly admitted:

> It was not always easy to abide by my decision. It had to be reaffirmed again and again. But I never regretted having made it. I believe I have done as well as most artists and have had much more fun. I had the satisfaction of being myself. [67] ✧

Acknowledgments
The following individuals and institutions have been extremely helpful in uncovering some of the long-buried material in this paper. For their generous help in facilitating my research, I thank Andrew Lee, librarian at the Tamiment Institute Library; Lynne Farrington, curator of printed books at the Annenberg Rare Book and Manuscript Library of the University of Pennsylvania; Mark Rosenzweig, chief librarian and archivist of the Reference Center for Marxist Studies, New York City; Mary Ryan Gallery, New York City; Judy Throm of the Archives of American Art, Washington, D.C.; and Dr. Marlene Park. I would not have been successful in locating many of my sources in Budapest without the help of architectural historian Dr. Sam Albert; Dr. József Sisa of the Institute of Art History at the Hungarian Academy of Sciences, Budapest; Dr. István Ihász, director of the Department of Recent History, Hungarian National Museum, Budapest; Zoltán Viszket, archivist, National Archives of Hungary, Budapest; and Eríka Pállfy, my research assistant, translator, and guide to the city of Budapest. My exploration of the connections with Mexican art was enhanced by the generous contributions of Lic. Antonio Saborit of the Instituto Nacional de Arte y Historia, Mexico City; and Lic. Raquel Tibol; by the assistance of Denise Muñoz and Itzel Vargas of the Instituto Nacional de Bellas Artes, Mexico City; and by the guidance of Dr. Edward Sullivan of New York University. For permitting me to reproduce the work of William Gropper and Louis Lozowick, I am grateful to Gene Gropper and the late Adele Lozowick. Guest Editor Joel Hoffman, and Wolfsonian staff responsible for *The Journal of Decorative and Propaganda Arts,* Jacqueline Crucet, Maria Gonzalez, and Leslie Sternlieb, deserve special thanks for their keen eyes and sound editorial advice. I am appreciative to Kimberly J. Bergen and Claudia Mendoza of the Wolfsonian registration department as well as photographer Silvia Ros for producing images of works in the Wolfsonian collection. Finally, like all scholars researching the interface of art with sociopolitical movements during the Modern period, I am indebted to Mitchell Wolfson Jr. for enthusiastically accumulating the valuable material preserved in The Wolfsonian–FIU.

67. Hugo Gellert, unpublished draft of speech, Gellert Papers, AAA.

Erika Doss

Looking at Labor: Images of Work in 1930s American Art

Erika Doss is professor of art history in the Department of Fine Arts at the University of Colorado, Boulder, where she is also director of the American Studies Program. She is the author of numerous articles and books on American art, including *Benton, Pollock, and the Politics of Modernism* (1991); *Spirit Poles and Flying Pigs* (1995); and *Elvis Culture* (1999). She conducted research for this essay as a Wolfsonian Fellow in 1995.

> I am the people — the mob — the crowd — the mass. Do you know that all the great work of the world is done through me? I am the working man, the inventor; the maker of the world's food and clothes.
> Carl Sandburg, *The People, Yes* (1936)

In 1997, design historian Victor Margolin remarked that a substantial majority of The Mitchell Wolfson Jr. Collection pertains to a time in European and American history "when the forces of nation-building were coalescing in strong cultural expressions of national identity" and "the idea of propaganda was defined through massive government-controlled campaigns of persuasion."[1] Preeminent among those nationalistic and propagandistic cultural expressions was an emphasis on labor and human productivity, and among The Wolfsonian's extensive collection of early modern and twentieth-century American paintings, sculptures, posters, prints, photographs, and decorative arts is a large number of images and objects focusing on work and workers. Paying special attention to the Wolfsonian collection, this essay considers how and why labor was visualized by American artists during the 1930s, the decade of the Great Depression.

Examples include Seymour Fogel's (1911–1984) *The Wealth of the Nation*, a color study for the 1941 mural *Industrial Life* (fig. 1). Fogel's mural was one of two panels commissioned by the Treasury Section of Fine Arts (the Section), a New Deal program established in 1934 to provide art for new federal buildings. It was painted for the interior lobby of the Social Security Board Building (now the Wilbur J. Cohen Federal Building) in

Detail of Dean Cornwell's Work for America!, 1918.

1. Victor Margolin, "Micky Wolfson's Cabinet of Wonders: From Private Passion to Public Purpose," *Design Issues* 13 (Spring 1997): 68.

232

fig. 1
Seymour Fogel,
The Wealth of the Nation,
study for the Section of
Fine Arts mural
competition for the Social
Security Board Building,
Washington, D.C., tempera
on paper, 23 x 33 cm,
1938. The Mitchell
Wolfson Jr. Collection,
The Wolfsonian–Florida
International University,
Miami Beach, Florida.

Washington, D.C.[2] In a December 1940 letter to Edward Rowan, who administered the Section's mural program, Fogel explained his "use of symbolic figures and objects" in *The Wealth of the Nation* and several other studies he rendered in preparation for the mural:

> The general theme of the sketches is built around forces that make for national security. The left panel is devoted to construction, industry, and scientific research. The driller [here depicted as two blue-collar workers] on the right carries the attendant ideas of building and growth. The scientist on the left with his microscope and test tubes suggests new frontiers for research both in pure science and in medicine. The large wheels in the center symbolize tremendous industrial power, while the man at the switch shows him to be in complete control.[3]

Fogel redesigned some portions of his color sketches for the final mural panels (changing the scientist on the far left of *The Wealth of the Nation,*

2. Some 375 artists competed for the Social Security Board Building murals, and commissions were awarded to Ben Shahn (to decorate the main corridor of the building), Philip Guston (for a three-panel mural in the auditorium), and Seymour Fogel. The latter developed several sets of color studies for his mural panels, including a pair in The Wolfsonian's collection and a pair, on extended loan from the Smithsonian American Art Museum, in the collection of the University of Maryland Art Gallery. The studies in The Wolfsonian are signed "Fogel 1938," indicating that he either signed the work later in his life and did not accurately remember the date, or he had originally intended them for another competition. See "Shahn Best of 375," *Art Digest* 15 (15 November 1940): 8; and Viriginia Mecklenburg, *The Public as Patron: A History of the Treasury Department Mural Program* (College Park, Md.: University of Maryland, Department of Art, 1979), 61–62.

3. Noted in Mecklenburg, *The Public as Patron,* 62.

for example, from a gray-haired figure to a younger man). But he retained his original emphasis on the links between labor, productivity, and "national security." Such themes acquired heightened symbolic significance during the years of the Great Depression (1929–1941), when widespread unemployment and an increasingly militant labor movement gripped the country. As historian Barbara Melosh remarks, Fogel's studies and his final mural panel intimated that "work is mastery, the vehicle to the planned future" imagined by President Franklin Delano Roosevelt and his New Deal advisors during the 1930s. "The drafting triangle, designers' compass, and laboratory apparatus are the tools and emblems of progress, wielded by men joined in the common labor of planning and building" a better American future, or at least one far removed from the exigencies of the Great Depression.[4]

Notions of work, and those of a moralizing work ethic, have been seminal to American understandings of self and national identity from seventeenth-century colonization to the present day. "Men are not valued in this country, or in any country, for what they *are*; they are valued for what they do," abolitionist Frederick Douglass remarked in 1853.[5] Work not only has a symbiotic relationship with the ideology of consumerism that characterizes the modern capitalist economy of the United States, but is central to American understandings of social standing, prestige, and self-esteem. Further, Americans have long tended to value work as a "calling," as a "practical ideal of activity and character" that is "morally inseparable" from their personal lives and that links individuals with the larger community of the United States.[6] As historian Daniel T. Rodgers argues, work has repeatedly been affirmed "as the core of the moral life" of the nation. Even as the nature of work was "radically remade" in the shift from a preindustrial economy of independent producers and skilled artisans (farmers, craftsmen, and merchants) to the mid-nineteenth-century burgeoning of a factory system composed of wage labor and capitalists, "the equation of work and virtue continued to pervade the nation's thinking."[7]

Yet, as crucial as work and the work ethic have been throughout the history of the United States, workers and specifically the American working class have been much more conflicted subjects. This was particularly true in the century following the Civil War—when the shifts from an agrarian to an industrial economy, and from local economies to a national market, were especially pronounced; when Karl Marx's arguments regarding the

4. Barbara Melosh, *Engendering Culture: Manhood and Womanhood in New Deal Public Art and Theater* (Washington, D.C.: Smithsonian Institution Press, 1991), 88–89.

5. Frederick Douglass, "Free Blacks Must Learn Trades," in *Frederick Douglass: The Narrative and Selected Writings,* ed. Michael Meyer (New York: Modern Library, 1984), 350.

6. Robert N. Bellah et al., *Habits of the Heart, Individualism and Commitment in American Life* (Berkeley: University of California Press, 1985), 66.

7. Daniel T. Rodgers, *The Work Ethic in Industrial America 1850–1920* (Chicago: The University of Chicago Press, 1974), xi–xiii.

fig. 2
Leo Raiken, *Rock Quarry*,
study for the Section
of Fine Arts mural
competition for the U.S.
Post Office, Westerly,
Rhode Island, oil on
canvas, 173 x 373 cm,
1939. The Mitchell
Wolfson Jr. Collection,
The Wolfsonian–Florida
International University,
Miami Beach, Florida.

economic and cultural value of workers and the inevitability of proletarian revolution were increasingly well known; and when distinct racial and gender divisions favoring white males were reinforced. Struggles over the definition and identity of industrial laborers—viewed either as independent and autonomous producers or as economic "hirelings" and wage slaves—greatly accelerated in the 1860s and 1870s. At this time American workers developed new and powerful labor organizations that aimed for living wages, better working conditions, and union recognition, and that linked labor with such tenets as equality, mutuality, and collectivity. Industrialists and business leaders fought back, angling for control of the nation's economy and its political directions with their own ideas about labor and the laboring classes, which centered on consumerism, marketplace supply and demand, and "the philosophies of laissez-faire and Social Darwinism."[8] As industrial capitalism further evolved in the late nineteenth and early twentieth centuries, tensions between labor and big business escalated, placing great strain on an idealized American work ethic—and on work itself.

Cultural anxieties about work and conflicted understandings of the working class are especially evident in the many representations of labor and laboring bodies produced during the Great Depression. Fogel's *The Wealth of the Nation,* for example, while seemingly an uncomplicated, if metaphorical, view of the significance of work in terms of "national security," posits a hierarchy of labor along class and gender lines. No women are seen in Fogel's picture. As Melosh explains, industrial labor was "manly" work, and women's work in 1930s art was generally relegated to depictions of family, farm, and fertility.[9] But the types of men and "manly" workers that Fogel chose to depict are highly revealing. The lab technician on the far

8. Bruce Levine et al., *Who Built America? Working People and the Nation's Economy, Politics, Culture, and Society* (New York: Pantheon Books, 1989), 560.

9. Melosh, *Engendering Culture*, 83–109 and passim.

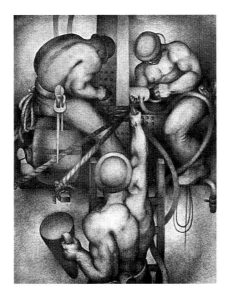

left and the engineer in the center of the panel, for example, are both white-collar professionals engaged in research and planning, whereas the muscular, shirtless guy in the back manning the switches and the pair on the far right preparing to follow orders are evidently blue-collar workers. Strong and brawny, these working-class males are icons of productivity and virility. Dressed in blue overalls or work pants, they are also spectacles of visual pleasure. Unlike the scientist and engineer, their faces are turned away from the viewer, thus making them anonymous, and ambiguous, laboring bodies.

Historian Michael Denning argues that during the 1930s there was a "laboring of American culture."[10] Popular and political references to laborers and the labor movement were common throughout the decade, as were terms such as work, industry, and toil. Working-class Americans assumed an increasing presence in culture and the arts—almost one-third of the artists who worked on New Deal art projects were from working-class backgrounds—and culture itself came to be seen in industrial terms: as product and production. This cultural laboring was not, however, seamless, nor was it without its own inherent tensions and conflicts. Fogel's bifurcated, all-male labor force, which opposed the professional-class experts of the New Deal's imagined national future with the eroticized and objectified bodies of working-class men, suggests the fracturing, rather than collectivity, of 1930s labor. Nor was Fogel's view atypical. Recurrent scenes reinforcing the difference between white- and blue-collar male workers (fig. 2), relying on symbolic (and stereotypical) images of "manly" workers (fig. 3), and depicting working men as eroticized objects of desire (fig. 4) reveal the degree to which 1930s visual culture embodied acute anxiety about the

10. Michael Denning, *The Cultural Front: The Laboring of American Culture in the Twentieth Century* (New York: Verso, 1996), xvii and passim.

changing nature of work and the meaning of the American working class. Such anxiety hinged, of course, on the economic crisis that enveloped the era, but it stemmed from longstanding and largely unresolved tensions regarding class, masculinity, and American identity that especially flourished during the Great Depression.

Prior to the 1930s, most American artists tended to avoid the subjects of work and labor. Although nineteenth-century artists were keenly interested in shaping and directing a distinct national culture, their most common visual trope was the American landscape, not the nation's burgeoning industrialism. On the one hand, industrial scenes were not uniquely American—the Industrial Revolution had swept throughout the entire Western world in the nineteenth century. On the other hand, serious artistic attention to wage labor would have forced painters, patrons, and audiences to reckon with issues of class, race, gender, and ethnicity, and thereby critically confront the myths of American independence and egalitarianism. Generally, terms such as "art," "culture," and "industry" shifted in meaning during the Gilded Age of the late nineteenth and early twentieth centuries. "Art" became synonymous with the fine arts of poetry and painting, "culture" with intellectual and artistic activity, and "industry" with factory production.[11] Art and industry were thought to occupy separate spheres, and artists, as the producers and guardians of culture, were generally expected to paint picturesque views of nature, not the slag heaps and working stiffs of manufacturing.

There were exceptions, of course, such as Robert Koehler (1850–1917), whose working-class background and sympathies were visualized in such nineteenth-century paintings as *The Socialist* (1885), apparently a portrait of his father, and *The Strike* (1886), a scene of labor struggle in Pittsburgh in 1877. Yet when most Gilded Age artists depicted industrial labor, they did so on romantic and allegorical terms, allied with the social and political objectives of their corporate, capitalist patrons. Such public sculptures and paintings glossed over the grueling contemporary realities of mass production by extolling preindustrial, artisanal notions of work and the work ethic, by idealizing their patrons, and by eroticizing working-class bodies. Consider, for example, John White Alexander's (1856–1915) mural cycle *The Apotheosis of Pittsburgh* (1905–1908), commissioned by Andrew Carnegie for the Carnegie Institute, and which included at its center a portrait of Carnegie as a knight in black armor. Or Douglas Tilden's (1860–1935) San Francisco sculpture, *Mechanics Fountain* (1901), made for industrialist Peter Donahue, depicting workers

11. Raymond Williams, *Keywords: A Vocabulary of Culture and Society* (New York: Oxford University Press, 1983).

in only leather aprons and skimpy loincloths.[12] Rarely, in fact, was labor even shown laboring. In Alexander's mural and in such paintings as Thomas Anshutz's (1851–1912) *The Ironworkers' Noontime* (1880–1881), the worker was depicted at leisure or posing beside his tools, a *symbol* of strength and productivity rather than a living, human force.[13]

Intractable to fine artists, industry became the purview of illustrators, whose wood engravings and lithographs helped promote the concerns of big business and focused on scenes of industrial architecture. Printmaker Joseph Pennell (1857–1926), for example, was awed by the dynamism of modern industry and produced hundreds of engravings that likened factories to cathedrals and almost entirely excluded the body of labor. Although in the 1880s he found no takers for a proposed illustrated study he called "The Picturesque Possibilities of Work," in 1916 he published *Wonder of Work,* a collection of highly expressive and celebratory illustrations of American foundries and steel mills. Disavowing any Progressive Era political or social intentions, Pennell remarked: "I am simply an artist searching for the Wonder of Work—not for morals—political economy—stories of sweating—the crime of ugliness. I am trying to record the Wonder of Work as I see it, that is all."[14]

Likewise, the Precisionist artists of the 1920s were far more attentive to the atmospheric effects of smoky factories and the compelling designs of modern industrial architecture than to the dehumanizing effects of industrial labor. They generally eschewed the assembly lines and other timesaving strategies extolled in efficiency expert Frederick Winslow Taylor's 1911 *Principles of Scientific Management,* the bible of mass-production industry. Paintings such as *Factory* (c. 1920) by Preston Dickinson (1889–1930), *Pittsburgh* (1927) by Elsie Driggs (1898–1992), and *My Egypt* (1927) by Charles Demuth (1883–1935), celebrated the order and beauty of modern American factories and grain elevators with little or no reflection on the human and environmental consequences (fig. 5). Similarly, interwar artists such as Louis Lozowick (1892–1973) exalted the functional geometry, dynamism, and efficiency of the machine (fig. 6). "The history of America is a history of gigantic engineering feats

12. Melissa Dabakis, *Visualizing Labor in American Sculpture: Monuments, Manliness, and the Work Ethic, 1880–1935* (Cambridge and New York: Cambridge University Press, 1999), 83–104; Janet C. Marstine, "Working History: Images of Labor and Industry in American Mural Painting, 1893–1903" (Ph.D. diss., University of Pittsburgh, 1993), ii–iv and passim; and Sarah J. Moore, "Constructing Cohesion on the Backs of Men: John White Alexander's Murals at the Carnegie Institute, 1905–08," in *Returning the Gaze,* eds. William Cowling et al. (Bloomington, Ind.: Indiana University Press, forthcoming 2002).

13. On Anshutz's painting, see Thomas H. Pauly, "American Art and Labor: The Case of Anshutz's *The Ironworkers' Noontime,*" *American Quarterly* 40 (September 1988): 333–358; and Randall C. Griffin, "Thomas Anshutz's *The Ironworkers' Noontime:* Remythologizing the Industrial Worker," *Smithsonian Studies in American Art* 4 (Summer/Fall 1990): 129–143.

14. Joseph Pennell, *The Wonder of Work* (1916), plate VIII, as noted in Anne Cannon Palumbo, "The Cathedral and the Factory: The Transformation of Work in the Art of Joseph Pennell," *The Journal of the Society for Industrial Archaeology* 12 (1986): 39–50.

fig. 6
(above)
Louis Lozowick, *Butte,*
oil on canvas, 76 x 56 cm,
1926–1927. Hirshhorn
Museum and Sculpture
Garden, Smithsonian
Institution. Gift of
Joseph H. Hirshhorn,
1966. Photograph by
Lee Stalsworth.

fig. 7
(above, far right)
Dean Cornwell, *Work for
America!,* oil on paper,
wood panel, 91 x 64 cm,
1918. The Mitchell
Wolfson Jr. Collection,
The Wolfsonian–Florida
International University,
Miami Beach, Florida.
Photograph by Silvia Ros.

and colossal mechanical construction," Lozowick remarked in "The Americanization of Art," an essay written for the 1927 *Machine-Age Exposition* held in New York. "The skyscrapers of New York, the grain elevators of Minneapolis, the steel mills of Pittsburgh, the oil wells of Oklahoma, the copper mines of Butte, the lumber yards of Seattle give the American cultural epic in its diapason," not the workforce — and no human beings appear in the series of paintings that Lozowick made in the mid- to late 1920s, based on these and other industrial cities.[15]

Labor was not entirely absent in American visual culture of the early twentieth century. If largely avoided in art, laborers did appear in popular culture. There were wartime propaganda paintings such as the 1918 *Work for America!,* in which illustrator Dean Cornwell (1892–1960) positioned a bare-chested "manly worker" in front of smoky factories, sturdy warships, and endless lines of ready-for-action infantry (fig. 7). Laborers also appeared in advertisements such as *Visit "The Workshop of America" by South Shore Line,* a brightly colored travel poster of 1926 that encouraged tours of Chicago's foundries and factories via regional railroads, with its imaging of two hardy steelworkers hammering away at a forge and below them, the plated "workshop" of Chicago

15. Louis Lozowick, "The Americanization of Art," in *Machine-Age Exposition,* ed. Jane Heap (New York: 1927), excerpted in Patricia Hills, *Modern Art in the USA: Issues and Controversies of the 20th Century* (Upper Saddle River, N.J.: Prentice Hall, 2001), 48–50.

fig. 8
(above)
Otto Brennemann,
Visit "The Workshop of America" by South Shore Line, chromolithograph,
109 x 76 cm, 1926.
The Mitchell Wolfson Jr.
Collection, The
Wolfsonian–Florida
International University,
Miami Beach, Florida.
Photograph by Silvia Ros.

fig. 9
(above, far right)
Clare Veronica Hope
Leighton, *New York Breadline*, wood engraving,
38 x 25 cm, c. 1932.
The Mitchell Wolfson Jr.
Collection, The
Wolfsonian–Florida
International University,
Miami Beach, Florida.
Photograph by
Bruce White.

industry (fig. 8). In such commercial illustrations labor was an abstracted symbol subordinated to larger causes: the war effort, the triumph of corporate capitalism.

Only with the advent of radical left magazines like *The Masses* (1911–1917), *The Liberator* (1918–1924), and *New Masses* (first published in 1926), were working-class subjects regularly visualized by artists and cartoonists who sympathized with working-class causes, including John Sloan, Robert Minor, Boardman Robinson, Art Young, George Bellows, Stuart Davis, and Hugo Gellert (1892–1985).[16] Yet their Social Realist views of labor were no less symbolic than those of John White Alexander or Dean Cornwell, and were often couched in equally simplistic and stereotypical styles and idealizing subjects. Some radical left artists drew on the social protest sensibility and sketchy graphics style of nineteenth-century French realists such as Honoré Daumier (1808–1879), typecasting labor as either the alienated victim of industrial oppression or as an icon of resistance. Sloan's *Ludlow, Colorado*, for example, which was featured on the cover of *The Masses* in June 1914, distilled a fifteen-month battle between coal miners and the Colorado Fuel and Iron Company to the image

16. Rebecca Zurier, *Art for The Masses: A Radical Magazine and Its Graphics, 1911–1917* (Philadelphia: Temple University Press, 1988), xvii and passim.

fig. 10
Reginald Marsh, *The Park Bench*, tempera on masonite mounted on panel, 61 x 91 cm, 1933. Sheldon Memorial Art Gallery and Sculpture Garden, NAA–Nebraska Art Association.

of a defiant, gun-wielding miner. Other Social Realist artists followed nineteenth-century, preindustrial conventions, casting labor on heroic, productive, and virile terms and commemorating the moral values of the work ethic.

For many artists and intellectuals, the 1930s were marked by nagging imperatives to reinvent labor imagery, to propose alternative representations of work and the working class that adequately embodied the changed circumstances of mass production within the realm of modern American art. Yet the manifestation of these ideals was fraught with complications. During the 1920s labor was visualized in terms of skyscrapers and factories; during the Great Depression many American artists shifted gears. With industry shutdowns and a dramatic slump in urban construction (by 1932, steel plants operated at only twelve percent of capacity and industrial construction had dropped from $949 million to seventy-four million dollars), Precisionist images of smoking factories and towering skyscrapers were no longer viable American icons. Because work was celebrated as the single most important factor in reviving the American economy, many 1930s artists turned to representations of the body of labor, albeit often on conflicted and contradictory terms that wavered between alienating victimization and hero worship.

Loss of work and financial destitution were repeated themes in the work of many depression-era Social Realists. Unemployment rose from 3.2 percent in 1929 to 24.9 percent in 1933, when one in four workers (thirteen million Americans) was out of a job. Those who were employed saw their wages drop forty to sixty percent. Many spent their days idly; others were forced to sell apples on street corners or to feed themselves in charity-organized food lines, as captured in Clare Leighton's (1898–1989) print of c. 1932, *New York Breadline* (fig. 9), its indigent subjects hunched beneath the skyscrapers of an elusive prosperity. Reginald Marsh (1898–1954) captured the resignation and stasis of the early 1930s in *The Park Bench*, which features black, white, male, female, and upper- and lower-class Americans crowded together in an urban park, awaiting the end of the Great Depression (fig. 10). "Go out into the street, stare at people. Go into the subway, stare at people… Lassitude, born of too little to eat, nothing to do and no place to go afflicts the occupants of *The Park Bench*," Marsh remarked.[17]

DAPA 24

17. *East Side, West Side, All Around the Town: A Retrospective Exhibition of Paintings, Watercolors, and Drawings by Reginald Marsh* (Tucson: University of Arizona Museum of Art, 1969).

fig. 11
(right)
Lewis Rubenstein,
Washington Bonus March,
watercolor on paper,
18 x 36 cm, 1932. The
Mitchell Wolfson Jr.
Collection, The
Wolfsonian–Florida
International University,
Miami Beach, Florida.
Photograph by Silvia Ros.

fig. 12
(below)
Paul Weller, *Scab,* oil on
masonite, 71 x 91 cm,
c. 1935. The Mitchell
Wolfson Jr. Collection,
The Wolfsonian–Florida
International University,
Miami Beach, Florida.

Yet anger and protest were also very much present in 1930s America, and socially and politically conscious artists ranging in stylistic diversity from Minna Citron (1896–1991) and Lewis Rubenstein (b. 1908) to Paul Weller (b. 1912), Anton Refregier (1905–1979), and Hugo Gellert were attentive to the era's general strikes, labor slowdowns, and calls to action. Rubenstein's 1932 watercolor *Washington Bonus March* depicts the scene when twenty thousand unemployed veterans marched on the nation's capital and demanded payment of promised World War I service bonuses (fig. 11). Weller's c. 1935 painting *Scab* shows striking coal miners humiliating a worker crossing the picket line (fig. 12). Refregier's *San Francisco '34 Waterfront Strike* (c. 1947)—a serigraph version of the mural entitled *The Waterfront–1934,* done for the Rincon Post Office in San Francisco, narrates California's history of labor strife. The words "STRIKE WON," printed in bold on the lower right, reference the success of organized labor (fig. 13).[18]

Similarly, Minna Citron's 1937 painting *Strike News* centers on seven factory workers reading about the impact of their industrial shutdown in a newspaper announcement (fig. 14). In a print of the same title, composition,

and year, she included the newspaper headlines "STRIKE CLOSES MILL" and "CIO," referencing the Congress of Industrial Organizations that formed in the 1930s and waged the nationwide offensive of union recognition and representation. And Hugo Gellert's many illustrations for *New Masses,*

18. Harry L. Katz, ed., *Life of the People: Realist Prints and Drawings from the Ben and Beatrice Goldstein Collection, 1912–1948* (Washington, D.C.: Library of Congress, 1999), 62–63.

**fig. 13
(above)
Anton Refregier, *San Francisco '34 Waterfront Strike,* serigraph, 46 x 71 cm, c. 1947. The Mitchell Wolfson Jr. Collection, The Wolfsonian–Florida International University, Miami Beach, Florida. Photograph by Silvia Ros.**

**fig. 14
(below)
Minna Citron, *Strike News,* oil on canvas, 64 x 76 cm, 1937. The Mitchell Wolfson Jr. Collection, The Wolfsonian–Florida International University, Miami Beach, Florida.**

The Liberator, and *Art Front* (the house organ of the 1930s John Reed Clubs, named after the journalist and founder of the American Communist Party), and for books such as *Karl Marx' 'Capital' in Lithographs* (1934), repeatedly focused on the working-class struggle.[19]

Social Realism has typically and somewhat simplistically been understood as an anti-modernist form of "documentary expression." Yet many of its 1930s practitioners crafted alternative, symbolist, and clearly modernist aesthetics that were far removed from traditional conventions of representational (or "realist") art. Fusing avant-garde art styles and strategies (especially figurative or dreamlike Surrealism and montage) with the particular subjects of depression-era social and political crisis, "social surrealists" such

as Luigi Guglielmi (1906–1956), Walter Quirt (1902–1969), James Guy (1910–1983), Peter Blume (1906–1992), and Arnold Wiltz (1889–1937) aimed to "transcend and rebuild modernism," making a new kind of modern American art marked by "revolutionary symbolism" rather than seemingly straight-forward documentation.[20]

19. On Gellert, see James Wechsler's essay in this volume and Anne Wise Low, "Hugo Gellert: Art on the American Political Front, 1914–1943" (Master's thesis, Department of Art History, University of Miami, 1995).

20. Denning, *The Cultural Front,* 122; on the centrality of documentary modes to 1930s culture, see William Stott, *Documentary Expression and Thirties America* (New York: Oxford University Press, 1973).

fig. 15
(opposite page)
James Meikle Guy,
Workers, serigraph,
51 x 33 cm, 1938.
The Mitchell Wolfson Jr.
Collection, The
Wolfsonian–Florida
International University,
Miami Beach, Florida.

fig. 16
(below)
Louis Guglielmi, *Phoenix,*
oil on canvas, 76 x 64 cm,
1935. Sheldon Memorial
Art Gallery and
Sculpture Garden,
NAA–Nelle Cochrane
Woods Memorial.

Debates about which art styles most appropriately embodied revolutionary politics were common in the 1930s; as critic Grace Clements observed in *Art Front* in 1936:

> Let us take a phenomenon of our present social system — a bread line — as a subject for a painting. Will the mere picturization or even dramatization of a bread line convey the *reasons* for its existence? We must answer — no.

The solution to the problem of visually conveying revolutionary social and political paradigms, Clements explained, lay in artistic manipulation of calculated and "cerebral" (rather than emotional) forms of modern art. This included Cubism and figurative Surrealism, and works that juxtaposed "two or more factors unlike in kind but united in idea."[21] James Guy's 1938 serigraph *Workers* seems to follow Clements's advice, featuring a colorful montage of figures — male, female, black, white, blue collar, white collar — normally separated but here united in the greater cause of working-class labor (fig. 15).

Luigi Guglielmi produced surreal fantasies and brooding, melancholy depictions of what he called "the darkness of industrial enslavement." His *One Third of a Nation* (1939), a dreary urban scene of run-down tenements and a deserted street strewn with coffins, referenced statistics that one-third of Americans lived in substandard housing.[22] Guglielmi's 1935 painting *Phoenix* more brightly imaged the historical progress from capitalism to revolution to socialism, moving from a factory in the far background, to a demolished brick smokestack and pile of rubble (out of which emerges the withered arm of a corpse) in the middle, to a portrait of Lenin propped against an electrical tower in the foreground (fig. 16). Arnold Wiltz similarly adopted the allegorizing, stage-set

---

21. Grace Clements, "New Content — New Form," *Art Front* 2 (March 1936): 8–9, as cited in Hills, *Modern Art in the USA,* 105–106.

22. O. Louis Guglielmi, "I Hope to Sing Again," *Magazine of Art* 37 (January 1944): 176. *One Third of a Nation* is in the collection of the Metropolitan Museum of Art, New York, and the play of the same name was written by Arthur Arendt and produced by the Federal Theater Project's Living Newspapers in the late 1930s. Walter Quirt also painted a mural, now lost, titled *One Third of a Nation* (1938); see *Walter Quirt, A Retrospective* (Minneapolis: University Gallery, University of Minnesota, 1979), 20–21.

fig. 17
(above)
Arnold Wiltz, *Liquidation*,
oil on canvas, 64 x 81 cm,
1935. The Mitchell
Wolfson Jr. Collection,
The Wolfsonian–Florida
International University,
Miami Beach, Florida.
Photograph by
Willard Associates.

fig. 18
(above, far right)
Alexander Z. Kruse,
A Boston Sunset,
oil on panel, 122 x 91 cm
framed, 1936. The
Wolfsonian–Florida
International University,
Miami Beach, Florida.
Gift of Kathreen Kruse.

compositions and fastidious brushwork of European Surrealists such as Giorgio de Chirico and Salvador Dali in paintings such as his 1935 *Liquidation* (fig. 17). This work oddly juxtaposes a fully dressed male worker operating a jackhammer with a nude woman amidst a fantasy of bombed buildings. A plane—perhaps the one that had just strafed this Italianate dreamscape—soars into the heavens.[23] In 1938 the arts monthly *Direction* called such work "Proletarian Surrealism," explaining that "a style of painting usually identified with extreme individualism and decadence takes on new vigor and meaning when it is used to express the moods and emotions of the dispossessed."[24]

Such meaning was clearly intended in Social Realist works by Alexander Z. Kruse (1888–1972), Harry Sternberg (b. 1904), and Carl Hoeckner (1883–1972), which linked labor with religious, specifically Christian, symbolism. In the 1930s Christ was often seen as a champion of the underclass, and Christianity was redefined along humanist lines. Some artists linked working-class figures with Christ's martyrdom. Alexander Kruse's 1936 painting *A Boston Sunset* shows labor crucified by capitalism and also references the 1921 trial and 1927 execution of Nicola Sacco and Bartolomeo Vanzetti—two Italian immigrant anarchists found guilty of murdering the paymaster and guard of a South Braintree, Massachusetts, shoe factory (fig. 18). Carl Hoeckner's *Steeltown Twilight (No. 12)* of 1936 features laborers being beaten by armed thugs while Christ is crucified (fig. 19), and Harry Sternberg's *Steel Town* of c. 1939, a composite of

23. Wiltz was born in Berlin in 1889 and was active in New York in the 1920s and 1930s. His painting *Spillway, Ashokan Dam* was exhibited at the Carnegie International in 1933; his watercolor *Road to a Village* (1929), owned by the Whitney Museum of American Art, was included in the *Exhibition of American Painting* held at the M. H. DeYoung Memorial Museum, California Palace of the Legion of Honor, San Francisco, in June 1935. The Smithsonian American Art Museum holds six of his works: *Spillway, Ashokan Dam* and five wood engravings.

24. "Proletarian Surrealism," *Direction* 1 (April 1938), noted in Denning, *The Cultural Front*, 122.

fig. 19
(right)
Carl Hoeckner, *Steeltown Twilight (No. 12)*, lithograph, 30 x 46 cm, 1936. The Mitchell Wolfson Jr. Collection, The Wolfsonian–Florida International University, Miami Beach, Florida.

fig. 20
(below, right)
Harry Sternberg, *Steel Town*, lithograph, 41 x 28 cm, c. 1939. The Mitchell Wolfson Jr. Collection, The Wolfsonian–Florida International University, Miami Beach, Florida.

sketches made in Pittsburgh, similarly contrasts hulking factories and industrial smokestacks with the signs and symbols of Christianity (fig. 20). As Sternberg remarked:

> In this print I tell the life cycle of the steel worker. His home was a company owned shack; the mill in which he worked, the bar in which he found recreation, and looming over this, his church circumscribed his life.[25]

Sternberg was deeply engaged in class struggle — later recounting that a vicious street battle between communists and New York City police in 1930 set him on a course of protest aesthetics throughout the Great Depression. His 1935 lithographic triptych *Dance of the Machine* more clearly catered to the "social surrealism" advocated by Clements and others (fig. 21).[26] Workers are chained to the giant cogs and wheels of mass-production industry in *The Present,* where the bony hands of management manipulate the time clocks, and assembly lines enslave labor. In the second print, *The Promise,* workers break free — a clenched fist rises out of a landscape of sprockets and gears. And in the final scene, *The Future,* time clocks and assembly lines have been replaced by the symbols of rational planning (an architect's triangle and blueprint and the framework of a well-designed industrial workplace in the background), intimating labor's liberation from the machine. As Sternberg later remarked:

> First of all, machines make wonderful subjects for picture making... the machine has been a key issue since the industrial revolution. There are two forces at play: the people who own the machine must make a profit, and the worker who works the machine must have a salary. Obviously, friction sets up as to how much a worker is paid. It was not too long ago that it was a twelve-hour day. It took union fighting, deaths, clubbings, all kinds of horrors — and I'm talking about America, not Russia — before the unions were victorious enough to bring about reasonable conditions for the workers.[27]

Interestingly, however, Sternberg's remembered specifics of working-class struggle and organized labor are only vaguely expressed in *Dance of the Machine.* The tools and designs he features in the final print of the series are reminiscent of those depicted in Fogel's mural panel *The Wealth of the Nation* (fig. 1), with its similar overture to the better national "future" imagined by the engineers, architects, and other experts of the New Deal.

25. Harry Sternberg, quoted in James C. Moore, *Harry Sternberg: A Catalog Raisonné of His Graphic Work* (Wichita, Kans.: Edwin A. Ulrich Museum of Art, Wichita State University, 1975), catalogue no. 144. For information on Hoeckner, a painter and illustrator who worked in Chicago, see the Carl Hoeckner Papers, microfilm roll no. 4048, Archives of American Art, Smithsonian Institution, Washington, D.C.

26. Harry Salpeter, "Harry Sternberg" unpublished 1945 manuscript, 2, Harry Sternberg Papers, microfilm roll no. D339, frame 225, Archives of American Art.

27. Malcolm Warner, "An Interview with the Artist," in *The Prints of Harry Sternberg* (San Diego: San Diego Museum of Art, 1994), 8–17.

fig. 21
Harry Sternberg, *Dance of the Machine*, lithograph triptych, *No. 1: The Present* (left), 61 x 43 cm; *No. 2: The Promise* (center), 61 x 28 cm; *No. 3: The Future* (right), 58 x 43 cm, 1935. The Mitchell Wolfson Jr. Collection, The Wolfsonian–Florida International University, Miami Beach, Florida.

As art historian Helen Langa observes, Sternberg and other "social viewpoint" printmakers—including Harry Gottlieb (1895–1992), Boris Gorelick, Elizabeth Olds (1897–1991), Riva Helfond, and Lucienne Bloch— "resisted" simplistic forms of documentation in favor of more complex visual narratives of labor. These narratives were often in a modern idiom and "addressed a wide range of themes from varied political and cultural standpoints." While their art differed on descriptive and prescriptive levels, such artists "actively engaged in imagining and representing labor's meanings within competing, overlapping, and intersecting ideologies of individual and societal responsibility."[28] Competing with radical left and communist views of labor during the Great Depression were those of the liberal New Deal. Early in President Franklin Delano Roosevelt's first term (begun 1933), the federal government came to recognize the value of labor imagery as a way of salvaging the nation's capitalist and corporate economy and of sustaining idealized notions of the work ethic. In developing art programs and projects that might advance these goals, the government turned to a great variety of American artists—including many, like Citron and Gellert, whose work often embodied more radical understandings of labor and working-class struggle. Appropriated for both leftist and liberal causes, the symbolic trope of labor acquired multiple and often contradictory meanings.

During the 1930s the federal government became the major patron of American art, fostering new public interest in American culture and providing nationwide emergency labor relief for the country's artists through the

28. Helen Langa, "Strength, Stress, and Solidarity: Imag(in)ing American Labor in the Depression Era," *Southeastern College Art Conference Review* 13 (1996): 1–13; see also Langa, *Reading the Fine Print: Labor, Social Justice, and Gender in the 1930s* (Berkeley: University of California Press, forthcoming 2002).

Works Progress Administration (WPA), Federal Art Project (FAP), Farm Security Administration (FSA), and other so-called alphabet agencies.[29] A diversity of artists—including painters Stuart Davis and Alice Neel, sculptors Louise Nevelson and David Smith, and photographers Gordon Parks and Dorothea Lange—found employment with federal art programs. So did many who gained art world acclaim after the Great Depression (Lee Krasner, Jackson Pollock, Willem de Kooning, and John Cage, to name a few). Wages were low (about twenty-five dollars a week), but so were the requirements of employment. Salaried artists in the WPA/FAP's easel project, for example, were allowed to paint whatever subjects they chose as long as they produced at least one painting a month.

The government employed thousands of artists and spent more than thirty-five million dollars during its depression-era art patronage from 1933 to 1943. Through the FAP, the FSA's photographic project, and the Section, New Deal support for American art resulted in some thirty-five hundred public murals; eighteen thousand sculptures; 108,000 easel paintings; 250,000 prints; two million posters; and hundreds of thousands of photographs. When these New Deal art programs were disbanded in the mid-1940s, much of this work was destroyed, auctioned, or donated to American institutions. In 1944, *Life* magazine reported that a New York junk dealer had purchased "bales" of WPA/FAP paintings and prints for four cents a pound at an auction in a federal warehouse.[30] The Wolfsonian's rich holdings of New Deal paintings, sculptures, mural studies, prints, posters, and books hint at the multitude of visual and material culture that was produced under the auspices of federal funding during the Great Depression.

New Deal arts patronage was hardly altruistic, of course, and centered largely on political and social desires to generate unity and restore confidence in American capitalism and democracy, both sorely tested by the strain of economic collapse and abiding unemployment. As evident in public murals by artists such as Seymour Fogel and Leo Raiken (1914–1972), an "iconography of labor" was courted by New Deal arts administrators, who recognized the propagandistic value of upbeat images of strong bodies and steady employment in the context of economic stagnation and malaise (figs. 1 and 2).[31] Designed for the Westerly, Rhode Island, post office,

29. Among reference works see Francis V. O'Connor, ed., *Art for the Millions: Essays from the 1930s by Artists and Administrators of the WPA Federal Art Project* (Boston: New York Graphic Society, 1973); and Richard D. McKinzie, *The New Deal for Artists* (Princeton, N.J.: Princeton University Press, 1973).

30. "WPA paintings bought from a junk-man are sold by N.Y. dealer," *Life* (17 April 1944): 85; see also "WPA Art Project director criticizes story on disposal of WPA paintings," *Life* (8 May 1944): 4.

31. Erika Doss, "Toward an Iconography of American Labor: Work, Workers, and the Work Ethic in American Art, 1930–1945," *Design Issues* 13 (Spring 1997): 53–66.

Raiken's 1939 *Rock Quarry* was among 1,477 entries in the Section's ambitious "Forty-Eight State Competition" of 1939, in which artists were asked to submit mural proposals for a number of new U.S. post offices.[32] Based on his firsthand observation of Rhode Island's granite industry, Raiken's painting clearly exalts "manly" workers and the work ethic, and symbolizes work itself in terms of shared experience and community. Yet, like Fogel's *The Wealth of the Nation*, Raiken's mural study bifurcates labor into separated hierarchies: blue-collar drillers and stonecutters, and white-collar engineers, architects, and project managers. However hierarchical they may seem, by emphasizing collectivity and avoiding the issues and concerns of contemporary industry — such as loss of skills, unionization, and strikes — these public images helped bolster liberal political and economic intentions to define labor on unified and essentially classless terms (in fact, few narrated working-class struggle). They further aimed to persuade American audiences of the benefit and inevitability of a national economy in which government and business were closely aligned: the culture of corporate capitalism.

These objectives were most evidently realized in the New Deal's more public art projects — in its Section murals, in the sculptures that were designed for government buildings, and in widely reproduced and distributed WPA posters. Prints, especially, became the locus of divergent subjects and styles, and printmaking became the medium of choice for many of the more

32. The Westerly post office mural competition was among the most controversial of the "Forty-Eight State Competition," especially after the Section chose a design by artist Paul Sample (1896–1974), which did not focus on Westerly's granite industry (and was not originally even designed for the Westerly post office). See "Speaking of Pictures: This is Mural America for Rural Americans," *Life* (4 December 1939): 12–13, which illustrates a number of the competition submissions; and Karal Ann Marling, *Wall-to-Wall America: A Cultural History of Post-Office Murals in the Great Depression* (Minneapolis: University of Minnesota Press, 1982), 161–170.

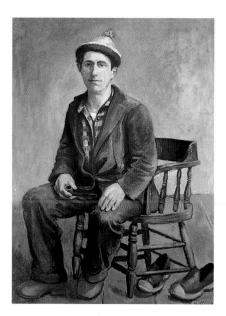

fig. 23
(above)
Harry Gottlieb, *Self Portrait*, oil on canvas, 101 x 76 cm, 1931. The Mitchell Wolfson Jr. Collection, The Wolfsonian–Florida International University, Miami Beach, Florida.

fig. 24
(above, far right)
Harry Gottlieb, *Next Shift*, color serigraph, 46 x 58 cm, 1938. The Mitchell Wolfson Jr. Collection, The Wolfsonian–Florida International University, Miami Beach, Florida.

politically and socially engaged artists in the 1930s. As Harry Sternberg remarked in 1936:

> The graphic arts have a special importance for the growing numbers of artists anxious to turn their talents to the service of the struggle against War and Fascism. No other medium has the adaptability of the print, which can be produced rapidly and inexpensively in large quantities, and can be distributed at low cost.[33]

Working for the WPA/FAP's Graphics Division from 1935 to 1936, and also teaching at both the Art Students League and the New School for Social Research in the 1930s, Sternberg played an especially "influential role in the New York printmaking world." In 1936 he received a Guggenheim Fellowship to study industrial labor in America. His lithograph *Coal Miner* stems from his research in the coal mines of northeastern Pennsylvania (fig. 22).[34]

Notions of creating affordable "art for the people" were common in the 1930s, and the serial capacity of prints—etchings, lithographs, woodcuts, serigraphs, and more—meshed perfectly with these ideals. Even before the WPA/FAP's Graphics Division was created in 1935, outfits such as the Contemporary Print Group, the Associated American Artists, and the American Artists Group had formed with the intention of providing "pictures for the masses."[35] Likewise, riling against the artist's popular

33. Harry Sternberg, from a paper on graphic art delivered at the First American Artists' Congress, 1936, in *Artists Against War and Fascism*, eds. Matthew Baigell and Julia Williams (New Brunswick, N.J.: Rutgers University Press, 1986), 137.

34. See Langa, "Strength, Stress, and Solidarity," 8, for an extended discussion of Sternberg's mining prints.

35. See Erika Doss, "Catering to Consumerism: Associated American Artists and the Marketing of Modern Art, 1934–1958," *Winterthur Portfolio* 26 (Summer/Autumn 1991): 143–167; and Bruce Robertson, *Representing America: The Ken Trevey Collection of American Realist Prints* (Seattle: University of Washington Press, 1995).

fig. 25
(above)
Harry Gottlieb, *The Strike Is Won*, color etching, 58 x 93 cm, 1938. The Mitchell Wolfson Jr. Collection, The Wolfsonian–Florida International University, Miami Beach, Florida.

fig. 26
(above, far right)
Elizabeth Olds, *Miner Joe*, serigraph, 41 x 30 cm, 1942. The Mitchell Wolfson Jr. Collection, The Wolfsonian–Florida International University, Miami Beach, Florida. Photograph by Bruce White.

reputation as "a playboy companion of the dilettante patron, a remote hero with a famous name," artist and arts organizer Ralph Pearson (1883–1958) urged the American printmaker to become "a workman among workers," noting of his ideal: "He prints his etchings, lithographs or woodblocks with hands which know ink and the rollers and wheels of his press. He works. He produces. He lives."[36]

Harry Gottlieb especially embodied Pearson's understanding of the artist as workingman. Raised in a working-class family in Minneapolis, Gottlieb studied with Robert Koehler (painter of *The Strike*, 1886) at the Minneapolis Institute of Art from 1915 to 1917. Gottlieb's *Self Portrait* of 1931 — in which he wears a knit cap, brown pants, and heavy boots — clearly posits his identity as a worker rather than an aesthete (fig. 23). During a Guggenheim Fellowship in Paris from 1931 to 1932, he mastered lithography. In 1936 Gottlieb was assigned to the Graphics Division of the WPA/FAP in New York City and produced numerous color lithographs of industrial labor. And in 1938, he and other WPA artists began experimenting with the more versatile and less expensive medium of color silkscreens, or serigraphs.[37] Two of his 1938 silkscreen prints, *Next Shift* and *The Strike Is Won* (figs. 24 and 25), cast laborers in heroic terms, as figures of autonomy and authority in the workplace, much like other contemporaneous silkscreen prints such as Refregier's *San Francisco '34 Waterfront Strike* (fig. 13) and Elizabeth Olds's 1942 *Miner Joe* (fig. 26).

36. Ralph Pearson, quoted in *America Today: A Book of 100 Prints* (New York: American Artists' Congress, 1936); reissued as *Graphics Works of the American Thirties* (New York: Da Capo Press, 1977), 10. See also Peter Welch, "The American League Against War and Fascism 1936 Calendar," in *Hot Off the Press: Prints and Politics,* eds. Linda Tyler and Barry Walker (Albuquerque: The University of New Mexico Press, 1994), 19–23.

37. Others who worked in silkscreen were Louis Lozowick and Elizabeth Olds. See *Harry Gottlieb: The Silkscreen and Social Concern in the WPA Era* (New Brunswick, N.J.: The Jane Voorhees Zimmerli Art Museum, Rutgers–The State University of New Jersey, 1983); and Ellen Sragow, "Harry Gottlieb: Artist, Printmaker, Political Activist, Gentle Radical, Friend," in *Hot Off the Press,* eds. Tyler and Walker, 25–32.

Active and dynamic, the "manly" workers these artists chose to depict are potent symbolic counter-images to the realities of depression-era America: the stasis of unemployment, the restricted conditions and hierarchies of wage labor in mass-production industry. As art historian Karal Ann Marling observed, 1930s murals were laden with images of fast-moving cars, trains, and airplanes that were, essentially

> cultural stereotypes that proclaim[ed] a hungry faith in the power of the machine-oriented, modern society to extricate itself from the dilemma of the present and to zoom miraculously away from the burden of hardship and failure.[38]

The repeated visualization of active and engaged labor in the 1930s follows the same "hungry faith." Retreating from the objective impulse of documentary expression, Gottlieb, Olds, Refregier, Sternberg, and other artists crafted compelling, mythical images of strong, muscular workers. These were idealized icons of an American working class, of labor in an imagined future when the working-class struggle had triumphed.[39] That such images were crafted under the auspices of the New Deal, whose labor policies favored corporate management and control, adds to their mythical and ironic character.

Symbolic understandings of labor, and similarly complex ideas regarding masculinity, are particularly evident in the many depression-era images, especially prints, but also paintings and murals, that center on the bodies of semi-nude American workers, including Arthur Murphy's (1906–1946) lithograph *Steel Riggers, No. 4, Bay Bridge,* and Francis De Erdely's (1904–1959) canvas *The Welder,* both mentioned earlier in this essay (figs. 3 and 4). While depicting men on a scaffold at a bridge construction site, Murphy's print (done with the WPA/FAP's Graphics Division in San Francisco) especially emphasizes their shirtless and well-muscled torsos. Likewise, while De Erdely dresses his working-class welder with the props of his trade — goggles on his head, bulky leather gloves on his hands, tools at his side — he also depicts him shirtless, his thumbs hooked into the belt buckle of his hip-hugging jeans, his sinuous body relaxed in a graceful *contrapposto.* Painted in 1942, De Erdely's "manly" worker is the male equivalent of the female pin-up, the "beefcake" to the "cheesecake," and the scantily clad strippers of girlie magazines like *Beauty Parade* (first published 1941), *Titter, Wink, Flirt,* and *Eyeful.*[40]

38. Marling, *Wall-to-Wall America,* 17.

39. Erika Doss, *Benton, Pollock, and the Politics of Modernism: From Regionalism to Abstract Expressionism* (Chicago: The University of Chicago Press, 1991), 85–87 and passim.

40. Burkhard Riemschneider, *The Best of American Girlie Magazines* (Cologne: Benedikt Taschen Verlag, 1997). Born in Hungary, De Erdely arrived in New York in 1939, lived in Detroit for four years, and then settled in Los Angeles in the mid-1940s; in 1945 he began teaching at the University of Southern California; see Susan Ehrlich, "The Jepson Group: The School, Its Major Teachers, and Their Drawings," in *Drawings and Illustrations by Southern California Artists Before 1950,* ed. Nancy Dustin Wall Moure (Laguna Beach, Calif.: Laguna Beach Museum of Art, 1982), 52–53.

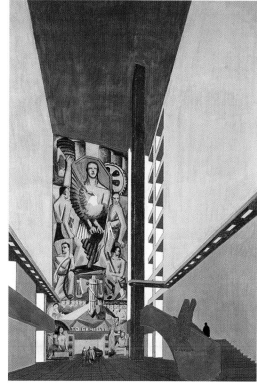

fig. 27
(above)
Leon Gilmour, *Cement Finishers*, woodblock print, 38 x 30 cm, 1939. The Mitchell Wolfson Jr. Collection, The Wolfsonian–Florida International University, Miami Beach, Florida.

fig. 28
(above, far right)
Seymour Fogel, *Mural Study for WPA Pavilion of 1939 New York World's Fair*, tempera and graphite on board, 61 x 38 cm, 1939. The Mitchell Wolfson Jr. Collection, The Wolfsonian–Florida International University, Miami Beach, Florida.

Leon Gilmour's (1907–1996) wood engraving *Cement Finishers* of 1939 and Seymour Fogel's mural study for the WPA Pavilion at the New York World's Fair of the same year similarly center on the semi-clothed bodies of working class men (figs. 27 and 28). Gilmour, a one-time laborer turned printmaker, depicts three strong bodies hard at work on a federal public works project; Fogel links the attributes of farm, family, and national unity with the muscular bodies of labor. Symbolizing work and the work ethic with images of stereotypically "manly" workers, these pieces further embody the deeply felt depression-era anxieties of many nonworking American men who defined themselves in terms of (their) labor. Simply put, work remained *the* key form of masculine identity in 1930s America, although concepts of masculine identity and self-actualization were obviously in crisis during the 1930s, when one-fourth of the American labor force was unemployed.[41]

Despite their efforts to change the nature of work (or, more accurately, to visualize such change) by using and developing diverse modern art styles, American artists remained loyal to this key construct. Even as they continued to guide American art along such modernist pathways as Surrealism and montage, American artists continued to rely on earlier conventions of the manly body and the heroic dimensions of work. This nostalgia contradicted realities of the 1930s, including mass production and the increasing professionalization of labor. Moreover, portrayed as the embodiment of muscle and might, the manly body of the Great Depression was also

41. Doss, "Toward an Iconography of American Labor," 60–66.

fig. 29
Jack Delano, *General
View of One of the
Factory Floors of the
Vought-Sikorsky Aircraft
Corporation, Stratford,
Connecticut,* **photograph
1940. Library of Congress,
Washington, D.C.**

defined in overtly heterosexual terms. As historian George Chauncey
explained, it was in the 1930s that "the now conventional division of men
into 'homosexuals' and 'heterosexuals,' based on the sex of their sexual
partners," really began to take place.[42] The shapes of the working-class
male body represented by many American artists in the 1930s paralleled
these sexual categories, and reinforced the stereotype of the muscle-bound
heterosexual he-man, the straight male worker.

Of course, the world of work is not exactly the most thrilling visual subject,
as apparent in FSA photographs such as Jack Delano's (b. 1914) *General
View of One of the Factory Floors of the Vought-Sikorsky Aircraft Corporation,
Stratford, Connecticut* of 1940 (fig. 29). Nor are artists welcome in the
workplace. Workers, after all, are supposed to be working, not posing,
and artists, particularly in periods of labor unrest, tend to be viewed with
suspicion as outsiders and rabble-rousers. This helps to explain the general
paucity of American art about work and workers. In a country wracked
by fears of cultural inferiority, art was meant to embody lofty ideals and
take the high moral ground. When nineteenth-century artists occasionally
touched on the subject of labor, they tended to either heroicize and
personalize independent workers (as did John Neagle in the 1826–1827
painting *Pat Lyon at the Forge*) or heroicize their bodies at moments of
leisure, as in Anshutz's *The Ironworkers' Noontime*. When the male American

42. George Chauncey, *Gay New York: Gender, Urban Culture, and the Making of the Gay Male World,
1890–1940* (New York: Basic Books, 1994), 13.

worker was imaged in the 1930s, he was made into a physical icon of national recovery: the body of the worker as an emblem of the well-bodied American economy.

But it is that very physicality that makes these images problematic. The semi-nude "manly" workers of 1930s art are especially vulnerable as objects of the American gaze. Clothes, after all, "are bearers of prestige, notably of wealth, status, and class. To be without them is to lose prestige," writes Richard Dyer. And nakedness reveals the inadequacies of the body. "It may betray," Dyer adds

> the relative similarity of male and female, white and non-white bodies, undo the remorseless insistences on difference and concomitant power carried by clothes and grooming. The exposed white male body is liable to pose the legitimacy of white male power: why should people who look like that… have so much power?[43]

In other words, while 1930s artists imaged labor in muscular and virile terms to connote the physical power of American working-class men, these representational conventions turned against them. Particularly at a crucial historical moment in the mid- to late 1930s, when the struggle between labor and capital was at its height, widespread representation of male workers as sexualized bodies — as passive objects of pleasure for others rather than the active subjects of their own autonomy and agency — advanced marginalization of the working class.

An "inability to imagine a completed narrative" characterizes the work of the depression-era cultural front, Michael Denning comments.[44] Indeed, a failure to develop alternative visual strategies in the 1930s that would effectively illuminate and transform the changed circumstances of work had the effect (however unintended) of helping to erase the working class from the larger purview of American historical and cultural consciousness. Habitual images that stereotypically cast workers as premodern symbols of the value of work and the morality of the work ethic, and as objects of erotic desire, helped define labor as "just a body." ✦

Acknowledgments

Thanks to current and former museum staff members Wendy Kaplan, Marianne Lamonaca, Pedro Figueredo, Francis X. Luca, David Burnhauser, and Anne Low for their generous assistance and advice with this project. Research also was conducted at the Smithsonian American Art Museum and the Archives of American Art, Washington, D.C., in fall 2000, and at the Sheldon Memorial Art Gallery, University of Nebraska, Lincoln, in spring 2001. I am indebted to the helpful staff at these institutions.

43. Richard Dyer, *White* (New York: Routledge, 1997), 146.
44. Denning, *The Cultural Front*, 119.

Susan Valdés-Dapena

"Painting Section" in Black and White: Ethel Magafan's *Cotton Pickers*

Susan Valdés-Dapena is an artist and art historian who specializes in public and community-based art. She has taught at Parsons School of Design, Hunter College, the University of Miami, and Florida International University. Valdés-Dapena has served as a gallery director and museum educator and has published art criticism in a number of magazines. She is currently completing a Ph.D. in art history at the Graduate Center of the City University of New York.

Over the postmaster's door in Wynne, Arkansas, hangs a mural of African Americans harvesting cotton (fig. 1). Only three people actually bend to pick the cotton, while others bring in full bags, weigh it, or look on. The painting, by the young white Colorado artist Ethel Magafan (1916–1993), was completed in 1939.[1] This Arkansas post office and the mural that adorns it were part of a New Deal initiative by the Treasury Department to develop federal buildings in towns across the United States. The painting was commissioned by one of the major New Deal art patrons, the Treasury Department's Section of the Fine Arts (the Section) (operated 1934–1943). Judging from the attire of the figures, we are meant to understand the scene as contemporary to 1939 rather than historical. No white people are depicted. How do we read this painting?

One major problem with analyzing Section murals, particularly with regard to complicated issues like gender and race, is that they are close enough in time to be familiar to present-day audiences. We assume that we can understand what the artist intended merely by looking at the works. It is too easy to forgo a carefulness that would be standard in analyzing older works of art. Because New Deal murals were part of a progressive economic and social agenda, historians have looked to them expecting to see progressiveness of one kind or another, writ, or rather painted, large. The scholarship of historians Barbara Melosh, Sue Bridwell Beckham, and Karal Ann Marling, in different ways, seems marked by their disappointment over progressive elements they sought in Section murals but did not find. Sometimes, even when progressive elements can be found in Section murals,

Detail of Ethel Magafan's full-scale cartoon of *Cotton Pickers*, 1939.

1. Ethel Magafan was active as an artist until her death in 1993, at age 76. Jenne, her twin sister, worked as an artist until her untimely death of a cerebral hemorrhage in 1952, at the age of 36. Unfortunately, Magafan's Wynne mural is now badly flaking. An exemplary Section work in every respect, it is in desperate need of restoration.

fig. 1
Ethel Magafan, *Cotton Pickers*, U.S. Post Office, Wynne, Arkansas, tempera on canvas, 1939. Photograph by Robert Jenkins.

we miss them because of the subtlety that was required to please local publics. Because of such compromise, Erica Beckh Rubenstein defined "painting Section" pejoratively in her 1944 Harvard dissertation, "Tax Payers' Murals," creating a bias that other scholars inherited. To Rubenstein, the Section mural was a "pleasant," highly professional, realistic, and dignified mural, "non-controversial and non-critical in theme, essentially an idealization of reality.... a portrayal of the community that would be pleasing to the Chamber of Commerce."[2] If we are to evaluate works done for federally supported arts projects, it is unreasonable not to consider the terms and demands of these projects. Although some Section murals included representations of race or gender that are problematic or backward, careful, nuanced studies of these subjects remain to be done. This essay conducts such a study on a small scale by looking closely at Magafan's *Cotton Pickers* within the highly mediated sphere of the Section commission and its broader historical context.

Is the painting racist simply because it connects African Americans and cotton? It was cotton and tobacco, after all, in their labor-intensiveness and profitability, that had driven the demand for the importation of more and more slaves from Africa. Even after abolition, cotton remained a locus for the subjugation of black Americans by white Americans. The latter not

2. The phrase "to paint Section" was adopted by New Deal artists themselves to sum up the thematic and stylistic approaches that the Section favored. Erica Beckh Rubenstein, wife of painter Lewis Rubenstein, introduced it to the public in "Tax Payers' Murals" (Ph.D. diss., Harvard University, 1944), 180–182. Rubenstein set the tone for later scholarship by pitting the FAP against the Section and expressing a clear bias for the former's democratic nature and openness to diverse styles. Karal Ann Marling, in *Wall-to-Wall America: A Cultural History of Post-Office Murals in the Great Depression* (Minneapolis: University of Minnesota Press, 1982), analyzed public response to Section murals, while perpetuating Rubenstein's bias in repeatedly describing them as "bland." Belisario Contreras's *Tradition and Innovation in New Deal Art* (London and Toronto: Associated University Presses, 1983) framed Cahill's and Bruce's projects as complementary and equally important. Marlene Park and Gerald E. Markowitz, in *Democratic Vistas: Post Offices and Public Art in the New Deal* (Philadelphia: Temple University Press, 1984), take a positive, although nuanced, approach to Section murals, relating them to other art and New Deal projects. Recent works include Sue Bridwell Beckham, *Depression Post Office Murals and Southern Culture: A Gentle Reconstruction* (Baton Rouge and London: Louisiana State University Press, 1989) and Barbara Melosh, *Engendering Culture: Manhood and Womanhood in New Deal Public Art and Theater* (Washington and London: Smithsonian Institution Press, 1991).

only controlled the means of production and the market value of cotton, but they often cheated black cotton pickers out of the little money they were due by rigging the scales or otherwise unfairly handling the weighing process. Likewise, the cotton field could become an embattled terrain where black workers were mistreated or degraded by white overseers.

During the 1960s, after Magafan's painting had been hanging in Wynne for more than twenty years, two young African-American men from nearby Jonesboro visited the Wynne post office, perhaps for the first time. They were members of the Jonesboro National Association for the Advancement of Colored People (NAACP). The men demanded that the postmaster have the mural painted over, feeling that it was demeaning to blacks.[3] Of course, the postmaster had no more authority to remove or cover the painting without permission from Washington than he would have had when it was first installed, which is what he told the men. Did the men from Jonesboro feel that the painting was demeaning because it repeated the old connection of African Americans to cotton picking, a menial job, or because cotton was an industry that had been among those responsible for African servitude and then for the continued oppression of African Americans? Or, did they think that Magafan's painting, specifically, showed black cotton pickers in a demeaning way?

A Wynne high school art teacher, Julia Gardner, had heard about the angry request for the painting's whitewashing, so she raised the issue at a town meeting. Such meetings had been scheduled so that black and white locals could get to know one another and amicably work through the difficulties of school integration. Gardner felt that the town should discuss the mural in case the issue was raised again. She had a fondness for Magafan's handsome and well-crafted work, and had often used it as a teaching tool with her art students. At the meeting, African-American residents were asked to discuss their feelings about the painting. Gardner recalls that the general attitude among the African Americans present was summed up by an elderly carpenter: it didn't do anything for him, but it didn't do anything against him either. Those at the meeting decided to keep the mural; there was no follow-up by the young men or the Jonesboro NAACP.[4]

The protestors from Jonesboro were not alone in the 1960s in showing their distaste for images of black cotton pickers, even when those images appeared in decades-old paintings. Sometime in the late 1960s, the faces of cotton pickers in a 1938 mural, *The Development of Western Civilization* by James Michael Newell (1900–c. 1985), were scratched out and spray painted over (fig. 2). The cotton picking was, significantly, the only scene in the large mural that was defaced. The painting, done under the auspices

3. Jimmie James, secretary, Cross County Historical Society, telephone interview with author, 31 October 1997; Jimmie James, correspondence to author, 10 November 1997; Julia Gardner, chairperson, Cross County Arts Council, telephone interview with author, 2 November 1997.

4. Gardner, interview.

fig. 2
(right)
James Michael Newell, detail of defaced cotton pickers, *The Development of Western Civilization*, Evander Childs High School, the Bronx, New York, fresco, 1938. Collection of the New York City Board of Education. Photograph by Alan Farancz.

fig. 3
(below, right)
James Michael Newell, detail of *The Development of Western Civilization* after 1999 restoration by Alan Farancz, Evander Childs High School, the Bronx, New York, fresco, 1938. Collection of the New York City Board of Education. Photograph by Alan Farancz.

of the Works Progress Administration (WPA) Federal Art Project (FAP), wraps around the library of Evander Childs High School in the Bronx. It is one of the rare New Deal murals done in true fresco — a difficult, time-consuming, and expensive medium — and an extraordinarily large example at that. For this reason alone, the mural is deserving of preservation. Other panels in the mural represent the most advanced scientific achievements being performed by white men, presenting an underlying racial (and gendered) world-view that may not sit well with us today. Nonetheless, the mural does not contain what would have been, in its time, any overtly racist imagery. The black cotton pickers appear in a section of the mural that shows various types of typical American labor of the day: farming, cattle driving, logging, mining, and railroad building. The African Americans, whose features were restored in 1999, are relatively dignified figures (fig. 3). While many artists depicted black workers as shirtless, shoddily

fig. 4
James Michael Newell,
detail of *The Development
of Western Civilization*,
Evander Childs High
School, the Bronx,
New York, fresco, 1938.
Collection of the
New York City Board of
Education. Photograph
by Alan Farancz.

clad, or anonymously bent in labor, Newell's figures have portrait-like faces that are clearly visible; their clothes are clean and whole. Nonetheless, cotton picking is all we see black workers doing, despite the variety of labor depicted in the scene. This racist slight would seem to be one born of oversight and naïveté on the part of the artist, for the adjacent panel in the mural features a pair of dark-skinned hands that wear manacles with broken chains and reach upward in an optimistic gesture (fig. 4). Between them is a book, opened to reveal a Walt Whitman verse: "And that where I am or you are this present day, there is the center of all days, all races. And there is the meaning to us of all that has ever come of races and days, or ever will come." The freed black hands and the text imply that Newell did perceive racial equality as an important aspect of the "development of Western Civilization," however incomplete his vision. Nonetheless, the graffitists, possibly racially radicalized students of Evander Childs High, found the image of the cotton pickers intolerable. Although we cannot assume the race of the graffitists, it is easy to see how black teenagers, after the assassinations of Malcolm X and Dr. Martin Luther King Jr., might not have been able to see a way forward in Newell's cotton pickers — dignified or not.[5]

What did images of African Americans picking cotton mean in the late 1930s, when Magafan's and Newell's murals were completed? During the years in which the federal government sponsored artworks through its various New Deal initiatives, 1933 through 1943, much of the United States was still largely rural and, prior to U.S. involvement in the war, a great number of Americans still worked in agriculture. The cotton and

5. Contreras, *Tradition and Innovation*, 156; *Adopt-A-Mural* (New York: The Municipal Art Society, 1991), 10–11; Michelle Cohen, "The 1930's: The New Deal Comes to Public Schools," a chapter from her dissertation in progress (CUNY Graduate School and University Center). The Whitman verse is from "With Antecedents," *The Leaves of Grass*. Restoration of Newell's mural was completed in 1999 by Alan Farancz.

tobacco industries, which represented a large share of the gross domestic product, were major employers for poor blacks and whites alike, who picked these crops by hand. Although a mechanized cotton harvester was patented in 1850, it was not used in commercial farming until the 1940s. Mechanized pickers were adopted last by growers in the South, where wages for pickers were the lowest of all the cotton areas, where farmlands had been broken up into small sharecroppers' lots, and where, prior to the development of new herbicides, high rainfall had produced a "weedier" crop that benefited from more careful handpicking. Until after the war, cotton picking by hand was a regular feature of life in certain regions of the country.[6]

Scholars have given much attention to distinguishing works produced under various New Deal arts initiatives, especially the two major ones, the WPA Federal Art Project and the Treasury Department's Section of the Fine Arts. The directors of these agencies, Holger Cahill (1887–1960) and Edward Bruce (1879–1943), had very different aims, and the projects were different from the ground up — in terms of organization, selection process, and payment. Edward Bruce, the director of the Section, wanted to promote an intrinsically American style of art. For him, this was painting that depicted a "return to the facts" of American life, or what is known as American Scene painting. Holger Cahill, director of the FAP, believed that "anything painted by an American artist is American art," and, unlike Bruce, he was open to all styles of art for public commissions, including abstraction.[7] Cahill had structured his organization more loosely than Bruce, giving more power to regional bodies; thus his own taste had less effect on specific commissions. Despite Cahill's openness, abstract murals were exceptional among works funded by the FAP. As historians Marlene Park and Gerald Markowitz have noted, regardless of whether muralists worked for the FAP or the Section, and many worked for both, most New Deal artists embraced a readable realistic style and represented what they believed to be typical American subjects.[8]

Dozens of murals that included cotton and cotton-related labor were sponsored by the Section. Sue Bridwell Beckham, in *Depression Post Office Murals and Southern Culture,* gives the number as roughly fifty cotton murals in Southern states plus one in Oklahoma and one in Texas.[9] My interest in Ethel Magafan's mural, however, is not primarily as an image of cotton-related labor but as an image of African Americans. Before we can analyze Magafan's *Cotton Pickers,* it is necessary to consider not only

6. Wayne A. Grove, "Farmers at the Technological Crossroads: Post-World War II Diffusion of the Mechanical Cotton Harvester," paper given at the ASSA Cliometric Society Sessions, January 1997.

7. Contreras, *Tradition and Innovation,* 101–103, 169.

8. The only quasi-abstract mural paid for by the Section was Lloyd Ney's *New London Facets* for New London, Ohio. Marling, *Wall-to-Wall America,* 293–328; Park and Markowitz, *Democratic Vistas,* 21, 168, 178–181.

9. Beckham, *Depression Post Office Murals,* 21.

other images of cotton picking and of African Americans, but also the function of the Section mural and the job of the Section muralist. The Section mural, after all, existed in neither a vacuum nor a museum. In towns that were generally far from Washington, and often from any large city, local constituents had the power to accept or reject murals. If the Section muralist's work were not hung, he or she would not be paid. What was an artist to do when the chairperson of a regional mural committee felt free to write this kind of criticism in official correspondence to the Section:

> Everyone who has seen the photo of the final production to be installed has commented on the excessive number of negroes in the picture, especially in the foreground... If it is not too late to change the color of some of those folk it would help a lot. After all, though there may be more of the negro race in our vicinity the whites *do* rule.[10]

A Quick Lesson on "Painting Section"

Unlike all other New Deal arts patrons, the Treasury Department's Section of the Fine Arts was not a relief organization, but one that awarded federal commissions on the basis of artistic merit. The Section commissioned paintings and sculptures for new federal buildings, mostly post offices and courthouses, for towns of all sizes across the country. Section director Edward Bruce's desire for permanence, decorum, and highly competent professional artworks was not unreasonable, given the decorum and permanence of their settings. These new edifices were often the first federal buildings in many towns and regions. As such, the buildings and the artworks that decorated them were local emissaries of Roosevelt's New Deal. Thus the unstated, but nevertheless real, goals that Bruce set for Section artworks and artists seem conflicting at best. During a time of unparalleled national financial crisis and unemployment, the Section mural was to reassure Americans of a productive and stable future, heralded by New Deal economic reforms (see Erika Doss's essay for more on this subject). At a time of unprecedented increase in the size of the federal government and its concomitant encroachment into local and individual spheres, Section murals were to celebrate characteristics of specific communities and establish their importance in national or universal terms. The ideal Section mural was also expected to nudge viewers toward the acceptance of agricultural, industrial, or social reforms consistent with the New Deal—but gently, in a way that would not alienate the more conservative among them. Finally, Bruce hoped to make his Section a permanent government agency rather than a Great Depression stopgap. This would have required Congressional support. Bruce's obsession with quality, which led him to overrule local committees, was at least partly fueled by a desire to hold up each Section mural as an example of the worth of his program. His fear of controversy, which often caused him

10. Lucille N. Henderson to Edward Rowan, 27 June 1939, 121/133, Vicksburg, Mississippi, in Beckham, *Depression Post Office Murals,* 80.

fig. 5
Ethel Magafan, *Cotton Pickers,* **full-scale cartoon, graphite on kraft paper, 122 x 366 cm, 1939. The Mitchell Wolfson Jr. Collection, The Wolfsonian–Florida International University, Miami Beach, Florida. Photograph by Silvia Ros.**

to bully artists, was probably also born of his desire to show Congress that Section works were as well liked as they were "good paintings." Ironically, a number of controversies occurred because of Bruce's unwillingness to surrender more control to regional committees. Despite flaws in the Section's procedures and Bruce's narrow vision with regard to appropriate themes and styles, his Section did lay the groundwork for later percent-for-art legislation and the National Endowment for the Arts.[11]

Large Section commissions were awarded to artists through anonymous national and regional competitions, which were judged by national or local committees of arts professionals. Bruce and his staff sometimes overruled committees' decisions, by selecting a different entry or, when they felt that the submissions were not of "sufficient quality," by selecting a muralist who hadn't entered the competition but had placed well in another, elsewhere in the country. In this way, the Russian-born Connecticut artist Simka Simkhovitch was awarded the mural for the Jackson, Mississippi, post office over any of the regional competitors and the recommendations of the committee — even though he hadn't competed for it.[12] Once a design was chosen, its subsequent development into a finished mural was likewise closely supervised at each stage by the Section, mostly by staff member Edward Rowan (1898–1946). Rowan relayed to the artist suggestions made by the committee or, usually, those of the Section staff itself.

To save time and money, the Section regularly awarded commissions for small post offices to artists who had done well in a competition for a larger commission but had not won. This created a loophole in the process through which the Section could reward artists who not only produced quality work but with whom it was easy to work — artists who had avoided controversy and worked well with local postmasters and publics, and artists who had complied with the Section's suggestions. Ethel Magafan was awarded three of her four small post office commissions based on

11. The last point has been made by Contreras and Park and Markowitz.
12. See Marling and Beckham.

competitions she had not won. Her first two, the Auburn, Nebraska, *Threshers* (1937–1938), and the Wynne, Arkansas, *Cotton Pickers* (1938–1939), resulted from her single unsuccessful entry in the Fort Scott, Kansas, post office competition (1937).[13] Although the Section believed Magafan's Fort Scott sketch was "one of the best compositions that was submitted," the local committee rejected it because she had chosen "a theme which the people of the locale are trying to forget." The Section "did not feel justified in overriding the committee on this point." Magafan's sketch featured the 1863 massacre of the citizens of nearby Lawrence, Kansas. The raid was the most infamous and brutal conducted by William Quantrill and his band of marauders, who terrorized anti-slavery sympathizers in Kansas, Missouri, and Kentucky—supposedly to return slaves to their owners. In reality, they were outlaws who took advantage of the Civil War to loot for personal gain. Magafan later said that she had naïvely chosen the "bloody" subject simply because of its potential for a dramatic composition.[14]

Ethel Magafan and her twin sister, Jenne (1916–1952), had studied at the Colorado Springs Fine Art Center under Boardman Robinson (1876–1952), Peppino Mangravite (1896–1978), and Frank Mechau (1903–1946), the last of whom was their mentor. All of these men had completed murals for the Section, and Robinson occasionally served as a Section judge. Ethel, Jenne, and another protégé of Mechau's, Edward Chavez (1917–1985), assisted Mechau with several murals. Mechau may have led Ethel Magafan to believe that a dramatic subject would yield a better composition that could succeed with the Section. Ethel was only twenty-one years old when she entered the Fort Scott competition. Her early rejection taught her the importance of pleasing the local population if she wanted to work for the Treasury Department's arts agency.[15]

Section artists were not paid hourly rates, like those working for the FAP. Instead, they were awarded a lump sum from which they had to deduct their materials and travel expenses. The artist received his or her first payment after the Section had approved the preliminary sketches; the second, after the Section had approved a full-size cartoon (such as Magafan's *Cotton Pickers,* fig. 5); and the final and largest of the three only after the Section had approved a photograph (made at the artist's expense) of the *installed* mural. Unlike FAP artists, who worked on projects in their own areas, mostly big cities, Section artists were expected to travel, often to

13. Edward Rowan to Ethel Magafan, 23 July 1937 and 20 August 1938, Ethel Magafan Papers, Reel NDA 14, Archives of American Art (hereafter referred to as EMP).

14. Rowan to Magafan, 23 April 1937, EMP; and Ethel Magafan, transcribed interview with Joseph Trovato, Woodstock, New York, 5 November 1964, Reel 3949, 1, Archives of American Art.

15. Ethel Magafan, taped interview with Karl E. Fortess, Woodstock, New York, 1960, Archives of American Art; Magafan, Trovato interview, 3; Bruce Currie, interviews with author, Woodstock, New York, 9 and 23 November 1997; "Edward Chavez, The Boy from the Golden West," *Art Students League News* (New York: Art Students League, n.d.).

small towns in different regions of the country.[16] This travel, at the artist's own expense, was to consist of two trips — one to determine what to paint, the other to install the mural. Long-distance travel, which was expensive and difficult during the depression, became even more difficult after the war began, since gasoline was rationed and trains were used for troop transport. Artists who could not travel to the site of their commission did research in their own local libraries, but these artists often encountered difficulties. An artist who researched tobacco farming in the library might find, when he submitted his sketches, that locals were outraged by his ignorance of the tobacco variety and growing techniques indigenous to their region. Muralists who worked directly on the wall moved to the area until the job was finished, but could get stuck waiting for months until the Section contacted them with final approval.[17]

Although Section commissions often paid less than they cost to complete, they carried a prestige that the relief arts projects did not. This was especially important to young artists, such as Ethel and Jenne Magafan and Ed Chavez, who parlayed their achievements for the Section into successful gallery careers after the war.[18] Because of the anonymous competitions, a higher percentage of women artists worked for the Section than were represented in galleries. (Based on name rolls, about nineteen percent of Section artists were women.)[19] Along with the Magafan twins, a number of women Section artists, such as Doris Lee and Andrée Ruellan, became successful gallery artists. It is impossible to tell from surviving records, which only list names, how many African Americans received Section commissions. Historian Barbara Melosh estimates there were three such artists, a meager showing, although she doesn't list them.[20] A number of prominent African-American artists such as Aaron Douglas, Augusta Savage, and Jacob Lawrence worked for the FAP. If few African Americans worked for the Section, it may have been due to the requisite financial and travel burdens.

Since Section artists were not compensated unless their works were installed, they were forced to work out any controversies that might prevent them from doing so. The award letter recommended a trip to the locale in order to design an appropriate mural and suggested contacting the postmaster. Beyond this suggestion, the Section did not establish any

16. The Section also required the artist to submit a color sketch before sending the full-size cartoon, although there was no remuneration connected with this step.

17. Cases in which artists misunderstood local agriculture and industries are legion; see Marling, Park and Markowitz, and Beckham.

18. See Magafan, Trovato interview. Ethel and Jenne's first New York exhibition was a "twin show" at the Contemporary Arts Gallery in 1940. Between 1950 and 1961, Ethel Magafan had thirteen solo exhibitions, seven of them in New York City. In 1951 she won a Fulbright grant to paint in Greece.

19. Park and Markowitz, *Democratic Vistas*, 8; Melosh, *Engendering Culture*, 220–227.

20. Melosh, *Engendering Culture*, 68, does not reveal how she arrived at this number. One of the Recorder of Deeds Building muralists was an African American (see press release, note 47).

procedures to facilitate the artist's interaction with the community. How the artist was to determine what theme would be most appropriate to the mural's immediate community remained vague. This was the area in which most conflicts arose. Section commissions were, perhaps, too often fulfilled by artists from distant parts of the country, who could be viewed as meddling outsiders. But even artists from the same region or state just as often "got it wrong," as far as locals were concerned. Because most artists lived in big cities, where art-related employment opportunities were concentrated, muralists were nearly always from "somewhere else" in a predominantly rural America. Even artists who were willing to travel and were open to suggestion could find postmasters uncooperative. Sometimes, the postmaster would convey only his own ideas for the mural, or the artist would become prey to an outspoken local historian or boosters from the chamber of commerce. Some artists were barraged with mail about the mural and didn't know which of the diverse or conflicting suggestions to favor. In best-case scenarios, the postmaster convened a committee to make suggestions, which more receptive artists used. Sometimes, the artist would respond to the expressed desires of a community, only to find that the Section found the theme to be inappropriate. Usually when the Section received complaints about a mural, it requested that the artist alter the mural to suit the town. Occasionally, though, if the Section believed that the work was of exceptionally high quality or if Bruce felt bullied by a local official, the Section would stand behind the artwork.[21]

Ethel and Jenne Magafan were two of the most successful women working for the Section. In fact, they received more Section commissions than most male artists, although many were for small post offices, which carried relatively small stipends.[22] Ethel did six murals for the Section and an early one that may have been for the FAP. Jenne did five Section murals and two that may have been for the FAP.[23] Ethel Magafan's extraordinary

21. For examples, see Marling.

22. According to Melosh, *Engendering Culture*, 222, only eighteen percent of women and twenty-three percent of men who worked for the Section had more than three commissions.

23. Ethel Magafan's six Section murals were for U.S. post offices in Auburn, Nebraska; Wynne, Arkansas; Madill, Oklahoma; South Denver, Colorado; and for the boardroom of the Social Security Board Building (in collaboration with Jenne) and the Recorder of Deeds Building, both in Washington, D.C. There is no official documentation for Ethel's early *Indian Dance,* which appears on lists as having been done for the Senate Chamber, Washington, D.C., and the Capitol architect has no record of it. An early mural for the National Home for Jewish Children may have been for the FAP. Jenne Magafan's Section murals were for U.S. post offices in Glenwood Springs, Colorado; Albion, Nebraska; Anson, Texas; and Helper, Utah, along with the Social Security boardroom collaboration with Ethel. Her two high school murals, which may have been FAP commissions, were for West High School, Denver, Colorado, and Grafton Junior High School, Worcester, Massachusetts.

fig. 7
(above)
Ethel Magafan,
Crossing the Panhandle,
competition panel for
U.S. Post Office, Amarillo,
Texas, tempera on
masonite, 17 x 92 cm,
1939. The Mitchell
Wolfson Jr. Collection,
The Wolfsonian–Florida
International University,
Miami Beach,
Florida. Photograph by
Silvia Ros. One of eleven
designs awarded
"runner-up" status.

fig. 8
(below, right)
Frank Mechau, detail
of *Long Horns,* U.S.
Post Office, Ogallala,
Nebraska, oil on canvas,
1938. Photograph by
Marlene Park.

fig. 9
(below, far right)
Ethel Magafan, sketches,
graphite on paper, c. 1940.
Collection of Bruce Currie,
Woodstock, New York.
Photograph by
Peter Valdés-Dapena.

number of Section commissions demonstrates that she knew how to "paint Section." She seems to have made the recommended two trips to the towns where her murals were to go: one for sketching and the other for installation. There are no records of how she determined during her first visit what subject she should paint. She, Jenne, and Ed Chavez generally traveled together to help install one another's murals. Ethel said that it was Chavez's "beat-up station wagon" that enabled the twins to work for the Section. Chavez noted, in a discussion of one of Jenne's murals, that the installation provided an important opportunity for artists who hadn't painted the mural on the spot to interact with the community. Ethel and Jenne were attractive young women in their early twenties. As identical twins, they were a striking pair atop a scaffold (fig. 6). They were enthusiastic and proud to be working for the Section. On her own cognizance, Ethel showed her completed *Horse Corral* mural to soldiers about to go overseas at a local U.S.O. before installing it in the South Denver, Colorado, post office. Edward Rowan praised Ethel's "imagination" for this smart public relations move.[24]

A number of elements, then, contributed to Ethel Magafan's success with the Section. She was sensitive to her audiences; she was enthusiastic and personable; she was amenable to changes that the Section suggested; and she was able to travel. Her craftsmanship was meticulous; therefore, her works were likely to have the permanence that Bruce desired. Raised in Colorado, Ethel's favorite subject matter was the terrain of the American West, a subject that corresponded to Bruce's ideas about themes appro-

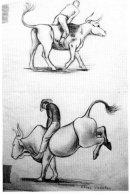

24. Magafan, Trovato interview, 7; "Edward Chavez, The Boy from the Golden West"; Currie interviews with author; Rowan to Magafan, 3 June 1942, EMP. Sometime after the completion of their studies, Ed Chavez and Jenne Magafan married. The three artists lived and traveled together until Ed enlisted in the U.S. Army.

fig. 10
Ethel Magafan, *Horse Corral*, competition design for U.S. Post Office, South Denver, Colorado, watercolor on paper, 38 x 76 cm, 1941. The Mitchell Wolfson Jr. Collection, The Wolfsonian–Florida International University, Miami Beach, Florida. Photograph by Silvia Ros. Mural was completed in 1942.

priate for American art. See, for example, her competition design *Crossing the Panhandle* (fig. 7).[25] Her style, too, corresponded to what Bruce desired — a realism that was modernized by a spareness of detail and a hint of the Streamline Moderne, influenced in part by her studies with Mechau (fig. 8). Especially as she matured, Magafan developed strong, simple compositions with solid figures that read well from a distance. In other words, her compositions were already visually scaled to the mural in a way that many painters who were primarily easel painters could not envision. Ethel's drawing skills were excellent, perhaps even stronger than her painting skills. Her style of rendering with beefy, confident contour lines gave her sketches a monumentality that made them look as if they should be murals (fig. 9). In cases where her competition submissions had drawing still visible, she fared well, such as her design for the South Denver post office, *Horse Corral* (fig. 10). In her choices of themes and manner of representation, Ethel Magafan displayed a thorough grasp of those contrary, unstated social goals that Bruce had set for the ideal Section mural. Nowhere is this more apparent than in her murals of African-American subjects, especially the Wynne, Arkansas, *Cotton Pickers.*

"Painting Section" in Black and White

The way that Section artists represented anybody, any community, or any local activity was a potential locus for public criticism. Communities, for example, were sensitive about being depicted as poor or backward, as in the famous uproar over Joseph P. Vorst's 1939 initial sketch of a sharecropper for Paris, Arkansas.[26] While criticisms over artists' lack of understanding of

25. Magafan later devoted herself almost exclusively to mountain scenes.

26. See Park and Markowitz, *Democratic Vistas*, 10–28; Melosh, *Engendering Culture*, 53–76; Marling, *Wall-to-Wall America*, passim. Joseph Vorst's unpopular sketch appeared in *Life* as one of the winners of the Section's Forty-Eight State Competition. See "Speaking of Pictures...," *Life* (4 December 1939): 12, 13, 15.

local crops or industries seem apt, many of the criticisms seem petty. Yet we can hardly blame people for not wanting the unpleasant truths of their daily lives immortalized within their post offices. If the Section mural was thus highly mediated terrain, this was perhaps nowhere more true than in depictions that included African Americans.

The history of public response to Section murals is based on newspaper articles and surviving letters to the Section. While one wonders how African Americans responded to a number of Section murals, there is little possibility of determining this now. If it is not explicitly revealed by a letter's content, there is virtually no way to tell the race of a letter writer. One of the few Section murals to inspire an organized African-American protest at the time it was painted was one of Gustaf Dalstrom's twelve panels for the St. Joseph, Missouri, post office. It features a fictional image of stereotypical, happy-go-lucky black minstrels making music on an equally fictional levee in St. Joseph. Unfortunately, the panel was completed as designed, despite the protest.[27]

Although African Americans appear in Section murals throughout the country, they figure most prominently in Section murals for the Southern states. In fact, African Americans were often used to represent the South in murals for other regions. In Ricard Brooks's *Decorative Interpretation of Unification of America through the Post* for Richland Center, Wisconsin, a stereotypical Aunt Jemima figure represents the South, just as the black cotton pickers in Newell's *Evolution of Western Civilization* represent Southern industry. It is important to remember that prior to World War II most African Americans still lived in former slave states—nearly seventy-six percent, according to the 1930 census.[28] Section murals that feature only blacks, and there are many of these, were a distinctly Southern phenomenon.

In the South, poor whites and blacks did exactly the same work, which was mostly agricultural, and many were sharecroppers. But early on, the Section was given to understand, via feedback from committees, postmasters, and viewers, that in the ideal world of the post office mural, Southern whites did not wish to be depicted in this manner, any more than they wanted to be shown poor or barefoot, regardless of the reality. Rowan's comments, particularly his policing against caricature, demonstrate that the Section preferred depictions of African Americans that were dignified and positive. Still, he passed on public concerns to Section artists about showing blacks and whites engaged in the same labor.[29]

27. This is described in Beckham, Marling, and Park and Markowitz.

28. The percentage is based on populations of African Americans in the eleven secessionist states plus Maryland and Kentucky. 1930 Census Data, United States Historical Census Browser, Inter-University Consortium for Political and Social Research (ICPSR), Ann Arbor, Michigan, http://fisher.lib.virginia.edu/census/, 24 March 1998.

29. Melosh, *Engendering Culture,* 71; and Beckham, *Depression Post Office Murals,* 192–197.

There were a number of solutions to this problem. The simplest was to show whites in authoritative positions. It is perhaps a testament to artists' progressive sympathies, or to pressure from Rowan, that relatively few artists took this route. Indeed, Section murals of agriculture or industry outside the South did not include overseers because they diminished the dignity of ordinary workers who were an important segment of the Section mural's audience. Some artists who depicted whites supervising black workers tried to make the blacks dignified nonetheless, as did Andreé Ruellan, in *Country Saw Mill* for Emporia, Virginia. Ruellan had done a number of sympathetic easel paintings and drawings of African Americans prior to her work for the Section. A handful of artists, such as Carl Nyquist, Arthur Covey, and Louis Raynaud, avoided dealing with the charged issue of black/white relations in their Southern paintings by depicting only whites doing agricultural labor in family groups, including the picking of cotton.[30]

A more common solution for artists who wanted to avoid portraying whites in authoritarian relationship to blacks was to depict only black workers. This would have been more acceptable to those Southern whites who believed that hard, menial labor, particularly the picking of cotton and tobacco, should be done by black workers, even though many whites also did these jobs. Some artists used other elements to make these depictions of African Americans more clearly positive. Jean Charlot included portraits of local individuals; Julien Binford's black workers were heroic and larger than life.[31]

Another favored solution to this problem was to show blacks and whites in the same painting but engaged in different labor, as did Doris Lee, when she associated a white couple with corn and a young black woman with cotton, in her Summerville, Georgia, mural. Southern artists H. Amiard Oberteuffer and Beulah Bettersworth also omitted white supervisors in favor of showing whites and blacks at different work. The African Americans in Oberteuffer's mural for the Vicksburg, Mississippi, courthouse are rendered with dignity and portrait-like faces. Nonetheless, her foreground is racially segregated into black and white halves, separated by a white man weighing cotton. Inequalities between these halves are apparent: a white mother assists her son with his math homework while her black counterpart sits idly by her children, who do nothing but stare.[32] Bettersworth's *Out of the Soil,* for the Columbus, Mississippi, post office, features a large

30. Nyquist's post office mural in Bolivar, Tennessee; Covey's in Anderson, South Carolina; and Raynaud's in Abbeville, Louisiana.

31. Post office paintings that depict only black workers include those by Ethel Magafan in Wynne, Arkansas; Joseph P. Vorst in Paris, Arkansas; Jean Charlot in McDonough, Georgia; Julian Binford in Forest, Mississippi; Robert Gwathmey in Eutaw, Alabama; Paul Rudin in Dunn, North Carolina; Paul Gill in Cairo, Georgia; and Charles Ward in Roanoke Rapids, North Carolina.

32. Park and Markowitz, *Democratic Vistas,* 90, note the ironic implications of the placement of Oberteuffer's mural over the judge's bench.

fig. 11
Simka Simkhovitch,
*Pursuits of Life in
Mississippi*, sketch for
Jackson, Mississippi,
post office and courthouse,
charcoal on paper,
57 x 76 cm, 1936.
The Mitchell Wolfson Jr.
Collection, The
Wolfsonian–Florida
International University,
Miami Beach, Florida.
Photograph by Silvia Ros.
Mural completed in 1938.

group of African Americans picking cotton in orderly rows in an abundant field. In front of them, plowing an altogether separate field in the foreground, is a lone white farmer. He is larger, more erect, and his face is visible. Yet we do not see a single facial feature on any of the twenty-five blacks depicted in the picture, since most are bent nearly in half, wear hats, and work with their backs to us. Unlike the white plowman, the black pickers do not seem to be individual people. Instead they are nothing but their labor, as reassuring in their abundance and orderliness as Bettersworth's field.[33]

It is probably not surprising that some of the most racially egregious Section murals are ones that include cotton, nor that the locus for this inequality, in art as in life, is its weighing. In Marion Sanford's *Weighing Cotton* relief for the Winder, Georgia, post office, two muscular black men, bare to the waist, with their lips sensually parted, proffer their cotton (and seemingly themselves) to a stern white male weighman in a suit coat and hat. This adds a sexual dimension to the racially charged act of a white man determining the value of the black men's labor.[34] A similar erotic dynamic is at play in the weighing scene in the foreground of Joseph Pistey Jr.'s *Agriculture and Industry of Claiborne Parish Louisiana* for the Haynesville, Louisiana, post office. Simka Simkhovitch's *Pursuits of Life in Mississippi* for the Jackson, Mississippi, courthouse (fig. 11) is

33. For Beckham, *Depression Post Office Murals*, 27–28, the division of workers into separate rows and the white farmer into a separate field merely reflects Southerners' tendency to acknowledge existing class and social barriers.

34. Sanford expressed her objectification of her African-American subjects clearly in correspondence that accompanied her Winder post office sketches: "The blacks lend themselves so well to sculpture that I couldn't resist using them in two of the sketches." Marion Sanford to Inslee Hopper, 2 December 1938, 121/133, in Melosh, *Engendering Culture*, 69.

divided into black and white halves, making one wonder if the justice dispensed beneath it will likewise be divided. While the "white half" depicts the judge and men of various occupations with portrait-like faces, the "black half" is dominated by cotton pickers, whose faces are obscured by their work. Only two men in the black precinct of the mural have unobstructed faces: a black banjo player who looks directly at the viewer and a lone white man who has "trespassed" to weigh the cotton.[35] Even the Social Realist Philip Evergood, who took the daring and progressive stand of showing whites and blacks working together in *Cotton — From Field to Mill,* for the Jackson, Georgia, post office, bowed to the convention of a suited white man overseeing the weighing, although a black man and a white man load the scales together. Still, in several of the "all-black" murals, including those by Magafan, Charlot, and Vorst, the African Americans perform the weighing as well as every other action in the painting. It is interesting to note that most of the artists discussed here, whose works were either too racially backward for the Section or too overtly progressive for local audiences, never received another Section commission.

The Wynne *Cotton Pickers*

The Section offered Ethel Magafan the mural for the Wynne, Arkansas, post office in August 1938. Correspondence from Rowan indicates that he received her two-inch-scale color sketch by 2 June 1939, and a photo of the completed mural by 8 November of that year. Rowan approved the mural early in December, and Ethel and Jenne installed it together the weekend before Christmas 1939.[36] Although Magafan was still living in Colorado when she received the commission, she had made the recommended sketching trip to Wynne. Cotton harvesting in Arkansas is a fall affair. Since the color sketch reached Rowan by June of 1939, Magafan must have visited Wynne for the fall harvest of 1938. Most of the aforementioned cotton murals were completed the same year as Magafan's or later, so she would not have had their "lessons" to draw on. It is unlikely that she knew any of the artists doing cotton or African-American murals at that time, although she became friends with Ruellan and Lee after the war. This was only Ethel Magafan's second mural for the Section. Her first, *Threshers,* had been well received in Auburn, Nebraska, where the president of a local art class had written a letter to Rowan praising it and placing it in the same league as Grant Wood's *Dinner for Threshers.* Magafan's payment for the Wynne mural was to be $560, less than the $620 for her first mural or the $750 she would receive for her third.[37]

35. Simkhovitch's mural was covered with a drape during the 1960s because it was deemed racially offensive.

36. Rowan to Magafan, 20 August 1938, 5 June 1939, 8 December 1939, EMP; "Mural Placed in Postoffice," *Wynne Daily-Star Progress,* 27 December 1939, Cross County Historical Society.

37. Rowan to Magafan, 23 July 1937 and 19 July 1938; Mrs. H. G. Harris to Rowan, 14 July 1938; Rowan to Harris, 19 July 1938, all EMP. Magafan's third Section mural, *Prairie Fire,* for Madill, Oklahoma, was awarded because she was a runner-up in the Amarillo, Texas, post office competition for *Crossing the Panhandle.* Rowan to Magafan, 12 September 1939, 14 September 1939, EMP.

fig. 12
(opposite page, top)
Ethel Magafan, detail
of *Cotton Pickers,*
U.S. Post Office, Wynne,
Arkansas, tempera on
canvas, 1939. Photograph
by Robert Jenkins.

fig. 13
(opposite page, center)
Ethel Magafan, detail
of *Cotton Pickers,*
U.S. Post Office, Wynne,
Arkansas. Photograph
by Robert Jenkins.

fig. 14
(opposite page, bottom)
Ethel Magafan, detail
of *Cotton Pickers,*
U.S. Post Office, Wynne,
Arkansas. Photograph
by Robert Jenkins.

This stipend was to cover two trips to Wynne and all materials—hardly a handsome amount.

Sue Bridwell Beckham believes that Northern artists often chose cotton as a theme for Southern murals because it corresponded to their preconceptions about the South and because they did not adequately familiarize themselves with other aspects of the locales.[38] This may have been true, but cotton was often a major industry in places where the murals were to go. Certainly, it was the main industry of Cross County, of which Wynne is the seat, where it employed everyone, blacks and whites alike. There is no surviving correspondence from Rowan informing Magafan that she should avoid depicting blacks and whites doing the same work, although he did pass on this advice to other artists. Whether Magafan received such a letter from Rowan or learned from other artists about the difficulties they had faced, she decided not to show blacks and whites working in the fields as equals. Rather than depict whites in powerful positions, she chose to depict only blacks. In the 1930s, African Americans constituted only one percent of the population of Colorado, where Magafan lived and had grown up, whereas they made up twenty-five percent of the Arkansas population. Like a number of artists who visited the South from other regions, she was probably interested in depicting African Americans, in part, because they were new and interesting subject matter.[39] Unlike Sanford and Pistey, however, Magafan did not treat her African-American subjects as exotic or other.

Most of the workers depicted in Magafan's *Cotton Pickers* (fig. 1) don't actually pick cotton but bring it in to be loaded onto a wagon and weighed. Only a few figures have been placed in the field, and one of these looks toward the viewer, shading his eyes from the sun. Most form a shallow frieze in the front of the composition. On the left, a man and a woman carry full bags of cotton toward the cart. They seem to form a family group with a little girl playing with a dog (fig. 12). On the right, two African-American men prepare to weigh a woman's cotton, while another man, his bag now empty, looks on (fig. 13). A middle-aged woman anchors the composition in the center (fig. 14). She looks back toward the direction from which the couple on the left has come. She seems to perform no action, and her stillness, her monumentality, and her column-like dress lend the composition grandeur and seriousness.

38. Beckham, *Depression Post Office Murals,* 182, for example, too often attributes differences or communication problems between artists and Southern publics to the Northern origins of the former.

39. James, interview; Gardner, interview. The fact that Ethel chose to depict only blacks because she knew she couldn't show blacks and whites doing the same work was related by Bruce Currie in our 9 November interview. See also 1930 Census Data. The phenomenon of white artists treating blacks as new and interesting subject matter is dealt with by Melosh, *Engendering Culture,* 67–76.

fig. 15
Ethel Magafan, detail
of *Cotton Pickers*,
U.S. Post Office, Wynne,
Arkansas. Photograph
by Robert Jenkins.

Magafan emphasized that her *Cotton Pickers* was drawn from life. It is possible that Magafan observed African Americans weighing cotton. Although it was not common on smaller farms, blacks sometimes did the weighing on larger ones.[40] This feature might have been merely an off-shoot of her decision to paint an "all-black" mural. Still, an unmistakable message that can be taken from the painting is that the competent African-American men weighing the cotton are entitled to evaluate the worth of their own labor. By choosing not to focus on the picking, Magafan avoided placing figures in bent-over positions, in which they become anonymous and less dignified, as in Simkhovitch's and Bettersworth's compositions. Instead, most of Magafan's figures are erect, their faces visible and portrait-like. All the adults wear shoes. Everyone has clean and neat clothes, and the women's attire is rather fashionable, especially their hats. The cloche hat of the woman on the left stands out particularly as atypical

40. Magafan emphasized this to the reporter of the *Wynne Daily-Star Progress,* "Mural Placed in Postoffice," and in a telephone conversation with Julia Gardner around the time of the NAACP objections to the mural. Information on local farming practices from the Gardner and James interviews.

in a scene of cotton picking. Whether this was the type of dress that Ethel observed or whether she chose to dress the figures this way to enhance their dignity, the effect is the same.

Beckham has described these figures as unhappy and broken in spirit.[41] Certainly, they are solemn. Even the little girl playing with the dog wears a serious face. Magafan's figures are fairly serious and static in all her Section paintings. Here, I think she may have erred on the side of "too serious" in order to show sympathy for the difficulty of the work, and because she wanted to make her depiction of African Americans as dignified as possible (no way to misinterpret these people as happy-go-lucky minstrels). These elements—the figures' faces, attitudes, postures, and clothes—imply that Magafan sought to create a positive image of African Americans. There is yet one more element that, in itself, is powerful enough to confirm this assertion: the proud, monumental woman at the center of the composition is a portrait of the African-American opera singer Marian Anderson, who was larger than life in 1939.[42] Although it is difficult to see from a distance or in small reproductions, Anderson is actually shown singing (fig. 15).

Having just returned from a successful concert tour of Europe, Anderson embarked on a tour of the United States in 1937, an event covered by *Life* magazine.[43] In 1939 Anderson was to perform at Constitution Hall in Washington, D.C., but the Daughters of the American Revolution (DAR) prevented her from singing there because of her race. During the public outcry that ensued, Eleanor Roosevelt and several other prominent women resigned from the Board of the DAR. "You had an opportunity to lead in an enlightened way and it seems to me that your organization has failed," said Roosevelt with her characteristically dignified and moral voice. The federal government invited Anderson to perform on the steps of the Lincoln Memorial. In what would become her most famous concert, Anderson sang on Easter Sunday, 9 April 1939, to seventy-five thousand people, and millions more heard her broadcast live on the radio.[44] This incident transformed the already-famous Anderson into a living legend and a cause célèbre for an end to Jim Crow practices. It also reminded the populace of the racially progressive ideals of the White House, particularly those of the first lady. Thus, Magafan's mural presented the Roosevelt administration's new racial agenda with a subtlety that enabled it to be accepted by diverse regional viewers.

41. Beckham's interpretation of this mural, *Depression Post Office Murals,* 197–200, begins with the erroneous premise that there is a white overseer, although there are no whites in the painting. Beckham is unaware that the "elderly woman" who peers "into a distance that does not offer a better life" is Marian Anderson.

42. During our 9 November interview, Bruce Currie told me that Ethel was pleased to have painted the central figure after Marian Anderson.

43. "A Great Negro Singer Tours America," *Life* (22 February 1937).

44. "Exhibit: Eleanor Roosevelt Letter," National Archives and Record Administration, http://www.nara.gov/exhall/originals/eleanor.html, 5 May 2001.

DAPA 24

fig. 16
Marian Anderson
at her 9 April 1939
concert on the steps
of the Lincoln Memorial.
Photograph by
Thomas D. McAvoy
(then a *Life* magazine staff
photographer)/TimePix.

The date that Rowan received Magafan's color design indicates that she was probably working on it when Anderson gave her triumphant April concert,[45] and I believe the concert inspired her to include Anderson's portrait. She might have used press photographs taken that day to help her with the likeness (fig. 16), many of which compare in pose and view with the central figure in the Wynne mural (fig. 14). Because of the events surrounding it, Anderson's concert was heavily covered by the press nationwide. Thus some Wynne viewers might have recognized Marian Anderson, despite her cotton picker disguise, particularly since the figures in the mural are nearly life-size.

There seem to have been no contemporary objections to Magafan's mural in Wynne. This could be attributed to the fact that Magafan's mural at once celebrated Cross County's agricultural contribution to the nation, dignified its African-American subjects, and respected its white viewers by avoiding a finger-pointing approach to race relations. The Section likewise had no quibble with *Cotton Pickers*, other than a few formal suggestions—one figure's head was too big, another not fully realized. A letter from Rowan dated 8 December implies a flurry of last-minute telegrams just as Magafan was readying to depart for Wynne to install the mural. The office of the Commissioner of Public Buildings appears to

45. Edward Rowan acknowledged receipt of the mural design in a letter to Magafan two months later, 5 June 1939, EMP.

have raised a question about "the appropriateness of the subject matter." Perhaps this was because in 1939 the Section had already fielded a number of complaints over murals involving cotton and African Americans. Whatever Magafan's answer, Rowan found it "entirely reassuring" and wired her to proceed.[46]

After the Wynne Mural

After the Wynne *Cotton Pickers,* Ethel Magafan was awarded four more Section murals: two for regional post offices and two for office buildings in Washington, D.C. Her last, awarded on 5 April 1943, near the end of the Section's history, was *Andrew Jackson at the Battle of New Orleans,* for the Recorder of Deeds Building in Washington. In it, Magafan again focused on African Americans in positive terms. Section commissions for Washington, D.C. buildings, unlike regional ones, were given unifying themes. Since Frederick Douglass had served as a recorder of deeds in Washington, D.C., and that office had continued to employ significant numbers of African Americans, all murals for the new building were to depict "The Contribution of the Negro to the American Nation." Thus Magafan's decision to focus again on African Americans was made in entering the competition, rather than being one she made on her own after being awarded a commission, as in the Wynne mural. It is clear, however, that Magafan very much wanted to win the Recorder of Deeds competition, since she submitted two ambitious designs for it. Both of her entries were historic battle scenes that required a good deal of research, particularly since each was from a different war.[47]

Of her two submissions, Magafan preferred *The Colored Regiment at Fort Wagner,* which featured the most renowned black regiment of the Civil War, the Fifty-fourth Massachusetts Infantry Regiment (fig. 17). The Fifty-fourth had made a brave, albeit unsuccessful, charge against the Confederates near Charleston, South Carolina. The leader of the Fifty-fourth, Robert Gould Shaw, was famous for demanding that his soldiers receive the same compensation and uniforms as their white counterparts. This subject was especially appropriate for the Recorder of Deeds Building, since Frederick Douglass's two sons had served in the Massachusetts regiment. Unfortunately for Magafan, she was not the only artist in the competition to choose this subject, and the rendition by Carlos Lopez was selected to adorn the building.[48] Magafan's other

46. Rowan to Magafan, 5 June 1939. Rowan referred to the telegrams in a letter to Ethel, 8 December 1939, EMP. See David W. Look and Carol L. Perrault, *The Interior Building, Its Architecture and Its Art* (Washington, D.C.: U.S. Department of the Interior, 1986), 113–114, for information on Mitchell Jamieson's later (1942) mural depicting Anderson's 1939 concert.

47. See Contreras, *Tradition and Innovation*, 219–234. Rowan to Magafan, 5 April 1943, EMP; Recorder of Deeds Building press release, U.S. Treasury Department Section of Painting and Sculpture, 7 April 1943, EMP; Park and Markowitz, *Democratic Vistas,* 34; Magafan, Trovato interview, 6.

48. Currie, 9 November 1997 interview; *The Shaw Memorial, A Celebration of an American Masterpiece* (Cornish, N.H.: Saint-Gaudens National Historic Site, 1997).

fig. 17
(opposite page, top)
Ethel Magafan, *The Colored Regiment at Fort Wagner,* competition panel for the Recorder of Deeds Building, Washington, D.C., tempera on board, 30 x 74 cm, 1943. The Mitchell Wolfson Jr. Collection, The Wolfsonian–Florida International University, Miami Beach, Florida. Photograph by Silvia Ros.

fig. 18
(opposite page, bottom)
Ethel Magafan, *Andrew Jackson at the Battle of New Orleans,* competition panel for the Recorder of Deeds Building, Washington, D.C., tempera on board, 30 x 74 cm, 1943. The Mitchell Wolfson Jr. Collection, The Wolfsonian–Florida International University, Miami Beach, Florida. Photograph by Silvia Ros.

composition, *Andrew Jackson at the Battle of New Orleans,* however, was chosen as one of the seven winning entries (fig. 18). It commemorated an episode from the War of 1812 in which six hundred free black volunteers successfully routed British forces double their number. As in Magafan's Wynne mural, the figures are dignified and serious. The resulting static quality was discussed by the committee, and one member compared Magafan's painting to a work by Renaissance painter Piero della Francesca.[49]

Both of Magafan's Recorder of Deeds compositions celebrated the bravery and integrity of African Americans, as well as their contributions to American life. Like her visual reference to Marian Anderson's 1939 concert in the Wynne mural, Magafan's focus on free black volunteer troops resonated, subtly, with the need to address persistent racial inequities in the United States. Some scholars have described Section murals as bland or, worse, hopelessly compromised, because they were meant to appeal to a broad audience. Yet, in cases where Section murals pushed local publics too hard, they were refused, covered with curtains, painted over, or eventually removed. Paintings that were progressive and subtle enough to be accepted, like Ethel Magafan's depictions of African Americans, were more likely to help alter people's preconceptions. This is what it could mean, in the most positive sense, to "paint Section." ✦

Acknowledgments

This article is dedicated to Dr. Marlene Park, with gratitude for her generosity as a mentor and for her continued friendship. Her work on the New Deal arts projects, particularly the Section, has laid the groundwork for all of us who follow. I am deeply grateful to Ethel Magafan's husband, Bruce Currie, and their daughter, Jenne Currie, for providing me with invaluable information and material. I would also like to thank Ted Cunningham, Julia Gardner, Jimmie James, Robert Jenkins, Rebecca Karamehmedovic, Lolly Shaver, Sally Webster, and, most of all, my husband, Peter.

49. Rowan to Magafan, 5 April 1943, EMP. See also G. M. Thornett, secretary, Board of Commissioners, Government of the District of Columbia, to Ethel Magafan, 11 June 1943, EMP; and Rowan to Magafan, 5 October 1943, 14 February 1944, and 15 March 1944, EMP.